A Walk in
Their Kicks

A WALK IN THEIR KICKS

Literacy, Identity, and the Schooling
of Young Black Males

Aaron M. Johnson

Foreword by Elizabeth Birr Moje
Afterword by Jay B. Marks

TEACHERS COLLEGE PRESS
TEACHERS COLLEGE | COLUMBIA UNIVERSITY
NEW YORK AND LONDON

Published by Teachers College Press, 1234 Amsterdam Avenue, New York, NY 10027

Copyright © 2019 by Teachers College, Columbia University

Cover design and illustration by Mya Thomas.

Library of Congress Cataloging-in-Publication Data is available at loc.gov

ISBN 978-0-8077-6105-2 (paper)
ISBN 978-0-8077-7733-6 (ebook)

Printed on acid-free paper
Manufactured in the United States of America

26 25 24 23 22 21 20 19   8 7 6 5 4 3 2 1

For my Blake—push on, brotha

Childhood poverty, the lack of early childhood education, and the denial of a college-preparatory K–12 education promoting critical literacies have contributed to producing what has been referred to as the school-to-prison pipeline. . . . Youth in underserved and underperforming schools that focus more on discipline policies as opposed to academic rigor would benefit the most if educational institutions adopted the view of literacy as a right. (Winn & Behizadeh, 2011)

Contents

Foreword *Elizabeth Birr Moje*   xi

Acknowledgments   xiii

Introduction   1
   How This Book Is Organized   10
   How to Use This Book   11

**PART I: NOTES ON THE STATE OF
   . . . DETROIT . . . EDUCATION . . . RACE . . . SCHOOLING
   . . . LITERACY . . . SOCIALIZATION**   13
   . . . on the state of the west side   13

**1. His Story: The History of School and Literacy
    Development of African American Males**   15
   Segregation, Jim Crow, and African American
     Academic Achievement   20
   School Desegregation   22
   The Great Migration   25
   School Busing   27

**2. Hustle and Flow:
    Student Literacy, Flow, Agency, and Motivation**   31
   Flow Theory   31
   Learning and Literacy as Social Constructs   32
   Agency and Identity   39

**3. Black Boy Fly: The Black Male Literacy
    Paradigm as an Instructional Framework**   43
   The Black Male Literacy Paradigm   43
   Home Versus School Language   45

Contextual Understanding   47

Culture and Socialization   48

Teacher Perceptions   56

Power, Agency, and Identity   57

Teacher Preparedness   58

Summary of the Black Male Literacy Paradigm   59

Literacy Assessment Instruments and Literacy Development   60

4. We've Got the Power: Culture and Socialization   **68**

Power and Contextual Understanding and the
   Relationship to Literacy   68

The Academic Achievement Gap Versus the Education Debt   70

Student Socialization   77

**5. You Mean I Can't Even Be Black in the Hallway?!?:
Discourse Communities and the Relationship
Between Power, Agency, and Identity**   **84**

Student Identities   84

Disidentification with School   87

Student Social Power and Valuing Students' Identities in School   92

**PART II: NOTES ON THE STATE OF
. . . BLACK BOYS**   **99**

Educator's oath   99

**6. Where I'm From: Teacher Identities and the
Impact on African American Male Students**   **101**

Understanding Literacy Through a Sociocultural Paradigm   101

Meet the Teacher Participants   103

Teacher Identities and the Roles They Play in Building
   Student Literacy   108

**7. A Walk in Their Kicks:
Understanding the Literacies of African American Males**   **117**

Engaging African American Males in Literacy   117

Teachers' Recognition of the Importance of Students'
   Connections to Teachers, School, and Texts   118

A Deeper Look at Turmoil: Home-Based and School-Based
   Adversities That Impact Student Learning Outcomes   142

8. Literacy Is . . . : Looking at Literacy Through a Different Lens **150**

Teachers' Expansions of Their Definitions of Literacy 150

The Necessity of Teachers' Use of Evidence-Based Instructional Strategies 157

Teachers' Improved Understandings of Students' Literacy Practices 158

9. The Choice Is Yours: "Giving a Damn" as a Strategy for Improving Student Outcomes **162**

10. Are We on Ten Yet?: Reconceptualizing Schools for African American Students **168**

Teachers' Recognition of the Importance of and Relationship to Students' Connections to Teachers, School, and Texts 169

Teachers' Expansions of Their Definitions of Literacy 170

Teachers' Improved Understandings of Students' Literacy Practices 171

The Necessity of Teachers' Use of Evidence-Based Instructional Strategies 172

The Education Debt . . . Revisited 172

Recommendations 177

Implications 178

Challenges to This Work 180

. . . until we meet again 181

Epilogue **184**

Afterword *Jay B. Marks* **187**

References **189**

Index **197**

About the Author **210**

Foreword

A Walk in Their Kicks by Dr. Aaron M. Johnson is a powerful book that is sure to open the eyes and hearts of many teachers. This book is powerful in its authentic voice; Dr. Johnson has lived the complex experience of an academically and musically gifted young African American boy who wanted to learn and excel, but also wanted to be part of his community. His willingness to open up his identities to the reader, to expose the struggles of dual consciousness he experienced and the sense of loss that a "subtractive education" can leave in a child, is a window into the psyches and the souls of Black boys across multiple U.S. education contexts. In sharing his experience, he reminds educators that he, a successful scholar and educator, was once an eager young Black boy sitting in a classroom, hoping for the opportunity to learn. He also reminds the reader that he could easily have been consigned to a lack of opportunity based on his race.

This book will also educate its readers in deep ways. Dr. Johnson writes a book for teachers and school leaders that respects their intelligence by inviting them into a discussion of the historical underpinnings of the [mis]education of African American children, with Detroit as an instructive case study. He does not shy away from citing research literature like so many texts written for educators do. He does not talk down to teachers. Instead, he insists that great teaching must be rooted in educators' understanding of history, psychology, linguistics, and literacy. He challenges his fellow educators to do the right thing by their students by learning from them and with them. He is a true pedagogue in that he teaches the reader both weighty education theories and relevant research findings, and then extends that scholarship into recommendations for practice.

Each section of each chapter provides deep historical or evidence-based analysis, bolstered by practical suggestions, such as ensuring that African American children are reading literature that they love and in which they see themselves represented, talking with Black youth to hear what they care about, putting African American students—especially boys—in leadership positions, engaging African

American children and youth in analysis of various discourse practices so that they become "metadiscursive," and showing students that you "give a damn" by respecting what African American children and their families bring to the learning environment and never, ever, giving up on them.

The book is also clear-headed about how hard the work will be, particularly if the readers do not first try to understand the cultural values, experiences, and practices of their students. As Dr. Johnson emphasizes, we must first see the potential and possibility in all our students if we are to invite them to reach for new potentials and possibilities. To do that, all teachers must overcome race-based assumptions or blinders (there is no such thing as "color-blindness") and recognize that we live in a racist and classist society, one that depends at some level on the subjugation of some groups to ensure the privilege of others. We also must deeply understand the histories that have led to "the way things are" if we are to counter them. And we must work collectively to challenge the assumptions that lead teachers to consign young people to educational categories that will determine their future opportunities.

This clear-headed perspective is made all the more believable by Dr. Johnson's impeccable credentials. He is not only the recipient of a doctoral degree but also a former teacher, school leader, and instructional leader. His work is all about nurturing both young people and their teachers to do their best work. He has, indeed, walked in their kicks—both those of students and teachers—and he knows from both ample research and practice that what he is sharing with educators will work if they open their hearts and minds to new ways of thinking, believing, and doing.

Read Dr. Aaron Johnson's book if you want to learn not only about systemic racial and economic oppression, but also about ways that educators can counter such oppression through everyday practice. Read his book if you care about the lives of countless young African American men and women who deserve the chance to achieve their dreams. Read the book if you care about young Black men and women who have much to offer our society if given the opportunity to learn—and to learn on their terms, with respect for their cultural values, experiences, and beliefs. Read his book if you want to walk in *his* kicks and be the kind of educator who makes a difference.

—Elizabeth Birr Moje
University of Michigan
September 17, 2018

Acknowledgments

When I was 12 years old, I started my first book of writing. In this book, I wrote mostly poetry, with some short stories. In one of the poems I wrote, "One day, my writing will sell." At first, I didn't believe that that dream would come true. Later, I thought, "Why not?" Literacy saved my life. Not in the literal sense, but books, poetry, that little book of my writing—they became my refuge. My 8th-grade English teacher, Mrs. Willie Bell Gibson, helped me hone my skills. Her Vocabulary Skill Building program (VSB) made me fall in love with words. It was in her class that I discovered books like *The Bluest Eye* and *Their Eyes Were Watching God*. I owe her a debt of gratitude.

I would like to thank my amazing family members, who contributed in their own ways to this work. I would like to thank my mother and my late grandmother, my first reading teachers. I want to thank my extremely patient wife, who supported me through the PhD process and the multiple iterations of my dissertation. Thank you, also, to my children, Kailyn, Aminah, and Blake, who are my inspiration for this work.

I want to thank Jean Ward for helping to make this project happen.

Last but not least, I would like to thank James Paul Gee. You read my book, and without even knowing me, you introduced me to a great publisher. Without your help, none of this would have been possible. You are a brilliant researcher and your discourse analysis was central to helping me comb through and analyze hours of recordings, writings, and conversations with teachers who were highlighted in this book. Thank you.

Introduction

Click-clack.

No amount of onomatopoeia can aptly describe the sound that a 9-millimeter handgun makes as it is cocked, aimed, and prepared to be fired. At the age of 10, for the first time in my life, I heard this sound as I stared down the barrel of his gun. I remember his countenance, the look in his eyes. He was calm.

"Check in dem shoes, homey!"

These were the words of the young Black man who was in the process of helping me understand the concept of preservation of one's own life over materialism. He requested my shoes as though he was asking me to pass him *his* shoes. The shoes he was talking about were the brand-new pair of Adidas Top Ten high-tops that my uncle had just bought me for getting good grades. I still remember the spongy tongue that was a little oversized for the shoe. The contrast of red, white, and blue was so sweet. These were my new kicks. I was a 5th-grader who, in the blink of an eye, was thrust into the world of pain, aggression, limited options, and angst of the young man who was robbing me. It wasn't until later in my life that I understood the significance of this event.

On that balmy spring day in 1985, I was also in the midst of dealing with my own pain. I was learning how to love myself. I was learning to love the nerd in me and attempting to accept the dual lives that I led. That dude never actually stole my shoes that day.

"What size shoe you wear?"

"Ten," I said.

"Yo feet too big," he said.

It turned out that my feet were too big for him to fit in my shoes. He walked away and pulled his gun on another kid on the playground and stole his Georgetown starter jacket (at the time, Patrick Ewing was our hero and we all wanted Georgetown jackets—I had one, too). He tried to steal my shoes, but he stole much more from me. He stole my innocence. He stole a little piece of my belief in humanity. He could not walk in my shoes, nor could I have walked in his. This was not the only thing that separated us as Black boys attempting to navigate our way in this society, facing similar, seemingly insurmountable odds. I never officially met the young man, but I would venture to say that his educational options were not enough to engage him in academic pursuits. I carried books. He carried guns. I played the violin and cello. He lurked around playgrounds. I solved equations. He robbed people. I was at school playing softball on the playground with my friends when he changed my life. He was not at school. I often wonder what he is doing. I wonder whether he walks in his own kicks and if anyone has ever attempted to walk in his. This is my attempt to walk in his shoes, if only just for a moment.

In our short encounter, he taught me something about our struggle as Black boys in America. He set me on a path to help me assuage my fear, anger, and guilt, and he inspired the Machiavellian idea within me that I could rise above the self-fulfilling prophecy that Black boys' lives are worthless and change this world for myself and for other Black boys like me. Our encounter was a fortuitous one that would help me choose the road less traveled at many different forks in many different roads. He helped me define and articulate the "why" about my purpose in the work of literacy, equity, and social justice.

I was raised in Detroit, Michigan, a city that, at the time, was plagued with crime, homelessness, a deteriorating public school infra-structure, and dilapidated housing and other building structures. The crack epidemic was at its apex. Currently, a massive gentrification ef-fort is happening in the city in the business areas, but many of the outlying neighborhoods remain untouched. Many young Black males living in the city and the region, as with any urban area in America for that matter, have experienced the negative impact of social and economic depression and repression and have lost their lives because of the deep-seated racist beliefs and perceptions about them. Ghettos are a manifestation of racism and economic depression, and although I love my city, I recognize that Detroit is home to some of the largest ghettos in the country, complete with dilapidated housing and eco-nomic and social repression. The so-called Black Gen-Xers are raising their Black sons in urban and suburban areas while they still fear for their lives, and their White counterparts are deciding whether or not to awaken themselves and acknowledge the racist beliefs and actions that are interwoven into the American psyche about Black maleness.

People around the world have witnessed the killings of Alton Sterling and Philando Castile at the hands of the police. The world has witnessed killing after killing of Black people, images and actions that are used to reinforce the subjugation of our bodies and our minds. We continue to mourn, be angered by, and resist oppression from the American conceptions about the value of Black lives; these same conceptions about Black lives guided the hands that killed Trayvon Martin, Michael Brown, Walter Scott, Tamir Rice, Oscar Grant, Amadou Diallo, Errol Shaw, and Malice Green. Racist sympathizers would justify the devaluation and degradation of Black lives by highlighting the lives of the victims. They might say: He stole something . . . so he was shot dead in the middle of the street. . . . He sold cigarettes illegally . . . so he was choked to death. . . . He refused to open his hand . . . so he was beaten on the head with flashlights. . . . He had a hoodie on as he walked home from the store to get iced tea and Skittles . . . so he was shot multiple times. . . . He was deaf and could not speak and was cognitively impaired and wielded a garden rake because he felt unsafe . . . so he was shot multiple times. . . . He reached for his wallet to show his identification . . . so he was shot 41 times with his hands up, with many of the bullets hitting him in his armpits. . . . He owed back child support and had warrants and ran away from the police officer . . . so he was shot in the back and a gun was planted on his dead body. . . . And on . . . and on . . . and on. Their bodies were not theirs.

This new generation of would-be game hunters are just like the old—they kill Black people, particularly Black men and boys, indiscriminately. They kill Black people regardless of education, class, or social status. Black men and women are not safe in cars with their significant others or children. We are not safe walking back from the store alone. We are not safe in groups. We are not safe in twos. We are not safe in cities or suburbs. Our children, many of whom are engaged in constructive experiences, are treated differently. The curators of treachery and oppression continually show us that they do not value Black lives.

Schools had long been believed to be refuges from the streets of many urban areas and have served as makeshift shelters for Black boys and girls to hide themselves from the crime that plagues many of their neighborhoods. Moreover, Black boys and girls have often used school for exposure to activities and sports, activities that many have used as a physical or emotional escape. However, schools have done much damage by way of destroying the Black mind and in purporting, sustaining, and maintaining the belief held by the dominant culture that Black boys and Black men are unintelligent and subhuman and thus not deserving of any value placed on their lives. In Ta-Nehisi Coates's book *Between the World and Me*, written as a letter to his son, Coates urges his son and, by proxy, other Black boys, men, women, and girls to take back their bodies and their minds. He stated:

> The streets were not my only problem. If the streets shackled my right leg, the schools shackled my left. Fail to comprehend the streets and you gave up your body now. But fail to comprehend the schools and you gave up your body later. I suffered at the hands of both, but I resent the schools more. (Coates, 2015, p. 37)

It is important to understand the gravity of Coates's (2015) statement. He resented the schools more, not because they were more dangerous. He resented them because the rules of engagement were unclear. Many Black families have the expectation that their kids will "get a good education and go to college." While this concept is noble, it does not take into account the deep-seated racist beliefs and practices embedded in the institution of school. Furthermore, if you were Black and lived in Detroit, the probability was high that your school did not have the resources to prepare you to read and comprehend at grade level, let alone prepare you for the rigors of a college or university. When one also considers the lack of access to basic survival needs, school curricula that is culturally irrelevant, and disproportionate discipline practices in schools, which are all manifestations of economic and social oppression, it becomes easier to understand how the sociocultural paradigm impacts progress in school. But to place the blame squarely on the shoulders of urban systems is tantamount to misrepresenting the whole of the problem.

The institution of school, the politicians, the federal and state governments, and well-meaning organizations have coined the term *achievement gap* to account for Black children's disassociation from school, school content, and school-based assessments. Viewing Black achievement in school through this lens evinces many of the same notions about the value of Black lives as those held by people who believe that Black lives are unimportant. The use of the term "achievement gap" allows us to continue the same type of deficit thinking that created it in the first place. When asked to address the achievement gap, although many educators cringe at the mention of its existence, viewing Black disassociation from school in this manner permits educators to identify Black children as the problem rather than the school environments themselves. Instead of reconceptualizing schools to meet the needs of students, to help them be places where variations and nuances in culture, language, and identities are valued, we have looked at Black children in American public schools as something to be fixed or to be acclimated to the culture, values, and mores of the school instead of the reverse. Admittedly, at one point in time, I also subscribed to this notion. The more I worked with Black children as a teacher and administrator, the more I understood that, in order to improve Black students' lives, schools have to make connections between race, socialization, and literacy in an effort to encourage them to take possession of their minds. Schools can help to make those connections by using a reimagined construct of school as the vehicle. This idea has particular significance for Black students because, as Coates (2015) pointed out, Black bodies can be taken at any time and for any reason. These facts, among others, make the concepts of opportunity and achievement gaps problematic because they do not delve deep enough into the conditions that brought them about.

I grew up in a neighborhood where, in the early to mid-1980s, the thing to have was a moped with an expensive sound system. I wanted one so badly. My parents and grandparents didn't have the money to purchase one for me, but they also knew that the mopeds were the tools of the drug dealers in my neighborhood. Young African American boys who were members of a crew ran drugs throughout the neighborhood and into adjacent neighborhoods. My parents and grandparents kept a tight rein on me and were concerned about my whereabouts, especially during the summer months. My family engaged me in constructive activities to the extent that they could afford it. I attended a magnet school across town from the 3rd through the 8th grade, rather than attending the nearby neighborhood elementary and middle schools. I attended a nationally recognized magnet high school rather than the nearby neighborhood high school. In contrast to Coates's (2015) experience, school saved my life, but it did not save the lives of many around me.

The neighborhood high school I would have attended was a school plagued by violence and drug trafficking. I often stayed in the house to read or practice my instrument rather than hang with some of my peers who participated in other activities. I would often stay inside and read through the encyclopedias that my family had purchased or other books my mother had in the house that were left over from the 1970s (*Black Boy*, by Richard Wright, and *Manchild in the Promised Land*, by Claude Brown). At the time, I often looked at these literacy practices as punishment because I was required to engage in them, but what I didn't realize was that they were preparing me for something greater. Literacy was literally saving my life by keeping me occupied and out of trouble. I was only allowed to communicate and associate with certain people. There were several houses on my street that were deemed "dope" houses, and I was given strict orders to stay away from and out of those houses. Many of my friends and neighborhood associates did not have the same support. My best friend, who lived directly across the street from me, fell in love with the notion of selling drugs. He often bragged about the money that he was making, and was going to make, because of what he was promised. While my interests were focused on school-related events, he spoke about smoking marijuana, selling crack, and making money.

The next time I saw my one-time best friend after the 9th grade was when I was an assistant principal and I searched for him on the state's felony offender website. There was my friend, in an orange jumpsuit, the attire that, as Black males, we all try to avoid. His image was a testimony to me that literacy has the potential to save lives and help Black boys take possession of their minds. Literacy had already saved my life. While some of my peers were known for participating in nefarious activities when we were young, I was known for walking home from the bus stop with a violin case, a cello, and a backpack full of books. The cello didn't keep me from getting beatdowns, nor was my backpack bulletproof, but I felt like I owned my own mind, and I still feel that way today.

As I stared at the picture of my friend on the computer screen, wearing his orange jumpsuit, I had an epiphany: Literacy can save one's life. As a young person, I spent countless hours in my room reading novels, biographies, poetry, encyclopedias, and treatises and writing my own poetry and prose. My friend's image reminded me about what I had once read in *The Narrative of the Life of Frederick Douglass* about how Douglass himself discovered the importance of literacy. At one point, Douglass, a child born into slavery, was learning how to read from his slaver's wife. After the slave owner heard about this, he addressed his wife about the issue and Douglass overheard the conversation. The slave owner told his wife that if she taught young Frederick how to read, he would never want to be a slave.

As the information on the state offenders' website stated, my friend was serving time in prison for possession and sale of narcotics. I had compared the prison time my friend was serving to the slavery that Douglass experienced. For Douglass, illiteracy represented slavery of the mind, and a life of literacy provided the freedom. Viewing my friend's image reinforced for me that participating in literacy and literate behavior could help one take possession of one's mind. Literacy had kept my mind focused on academic endeavors and kept me out of trouble. As I stared at the image of my friend, I wept. I wept for the countless numbers of Black boys and men who had fallen victim to the lure of the drug trade. I wept for the Black boys and men who were victims of senseless violence at the hands of their peers or the police. I wept for the young man who drew a gun on me when I was 10 years old on my school playground. I wept for those whose masculinity had been misread and stolen by the dominant American culture and who were forced into a life absent of the promise that literacy could provide.

This book will outline how we can better understand the lives of African American males, which will lead to enhanced understandings of how they view the world and the literacy in which they engage for themselves. It will also engage readers in a critical analysis of race as it relates to literacy specifically and the institution of school in general. Race is a critical element in how teachers perceive their students; thus, the idea of how racial paradigms impact the connection to literacy expected by the dominant culture, and the consideration of race as it pertains to how African American boys are allowed to navigate schools, have a significant impact on how they are engaged in school-based literacy. Tatum (2005) found that there was a correlation between the perceptions of the in-school and out-of-school literacy events and practices of African American students and the curricular and pedagogical decisions that are made for them. Teachers' perceptions of the literacy and academic abilities of African American students manifest themselves in their text selections for these students, the instructional strategies and assessments they use, and the literacy interventions they employ. I do not intend to replicate the work already done by Tatum and others —there is other research that supports thinking that builds upon his work about the problems of literacy development and underachievement. Rather, I am interested in focusing on how sustained dialogue and an understanding of the sociocultural nature of literacy can provide readers of this book with ways of thinking that contribute to changes in classroom literacy practices and improve the academic success of African American males in school classrooms. Furthermore, my goal is to engage educators, politicians, parents, students, clergy, businesspeople, activists, and laypeople in dialogue and reflection about how America's schools can be revolutionized to become institutions of discovery and learning and to fulfill the promise of a relevant and equitable, free and public education.

The practical implementation of the idea of using literacy to help African American male students reclaim their minds can provide opportunities for them to see a positive life trajectory through access to relevant and challenging reading materials. When students have access to relevant texts, relationships can be built between African American male students and educators (and other adults) who are willing to dedicate their lives to the pursuit of improving educational outcomes. Tatum (2005) spoke of books that were given to him by his teachers, and it was his belief that these teachers helped save his life. Texts such as *The Autobiography of Malcolm X* by Malcolm X, *Black Boy* by Richard Wright, *Manchild in the Promised Land* by Claude Brown, and more recently, *The Beautiful Struggle* and *Between the World and Me* by Ta-Nehisi Coates have provided real-world stories about how literacy saved the lives of the African American males depicted in these narratives. I believe that the life of my friend could have been directed down a different path if someone would have encouraged him to read texts that depicted African American males triumphing over their circumstances. He could have been encouraged to take possession of his own mind through literacy. No one attempted to walk in his kicks.

Through this book, I hope to generate thoughtful discussion and opportunities for critical reflection about perceptions and beliefs regarding African American males. I also hope to encourage the readers of this text to make connections between their own biases and the critical role that those biases play in curricular and pedagogical decision making, cultural understanding, and how turmoil impacts the lives of African American males. I hope to urge teachers and other educators to align classroom instructional strategies and text selections to students' real-world experiences.

I will highlight theoretical frameworks that are central to improving the lives of Black male students and how those connect to their literacy development. I will introduce research that is pragmatic in nature and aimed at delving into the core of the being of Black males, and I will start dialogue about how to fully engage them in school-based literacy. I will make connections to the theories that undergird this work and discuss how and why African American students reject school as an institution and school-expected literacy, which often supports the dominant American culture. The social constructs of race, economics, and human socialization, all of which have an impact on the literacy of African American male students, will be examined through the lens of historical implications, school organizational structure, school educational and social practices, and their connection to Black male achievement, negative racist perceptions, and the literacy engagement practices of African American males.

The connections between themes of culture, race, gender, and pedagogy and literacy development are well documented by researchers like Tatum (2005), Lewis (2001), Smith and Wilhelm (2002), Newkirk (2002), Ladson-Billings (2006), and Lewis, Enciso, and Moje (2007). The research speaks not only of these themes' connections to literacy development itself but of the need to address the literacy and schooling of African American males through a sociocultural lens. Literacy is the most important skill a person needs to participate fully in a democracy, to make sense of the world, and to develop a positive identity about oneself. Recent events have proven that negative perceptions of African Americans persist and are supported, refined, and reinforced in schools, mostly through texts that are rooted in the dominant cultural context.

As a high school–age student, I would have been inspired had I been encouraged to read the likes of Dr. Frances Cress Welsing, Amiri Baraka, David Walker, Toni Morrison, James Baldwin, or Paulo Freire. I would have understood the pain, fear, and anger of the young man who tried to rob me had I been exposed to, or been encouraged to read, *The Wretched of the Earth* by Frantz Fanon, or if I knew what the psychology of oppression was.

This book is about Detroit, but it is also about Newark, Baltimore, South Central Los Angeles, Chicago, Miami, and Queens. It is also about Birmingham, Michigan; Berkeley, California; Oak Park, Illinois; and Madison, Wisconsin. It is about the schooling of Black children, with a focus on male students, in urban and suburban settings and how their education has led to what Carter G. Woodson (1933) called "the mis-education of the Negro." The topics addressed within this text represent a rebellion against the broader national view, that the dilemma that many African American males face is one that is a self-created, communal manifestation of the disassociation from school, society, and their values. This book challenges perceptions of Black males through an analysis of history, racism, and the construct of school, and it asserts that the institution of school is a machine to maintain the status quo of the dominant culture. The literacy development and schooling experiences of Black male students are highlighted using several metrics.

This text highlights the need for increased conversation and action about how to engage African American male students in school-based literacy. The need for these expanded conversations about how to center African American learners in the schooling context exists nationwide. There are a few premises that undergird the examination of race, socialization, and literacy that occurs throughout this book:

1. African American male students have lower graduation rates than their White counterparts.
2. African American students often reject schools and school-based literacy; however, standardized assessments measure their assimilation and acceptance of the very texts that they reject.

3. There is a connection between the literacy of African American males and their success in school and in life.
4. Schools, the U.S. government, and social organizations have not found the solutions to address the specific needs of African American males; in fact, these institutions have often represented or perpetuated the turmoil experienced in other parts of their lives.

This text sets the goal of helping teachers to help Black male students engage with literacy and encourages them to help their Black male students take possession of their minds by seeking to understand their lives and how they are socialized. When African American male students are encouraged to take back their minds, the space is created to construct a multifaceted approach that affirms their humanity. This book is rooted in real-world, historically documented educational and social occurrences, and it has the potential to open further dialogue and action around the issue of African American male literacy.

HOW THIS BOOK IS ORGANIZED

In Chapter 1, I give a brief history of schooling in the United States, particularly as it relates to African American children. I take readers through the history of segregation and desegregation, Jim Crow, and the implications for literacy and schooling for African American males. In Chapter 2, I discuss flow theory (Csikszentmihalyi) and how teachers can use that and other theoretical frameworks, such as social development theory (Vygotsky), social learning theory (Bandura), and the transactional theory of reading and writing (Rosenblatt). I encourage teachers to use their understandings of student agency and motivation, specific to African American students, and to think about how they can build appropriate literacy instruction to engage those students, while simultaneously using their understandings of the historical implications of schooling that were highlighted in the first chapter. In Chapter 3, I introduce the Black Male Literacy Paradigm, which provides educators with a framework to engage African American males in school-based literacy. Chapter 4 talks about the impact of culture and socialization on the engagement of African American males, and Chapter 5 takes those understandings and clarifies for educators the connection of culture and socialization to power, agency, and student identity. Part II of the text starts with Chapter 6, which introduces a study that sought to understand teachers' identities and how their personal identities influenced their perceptions of African American students. Chapter 6 also explores how teachers' perceptions of African American male students influence their text selections and instruction. Chapter 7 is robust with information regarding teachers' thoughts on how African American students connect to literacy, the themes that emerged during a study I conducted regarding what conditions need to be present to engage African American male students in school-based literacy, and the impact that trauma has on the lives of African American students. Chapter 8 encourages readers to reconceptualize their definitions of literacy and to think of literacy as a set of inter-connected processes, rather than just a cognitive one. Chapter 9 goes in-depth on a strategy that one teacher called the "give a damn" strategy. It encourages educators to help African American male students connect to the institution of school by genuinely caring about their well-being. Chapter 10 outlines how educators can transform schools to be environments that are free of racist behaviors and pay the education debt owed to African American children. The chapter also provides recommendations, implications, and challenges to engaging in this work.

HOW TO USE THIS BOOK

At the end of most of the chapters in this book are sections titled "What Teachers Can Do Right Now" and "What Administrators Can Do Right Now." These sections are meant to be used as recommendations for educators as they plan and build their instructional environments. While the content within the chapters has both theoretical and pragmatic foundations, the lists at the end of the chapters provide easy-to-implement, practical tools. Teachers can use the recommendations at the end of each chapter to plan lessons for their students, build equitable and identity-affirming classroom environments, and foster positive relationships with all students, particularly African American males. Administrators can use the recommendations at the end of each chapter to build schoolwide affinity groups, implement and change policy, and plan alongside their teaching staff. *A Walk in Their Kicks* helps educators be intentional about how to improve teaching and learning for African American males. This text uses several evidence-based theoretical foundations, real-world occurrences, and data from conversations with teachers to support its conclusions. Educators can use the content from the chapters and the recommendations that follow immediately after reading.

While this book can be used by K–12 teachers and administrators, it is extremely versatile and should also be used at the collegiate level. Instructors who teach undergraduate and graduate students will find that this book gives them a roadmap and a framework to prepare pre-service and practicing teachers to engage their African American students in school-based literacy. This book can be used at the elementary, secondary, and collegiate levels in the following types of courses and groups:

- K–12 professional development (teachers and administrators)
- Educator book clubs
- Superintendent preparation
- Professional Learning Communities (PLCs)
- Undergraduate methods courses
- Undergraduate reading courses
- Graduate courses for students obtaining their master's of arts in reading or education leadership, or their PhD/EdD in curriculum and instruction, leadership, or education policy studies
- Any graduate or undergraduate course that seeks to engage students in literacy, that helps teachers understand the unique history of African American students and the institution of school, and/or that puts the African American learner at the center of school-based policy, curriculum, and instructional practices

Part I

NOTES ON THE STATE OF

. . . DETROIT

. . . EDUCATION

. . . RACE

. . . SCHOOLING

. . . LITERACY

. . . SOCIALIZATION

. . . on the state of the west side

i was born into a ghetto haze
into the drunken rage
of a Black man full of angst
from being trapped in a cage
taught to be ashamed
in the presence of those who claim
to be superior over most
we were never taught how to boast
cuz DTE's energy is not kinetic
all i know is bad habits and bad credit
got a deep cut
and my heart needs some antiseptic
i wonder if 7 mile broke my smile
or if it was Daddy O'shea's bad ass sons
    running wild
always been a part of the rank and file
the proletariat
nothing you can scare me wit
i ride like i'm in the belmont stakes
with a chariot strapped to secretariat

ain't no one who you can pair me with
compare me with
anyone with a tongue and a frontal
    lobe
and i'll flow like 75% of this liquid
    stuff that makes up our globe

i was born into the
click-clack
of the rack of a 12 gauge
shot into the pitch-Black
night
on december 31
we knew to get back
into the house
as neighbors rang in a new 365
wasn't with noisemakers and other
    knick-knacks
i need a prophylactic
in my backpack

i carried a sack . . . lunch
and a hunger for something more
i heard thunder and saw lightning
on dry nights
no video recorders to play back
the ghetto olympic highlights
prayed for dry eyes
flew thru neighborhood school
like high kites
in march
the urban child's brain
shall be split into two hemispheres
one to stay parched
one for manual labor
unless the boy can read with speed
with a wit sharp like a saber
and can do math like a pharaoh
or claudius ptolemy
that was me
but i never claimed to have a halo
but i met a few angels
along the path
they blocked bullets, opened doors,
    guided my hands
as i perfected my craft
checked my swag
and Black dialect
at the front doors of
universities and city limits

but I opened up my soul
and buried it deep within it
I pivot between shards of darkness
and rays of light
never really taught how to fight
but intellect high like
stealth missions
i grew up in blood thirsty urban
    coliseums
cheered on by apparitions
got love with no conditions
work towards manumission
still fishin for my religion
no scales in my kitchen
i eat whales in small bites
great whites in big gulps
still looking for another human to trust
no fiction, no pulp
a dreamer committed to folly
looking for a state to reside
outside of this perpetual melancholy
on my knees
to pray
then crawled up out of the gutter
midday
with a dream
and a stick of butter

in my pocket

—aaron m. johnson

CHAPTER 1

His Story

The History of School and Literacy Development of African American Males

> One ever feels his twoness—an American, a Negro; two souls, two thoughts, two unreconciled strivings; two warring ideals in one dark body, whose dogged strength alone keeps it from being torn asunder.
>
> —W. E. B. Du Bois

It is important to first contextualize the history of public schooling as it relates to African Americans and literacy by providing a brief outline of the organizational structure of the institution of school and the purpose of education in the United States. This context is by no means meant to be a comprehensive account of race, schooling, or the confluence of the two. However, starting with the foundation of the institution of school will allow readers to understand how major historical events still impact the learning of African American students today. The institution of public schooling is rooted in the fabric of this country and was built to reinforce the ideals and the values of the newly formed republic. However, those ideals were never developed with Black people in mind (or even poor White people). The prevailing thought was that Africans did not have the capacity to learn; thus, they should not have the opportunity to learn. With this circular logic embedded into ideas about who schooling was for, African Americans were systematically subjugated to a life of illiteracy and the denial of access to schooling and life, liberty, and the pursuit of happiness. So, to understand African American students' relationship with the institution of school is to understand the purpose, beginning, and evolution of public schooling in this country. This book sets the stage for the idea of reconceptualizing schools to fit the needs of African American students.

Thomas Jefferson (1781), our nation's third president, introduced the idea of public schooling and set the background and template for it in his *Notes on the State of Virginia*. In this document, Jefferson outlined a process by which students would attend schools in their home communities, which would be divided into what he called "hundreds" (p. 203). A hundred was a county or area where the students resided that would dictate where they attended school. In these hundreds, young boys (girls were not included) would attend schools free of charge for 3 years, after which their families would decide whether or not to continue their schooling privately. Jefferson (1781) stated:

> Of the boys thus sent in any one year, trial is to be made at the grammar schools one or two years, and the best genius of the whole selected, and continued six years, and the residue dismissed. By this means twenty of the best geniuses will be raked from the rubbish annually, and be instructed, at the public expense, so far as the grammar schools go. (p. 156)

Not only does Jefferson mention the process for the beginning of public education throughout the document, but he posits that the purpose of education is to

> teach them how to work out their own greatest happiness, by showing them that it does not depend on the condition of life in which chance has placed them, but is always the result of a good conscience, good health, occupation, and freedom in all just pursuits. (p. 157)

In Jefferson's (1781) document, he goes on to state that education in reading, writing, and arithmetic is a means to "cure idle minds" and that everyone should be literate in order to participate in the democratic process (pp. 158–159). During Jefferson's era, the United States, a newly formed and recently liberated nation, was still fighting against the rule and influence of Great Britain. One lingering British influence on American schooling was the notion that education should serve as a means to develop character and morality in students from the perspective of the Bible. From an educational perspective, Jefferson felt that instruction in the Bible and other religious doctrine would be ill-placed in his plan for schooling and that children were not mature enough to grasp the complexity of religious thought. His outline for schooling included funding for boys whose families could not pay as well as instruction in Greek, Latin, mathematics, history, and reading as a means to prepare students for study at institutions of higher learning. Jefferson also proposed a constitutional amendment stating that education should be public and supported and funded by the government.

As Jefferson suggested, after the boys who showed intellectual promise and genius were identified, "the rubbish" should be raked away. By introducing this thought, he set the stage for the philosophy of education to support a meritocracy within the institution, a practice that we continue today. For the sake of analysis, it is necessary to dwell on this idea of human beings regarded as rubbish for a moment. First, the obvious members of this group of human beings regarded as "rubbish" were Black people (most of whom were enslaved at the time) and women of all backgrounds, since they were excluded from Jefferson's vision. In addition, poor White people or other White families without any social power, or those who were not landowners, were included only in the sense that, if the student came from a poor family, he had to show intellectual promise or genius (how this was determined is unknown) to be considered for further inclusion in Jefferson's dream for public schooling. Even among those included in Jefferson's vision for public schooling, it was unclear how Jefferson planned to identify the boys with intellectual promise and genius; thus, the groundwork was laid for a system of arbitrary assignment of student achievement. Our contemporary measures for identifying students' future performance start prior to elementary school. Schools begin to sort and select students as early as preschool by using standardized testing, teacher recommendations, and classroom assignments. Students are stratified into in-class reading and math groups, which often divide along racial lines. There are also cases where students in the 3rd, 4th, and 5th grades are sent to classes other than that of their main teacher to receive more rigorous instruction. If one were to peek into those so-called advanced classes, one would find a preponderance of White males assigned to them. At the middle school and high school levels, honors and advanced placement classes are often used to achieve Jefferson's goal of finding intellectual promise and raking the rubbish away.

To further separate African American students and seal their academic fates, schools have disproportionately identified students, particularly African American boys, for special education services as early as 3rd grade. Students' reading performance on standardized reading assessments or recommendations given by their teachers (I will speak about teachers' involvement in students' disconnect from school in subsequent chapters) account for a large part of how African American students are identified for special education or remedial classes. Schools and districts rarely look at how their institutional practices often serve as barriers between African American students and literacy development.

The current structure and foundation of public schooling followed the model outlined by Jefferson (1781), which made a few things clear: (1) Public schools were meant only for White male students; (2) even for White male students, only the top percentile would be identified for further schooling; and (3) instruction was to be used to support reading, mathematics, and philosophy, all ideals that would be taught from the European perspective (Johnson, 2016). This point is important to understand as it supports the premise of this text.

Jefferson's outline for schooling has direct connections to modern-day organizational structures for public schooling. Within schools' organizational structures, the teacher is the central figure and purveyor of knowledge, while children are expected to receive instruction. However, contemporary research confirms that children learn best when they are allowed to explore, analyze, and connect with new knowledge that builds on their cultural and academic schemas. Furthermore, since schools still view reading, science, and mathematics as the essential content areas, as Jefferson did, what students are expected to know and be able to do is determined by state and local boards of education, administrators, and teachers. As a result of the beliefs about what content students should know, the canon of course content that is taught, as well as the physical plant of schools themselves, are built to support the antiquated organizational and instructional structure. Thus, when schools continue to apply antiquated methods of instruction, frequently the most vulnerable, marginalized, and disenfranchised students within that structure are more likely to fail. The implication for Black children, particularly Black boys, is that they are expected to learn in inequitable school structures that were not built for them to be successful in the first place. It is critical that educators and administrators view the school as a place where the voices of Black male students are given privilege.

When considering how justice in American public education could be made manifest, two prominent education scholars come to mind, John Dewey and Horace Mann Bond. Dewey, who wrote *Moral Principles in Education* (1909) and *Democracy and Education* (1916) and set the foundation for contemporary education philosophy, spoke about issues of equity, effective instructional practices, and school organizational structure. Bond, who wrote *The Education of the Negro in the American Social Order* (1934/1966), spoke about the need to consider the historical implications and unique academic needs of African American students when seeking to improve the institution of school. Dewey (1909, 1916) and Bond (1934/1966) agreed with Jefferson that knowledge of history, mathematics, science, and reading were more important than the teaching of character and morality. Accordingly, the modern school context was built on the idea that development of content knowledge, intellectual thought, and new ideas, rather than religious rhetoric, is the purpose of education.

Bond (1934/1966), however, disagreed with Jefferson about who the benefactors of a public education should be and how those parties should benefit. Again, Jefferson (1781) asserted that boys (girls were not mentioned) should be the beneficiaries of public education—more specifically, boys who "showed intellectual promise" or "genius." Moreover, since the White economic elite in Jefferson's era not only built, supported, and expanded the institution of chattel slavery (Jefferson himself was a slaveowner), we can reasonably and confidently assume that Jefferson's vision for public schooling did not include enslaved Africans. Bond (1934/1966) provided critical analysis of Jefferson's vision when he wrote about African American children being the beneficiaries of education, just as their White counterparts were proposed to be. He wrote:

> It is the opinion of the writer that there is not a great difference between the activities which are best suited to translating our common ideals into teachable form, where Negro and White children are concerned. Most of the different "needs" are those of economic dissimilarities, and not of race. The activity curriculum for the attainment of health, the fundamental processes, occupational efficiency, worthy home membership, and other objectives would hardly be different for the children of Negro tenants on Southern cotton farms. (p. 9)

Bond went on to advocate that African American children be taught the same things as White children, and he fought against the opinion of his time that African American children were incapable of learning certain subject matter.

As African Americans were seeking to enhance their connection to literacy during the time of slavery and during and after the Reconstruction Era (1865–1877), they were continually denied participation and access to democracy and the democratic process. American democracy is built upon the notion that the citizens of this country can read, understand, and analyze their rights, all set forth in the Constitution of the United States. Without being able to read and understand the Constitution, one cannot fully grasp one's place in society. It is my belief that Jefferson knew this, and he proposed the institution of public school (which would grant the right to literacy only to White males) to reinforce the ideals that the Constitution outlined and supported.

Dewey (1956) also believed that the institution of school was strengthened by the fact that school set the foundation for democracy. He stated, "All that society has accomplished for itself is put through the agency of school" (p. 7). When one then contemplates the purpose of school, it can be further argued that education sets the foundation for members of society to participate in the democratic process. Giving students the opportunity for further study in math, science, and reading gives them the background to be able to create, innovate, and develop and analyze philosophy. With this in mind, it then becomes even more necessary to support students in gaining a proper foundation in the development of literacy. If we believe the premise that a proper education prepares students to participate in the American democratic process, then we have to understand that the disenfranchisement of African American students from the institution of public school also represents a disenfranchisement from participating in the American democratic process, of which literacy is an essential component. Literacy is important because one's understanding of one's rights is dependent upon it, and the process of building literacy is the foundation upon which all other disciplines are built. Thus, we would have to conclude that literacy is a civil right and that by not engaging students in literacy to fully participate in the democratic process, we are, in fact, denying them their civil rights.

SEGREGATION, JIM CROW, AND AFRICAN AMERICAN ACADEMIC ACHIEVEMENT

The development of African American literacy that began during the time of slavery continued during the Reconstruction Era after the Civil War. Bond (1934/1966) estimated that between the years of 1870 and 1920, the percentage of African American people who were of school age and actually attended school rose from 9.2% to 54%. Although slavery was outlawed in 1865 with the passing of the 13th Amendment to the Constitution, many southern states enacted a series of laws dubbed Black Codes (Johnson, 2016), a set of oppressive laws that sought to keep African American people in a subservient status. The oppressive laws of the South and the North made it even more necessary for African American people to develop literacy skills to participate in the democracy to which they were given legal rights.

In 1896, the landmark U.S. Supreme Court decision *Plessy v. Ferguson* laid the legal foundation for supporting the Black Codes and the Jim Crow Era's nefarious "separate but equal" doctrine. *Plessy v. Ferguson* set the stage for legalized segregation across the country. In 1892, Homer Plessy and a group of activists in the state of Louisiana decided that they would intentionally violate the state's law requiring segregation on trains. Plessy, a member of New Orleans' French-speaking Creole community who described himself as having 1/8th African heritage, was considered to be "colored" in the state of Louisiana at the time. After sitting in a rail car marked for Whites only and refusing to move, he was arrested and arraigned at a criminal court in New Orleans before Judge John Ferguson. Ferguson and the Louisiana Supreme Court ruled that no laws had been broken and that rail companies could maintain separate rail cars for Black and White citizens. The ruling was challenged and it was eventually heard before the U.S. Supreme Court.

Plessy's lawyers argued that the Thirteenth and Fourteenth amendments of the Constitution were being violated on the basis that segregation on rail cars was continuing to perpetuate a badge of servitude, much like the institution of slavery, and that Black citizens were not being afforded the same rights given to White citizens. The Supreme Court ruled that states could racially segregate rail cars for intrastate travel as long as Black citizens were provided accommodations that were equal to those of Whites. The ruling in the *Plessy v. Ferguson* case laid the legal groundwork for the expansion of segregation in other public facilities, including schools.

For instance, in 1899, the Supreme Court ruled in *Cumming v. Richmond County Board of Education* that school districts could maintain separate school facilities for White and Black citizens and that the school district was not financially responsible for providing equal and separate facilities. The plaintiffs of the case (African American citizens of Richmond County, Georgia) maintained that because citizens were taxed irrespective of their race, their tax dollars should be used to maintain proper high school facilities for their children, just like those provided for White students who were of high school age. The Supreme Court supported the lower district court's decision to support the ruling of the Richmond County school board, which claimed that it could not financially support a high school for White students, a primary school for about 300 African American students, and the proposed new high school for African American students (*Cumming v. Richmond County Board of Education*, 175 U.S. 528, 1899). The school board agreed to maintain the primary school facility for African American students but said that if the African American parents wanted their high school–age students to continue receiving instruction, they should enroll them in private schools.

Those who supported the practice of "separate but equal" never engaged in conversation about how to define it. Thus, because of the ambiguous meaning of the word *equal*, the application and interpretation of several federal rulings were left up to local and state governments. In public spaces across the North and the South, separate never meant equal, even after the practice of "separate but equal" was outlawed with the passage of the Civil Rights Act of 1964.

SCHOOL DESEGREGATION

With regard to education, the legal precedent that was set with the *Plessy v. Ferguson* ruling meant that states could set up a system where African American students would not be allowed to attend the same schools as their White counterparts. As a result, many aspects of American social and public life, particularly in the Southern states, were segregated. African American children were forced to attend schools that were in disrepair and lacked basic supplies and books, while many White students attended schools that provided them access to much more. Although segregation in schools was a main factor in the disconnect between school and academic endeavors and African American people, African Americans also faced the threat of legalized terrorism on a daily basis. Many would like to reduce the terrorism that African American people faced to the actions of racist groups such as the Ku Klux Klan; however, terrorism was carried out by everyday people, every day. They faced social, economic, psychological, and physical terrorism, as well as the threat of death, if they committed even the slightest transgression against the racist Black Codes and Jim Crow laws—and children were no exception.

As the movement for integration between Blacks and Whites was brought forward by the idea that schools should be integrated first, it had implications for the broader societal context and the growing movement for civil rights. Even if racist Southerners could not or would not articulate it, they inherently knew that the foundation for society and socialization is built through the institution of school. Federal and state dollars were being used to perpetuate racist beliefs; thus, school integration was about more than just equal access and opportunity. It was about the unequal access to sociopolitical power for Black students and the federal government's support of such inequality, which was carried out by local governments and school boards.

In 1954, the U.S. Supreme Court ruled in the case of *Brown v. Board of Education of Topeka*. Thurgood Marshall, who would later become the first African American to sit on the Supreme Court, was a lawyer arguing on behalf of *Brown* and the other petitioners. Although the *Brown* case was argued on its own merits, it was also a collection of consolidated cases from around the country and highlighted the vastness of segregation in the South and North. The Supreme Court ruled that "segregation of children in public schools solely on the basis of race deprives children of the minority group of equal educational opportunities, even though the physical facilities and other 'tangible' factors may be equal" (*Brown v. Board of Education*, 1954, p. 483). The Supreme Court took into consideration the fact that Black people had faced many academic obstacles during and after their emancipation from slavery. Furthermore, in the court ruling, the justices specifically mentioned the importance of literacy among African American students.

The language from the Fourteenth Amendment played a significant role in the *Brown* decision and many other key civil rights legal victories. The Fourteenth Amendment states:

> No state shall make or enforce any law which shall abridge the privileges or immunities of citizens of the United States; nor shall any state deprive any person of life, liberty, or property, without due process of law; nor deny to any person within its jurisdiction the equal protection of the laws. (U.S. Constitution, Amend XIV, §1)

In the ruling, the justices asserted that "the history of the Fourteenth Amendment [was] inconclusive as to its intended effect on public education," citing then-existing practices of racial segregation as well as the widely divergent views surrounding the scope of the amendment from both proponents and opponents at the time of its ratification. The justices wrote that "an additional reason for the inconclusive nature of the Amendment's history, with respect to segregated schools, [was] the status of public education at that time":

> In the South, the movement toward free common schools, supported by general taxation, had not yet taken hold. Education of White children was largely in the hands of private groups. Education of Negroes was almost nonexistent, and practically all of the race were illiterate. In fact, any education of Negroes was forbidden by law in some states. (pp. 489–490)

Research in the early 20th century by pioneering African American scholar Carter G. Woodson, *The Mis-Education of the Negro* (1933), provided evidence to help make the point that literacy was developing for African American in the years after the Civil War, in spite of the barriers presented by laws designed to prevent African Americans from being literate. Woodson estimated that by the end of the 19th century, about 15–20% of African Americans could read. A more-recent study by Anderson (1988) estimated that by 1900, the percentage of literate African Americans was about 20–30%. While some might not consider these percentages of African American literacy to be significant, when one considers that reading was illegal in many states for African Americans 20–30 years prior, this represents monumental growth in a system that prevented them from being literate in the first place.

In the Brown decision, the court made explicit reference to the considerable change that had taken place in American education in the first half of the 20th century, which made providing equal access all the more important:

> Today, education is perhaps the most important function of state and local governments. . . . In these days, it is doubtful that any child may reasonably be expected to succeed in life if he is denied the opportunity of an education. Such an opportunity, where the state has undertaken to provide it, is a right which must be made available to all on equal terms.
>
> We come then to the question presented: Does segregation of children in public schools solely on the basis of race, even though the physical facilities and other "tangible" factors may be equal, deprive the children of the minority group of equal educational opportunities? We believe that it does. (p. 493)

The *Brown* ruling overruled the 1896 *Plessy* ruling (and others) and put an end to lawful segregation in education. Still, it took several decades for this change to be accepted, adopted, and supported; during that time, the terrorizing of Black children continued, with school-age children being the main targets.

The *Brown v. Board of Education* decision forced school districts to develop desegregation plans that involved eliminating one-race schools or schools that were segregated by rule of law. One such school district that insisted upon operating single-race schools was the Charlotte-Mecklenberg school district in North Carolina. The district was found to be out of compliance with federal law as it had not developed an acceptable plan that successfully created non-one-race schools (*Swann v. Charlotte Mecklenberg*, 402 U.S. 1, 1971). To comply with this order, the Charlotte-Mecklenberg schools enacted a plan to transport students who lived in all-Black neighborhoods to schools that had large White populations. Charlotte-Mecklenberg's "Finger Plan," named after Dr. John Finger, the Supreme Court–appointed expert sent to help the district develop a desegregation plan, bussed students from all-Black neighborhoods to all-White schools as a solution to desegregate the schools.

THE GREAT MIGRATION

Before and during the time of the *Brown v. Board of Education* ruling, many African American families were fleeing the South to pursue opportunities in the northern cities. Families fled to escape poverty and the daily terrorism that they faced as a result of the the Black Codes and the oppressive laws and practices of the Jim Crow South. Black people also moved to the North for access to better education for their children. The Great Migration started around 1910 and continued through the 1970s (History.com, 2018). While the promise of better-paying jobs and better opportunities for schooling were some of the key factors that helped many families decide to move during the migration, others were seeking refuge from the many dangers that African American men, women, and children faced in the southern states. Many northern and western urban metropolises and metropolitan areas—including Detroit, Chicago, New York, Los Angeles, Newark, Pittsburgh, Oakland, and Boston—experienced a surge in their African American populations during this time.

With the migration to the North and to the West, many African American children who had experienced interrupted schooling, schools with limited resources, and the promise of separate but equal facilities faced new challenges. African American children who fled to the North still faced some of the same inequities they had faced in their schools in the South. However, in the North, African American students were farther away from their support base of Historically Black Colleges and Universities that were mainly based in the South. The Historically Black Colleges and Universities, many of which were created during Reconstruction, understood and took into account the fact that African American children had received inadequate education, and they worked to help students acquire a secondary and postsecondary education. Additionally, as more southern Blacks migrated north, many White northerners sought refuge from the influx of Black people moving into the cities by moving out to surrounding suburbs and establishing suburban school districts. This suburbanization created all-White communities with school districts that were also virtually all White, which continued and expanded the segregation of schools and communities.

There were a number of implications of the *Brown v. Board of Education* ruling. One implication was that the federal government began to force schools and other public institutions to desegregate their facilities. In the South, Army and National Guard troops had escorted African American students into previously all-White schools to protect them from violence and ensure that students were permitted to enter the buildings (although troops could not enforce equitable access to content and literacy for African American students). Many courageous young girls and boys faced the vitriol and hate of peers, parents, teachers, politicians, and administrators. The most infamous of such clashes occurred in Virginia and Little Rock, Arkansas, immediately after *Brown*.

The *Brown* ruling had different implications in northern cities like Detroit, where a lawsuit challenging school segregation would go on to have a national impact. As school districts around the country were forced to comply with the federal school desegregation mandate, many districts and families disagreed with how desegregation plans should be carried out. In 1970, the Detroit Board of Education sought to implement a desegregation plan that would meet the mandate of the federal government. Before the desegregation plan could be implemented, the Michigan state legislature enacted Public Act 48, which dismissed the Detroit Board of Education plan and gave control over school districts to local neighborhoods.

Vera Bradley, an African American woman who had two sons enrolled in Detroit Public Schools at the time and who believed that her children were victims of an inferior education, contracted the services of the Detroit branch of the NAACP. In 1970, Bradley, along with other families and the NAACP, sued Michigan Governor William Milliken, the Detroit Board of Education, the Detroit superintendent of public schools, and State Superintendent John Porter for participating in de jure segregation. De jure segregation is the legal segregation of groups in society, usually by race or religion. At the time, the Detroit metropolitan area and Detroit Public Schools had been regarded as the most segregated region and school district in the country (Freeman, 2011). In 1970, the case was heard by the U.S. Federal District Court, which ruled that the state of Michigan's actions through Public Act 48 were unconstitutional and that the Detroit Public Schools' original plan of desegregating the schools by including 53 of 85 surrounding suburban school districts in its desegregation plan should be enacted (Freeman, 2011; Meinke, 2011; *Milliken v. Bradley*, 418 U.S. 717, 1974).

Milliken et al. v. Bradley et al. reached the U.S. Supreme Court in 1974. The court ruled that although Detroit Public Schools was found guilty of practicing de jure segregation in its public schools, the surrounding suburban school districts could not be included in the desegregation plan of Detroit Public Schools because none of the 85 surrounding districts had been charged or found in violation of any federal law. Therefore, Detroit Public Schools had to implement a desegregation plan that involved only schools within the district. Some argued that there would be no way to desegregate the schools because of the high concentration of African American citizens who lived within the city boundaries and the high concentration of White citizens living in the surrounding suburbs. Olzak, Shanahan, and West (1994) argued that the Supreme Court's actions in the *Milliken* case gave voice to opponents of busing and put an end to many school desegregation plans nationwide.

SCHOOL BUSING

It is safe to characterize those who opposed the busing of students across city and neighborhood boundaries as being opposed to desegregation efforts and the mandate from the federal government (Johnson, 2016). The campaign against busing and integration had two major elements that were underlying causes of opposition during the time of the movement. The first element of the anti-busing and anti-desegregation movement was that, in regions like the Detroit metro area, many African American citizens lived within the city limits, and intra-district busing did not present a solution to the problem of segregation across municipalities and districts.

Most school districts across the country required students to live within the boundaries of the city or municipality or within the boundaries of the school district, which are often concurrent. The movement toward suburbanization provided cover for claims that the districts had purposefully excluded Black students. Furthermore, researchers of school desegregation contend that the *Milliken v. Bradley* case put an end to federal desegregation lawsuits in the North while protests by desegregation opponents increased (Olzak, Shanahan, & West, 1994; Welch & Light, 1987). In areas like Detroit, where residential areas were segregated along racial and socioeconomic lines, both African American and White students were consigned to attend racially segregated schools (Olzak, Shanahan, & West, 1994).

The second major element in the matter of the opposition to school desegregation dealt directly with the issue of race. A study conducted by Olzak, Shanahan, and West (1994) found that those who opposed desegregation felt a sense of competition with African Americans. Their study used a definition from Blalock (1967) that defined competition as "a situation where groups or individuals are striving for the same limited resources" (Blalock, 1967, p. 73; Olzak, Shanahan, & West, 1994, p. 201). James (1989) contended that the competition between ethnic groups was increasing immediately post-*Brown* to 1977 (the conclusion of the *Miliken v. Bradley* case) while desegregation mandates were being reinforced and residential areas were growing more integrated. As more African American families acquired the financial resources to be able to move into suburban areas, White citizens felt that they would have to compete against these newcomers for educational, political, and social resources (James, 1989; Olzak, Shanahan, & West, 1994). Olzak, Shanahan, and West (1994) asserted: "The mechanism that underlies racial conflict involves perceived and actual threats to Whites' dominance over African Americans" (p. 232). Hence, opponents of desegregation did not want to relinquish the social and political power afforded to their children and their communities, and they used the exclusion of African American students from an equitable education as the major weapon in this fight.

Opposition to the integration of schools further marginalized African American students and served as a barrier to their development of in-school literacy practices. Schools' expectations of student literacy inherently involve an understanding and acceptance of the language of the dominant culture and the mores of school, and the school environment itself is a microcosm of the broader American cultural context. Because several researchers, including Tatum (2005), Lewis (2001), Ogbu (1991), and Steele (1992), have made reference to this notion of dominant culture, it is important to define it with reference to how it may affect how African American students connect to school-expected literacy.

The dominant culture can be defined as the collective ideas, language, actions, notions of power, social codes, and values subscribed to by the majority of Americans. It can be argued that African American male students reject school-expected literacy not because they dis-identify with school but because school texts represent the values of the dominant culture, which are different from or devalue their own. Delpit (1996) asserted that, given the opportunity and guidance by their teachers, students can learn to morph their identities to connect to in-school literacy even when that literacy represents the values of the dominant culture.

Along with the historical, systematic denial of access to school, African American students have also been denied access to the cultural mores, values, and language of the dominant culture, which were and still are expected in school literacy. Furthermore, students have lacked access to the diversity of experiences with other students, teachers, and thought processes that they would have been privy to through full school integration. Thus, African American students have continued to find themselves at a disadvantage when it comes to trying to connect with expected in-school literacy.

The history of schooling in the United States and its implications for African American people is much more vast than what is accounted for here; however, it was necessary to provide a brief background to set the context for public schooling for African American children today. Even when it was against the law to teach Black people how to read or engage them in any type of academic pursuit, African American people found ways to practice literacy in many other forms. Through a rich tradition of oral storytelling, Black people learned about their heritage and ancestry, heard stories of triumph and freedom, and learned how to develop and decipher coded language. Black people also communicated with one another through music and biblical teachings. This background is important to dispel the myth that African American people do not or have not participated in literacy events.

Knowing that there has been an ongoing marginalization of African American literacy practices, it is easy to see how the institution of school has historically and systematically devalued African American people's literacy development and participation in literacy events. As a result of African American children being disenfranchised from the institution of school, they have been disconnected from what is traditionally expected in terms of school-based literacy and thus disconnected from the institution of school itself.

WHAT CAN TEACHERS DO RIGHT NOW?

- Engage in research regarding the history of African American people in the United States (see references to access relevant research).
- Build lesson plans that address African American students' social and cultural history.
- Challenge the resources provided if they do not meet the needs of all students.
- Engage in authentic activities that seek to get to know the perspectives of students of color.
- Form book clubs with other teachers to engage in inquiry about the identities of African American children and the relationship to schooling. Some possible books to read include the following:
  » *Teaching Reading to Black Adolescent Males*—Alfred Tatum
  » *Other People's Children*—Lisa Delpit
  » *Between the World and Me*—Ta-Nehisi Coates
- Track classroom data that look at how many times children of color are referred to the office for minor offenses compared to their White peers.
- Use restorative and affirming language in classrooms.

WHAT CAN ADMINISTRATORS DO RIGHT NOW?

- Help students of color (particularly Black males) build schoolwide affinity groups.
- Intentionally connect students of color in need of more supports with teachers who have a proven track record of success in creating relationships with African American children.
- Analyze data—be sure that teachers and all stakeholders have a clear picture of how students are performing in their schools, districts, and states.
- Intentionally choose Black male students to serve in leadership roles.
- Analyze the history of African Americans in school and promote equity *and* equality. Understand that fair is *not* always equal.
- Engage parents in conversations about their children's experiences in school.
- Look at the behaviors of African American students as being shaped by ongoing racism and oppression rather than strictly as deviations from a White dominant cultural norm. Discipline students according to an improved understanding.
- Be honest and open about the state of your school, and acknowledge the need for change, particularly with regard to the literacy of Black males.

CHAPTER 2

Hustle and Flow

Student Literacy, Flow, Agency, and Motivation

The best moments in our lives are not the passive, receptive, relaxing times. . . . The moments usually occur when a person's body or mind is stretched to its limits in a voluntary effort to accomplish something difficult and worthwhile.

—Mihaly Csikszentmihalyi

FLOW THEORY

As with any other process in which we human beings spend our time, when we engage in literacy events, we need to experience a level of enjoyment that allows us to escape the activities occurring around us. The same holds true for the process of learning. The concept of flow was first recognized and documented by Mihaly Csikszentmihalyi in the 1960s. He expanded upon it during the 1970s and 1980s, and his theory reached its culmination in his book *Flow* in 1990. Flow theory puts a name to the phenomenon that human beings experience as they look for enjoyment in their work or play. Individuals experiencing flow become so engrossed in the activity in which they are engaging that they may lose awareness of what is happening around them. Csikszentmihalyi (1990) found that artists, poets, researchers, and others who were working on projects often ignored their physiological needs as they participated in their work.

With regard to literacy, Smith and Wilhelm (2002) said that in order for boys to connect to in-school literacy, they need to experience flow. Smith and Wilhelm (2002) and Tatum (2005) asserted that boys should be given opportunities to connect their out-of-school flow experiences to their in-school literacy in order to find enjoyment in reading. Students' flow experiences are especially relevant to their agency in that, in order for one to be motivated to participate in an activity, one has to recognize the activity's relevance, one has to experience enjoyment while participating in the activity, and one has to believe that success can be achieved by participating. The concept of helping students experience flow and connect their flow experiences to in-school literacy should be central to how teachers plan instruction for their students. This has particular importance for helping African American students to connect out-of-school literacy to in-school literacy.

Literacy interventions that incorporate the social component of learning, outlined by Vygotsky (1978) and Bandura (2001), allow students to experience flow. These interventions have the ability to respond to students' sociocultural needs as outlined by Tatum (2005) and Kucer (2009) and teach students how to assert their identities and allow those identities to become malleable between cultural spaces as outlined by Gee (2001) and Lewis et al. (2007). The idea of how students' identities impact their connection to school-expected literacy will be explored later in this book. The hope is that this book will encourage teachers to engage in conversations that help them recognize African American boys' flow experiences and use their knowledge of their students' experiences to help with literacy intervention planning.

LEARNING AND LITERACY AS SOCIAL CONSTRUCTS

Before speaking directly to the achievement of African American students and its relationship to literacy development, it is necessary to provide a definition of learning. For our purposes in this book, I am using Merriam-Webster's definition of *learning*: "the activity or process of gaining knowledge or skill by studying, practicing, being taught, or experiencing something: the activity of someone who learns" ("Learning," n.d.).

For many years, learning was approached from a behavioral perspective. Behavioral theorists and researchers like Skinner and Pavlov believed that learning occurred when a stimulus was applied to a being, whether human or animal, and the being changed its behavior as a result. The behavioral perspective of learning stands in opposition to the idea of learning as a social construct. The behavioral perspective represents a fixed perspective about learning and tries to measure it quantitatively. The social construction of learning was aptly defined by Vygtosky (1978) and expanded on by Bandura (2001). Vygotsky and Bandura agreed that learning occurs socially as human beings interact with one another, learn from one another, and adjust their perspectives as a result of their interactions. This conceptualization of learning as being constructed socially supports the notion that, just as it is difficult to quantify human experiences such as pain or fear, it is equally difficult to quantify how much learning has occurred within a given period of time.

Educational theorists like Koffka (1935), Vygotsky (1978), and Bandura (2001) theorized that the process of learning began with, and was connected to, human social development. Koffka (1935) developed the gestalt theory based on his work in psychology. Koffka's theory supported the notion that learning occurs neither before development nor simultaneously with development. Instead, he theorized that learning was a subset of development and maturation, and that humans learn naturally as a result of proceeding through the maturation process (Koffka, 1935; Vygotsky, 1978). The core of gestalt theory claimed that the knowledge of one fact led to the inevitable knowledge of many facts. Thus, Koffka theorized that when humans showed the capacity to know and understand information pertaining to a particular intellectual pursuit, that capacity could be used to understand several other funds of knowledge. Koffka's theory suggests that the immersion of teachers in dialogue that is designed to help them intentionally develop and build knowledge and ways of thinking to connect students' out-of-school literacy practices to expected in-school literacy can improve students' overall schooling experiences. If gestalt theory can be used to explain literacy and its relationship to overall student achievement, then one might support the immersion of teachers in evidence-based literacy interventions using a sociocultural paradigm as one of several viable components of a theoretical framework for improving African American male students' achievement and literacy.

Vygotsky (1978) introduced social development theory and the zone of proximal development as concepts. Social development theory proposed that learning and development were not mutually exclusive as had been previously theorized. The prior theoretical foundations of behavioral theorists like Piaget and Binet posited that learning came after the developmental maturation processes and that they were not connected. Vygotsky believed that development, maturation, and learning occurred simultaneously. Vygotsky's (1978) *Mind in Society* introduced the zone of proximal development, or ZPD, which expanded on his framing of the processes as interconnected. He proposed that in order for humans to develop, mature, and learn, they had to do so in social situations, have exposure to more knowledgeable others, be challenged within their expected trajectory of acquirable knowledge, and allow their perspectives to be changed based on new information (Vygotsky, 1978, pp. 84–90).

Bandura (2001) introduced thoughts about cognition, human interaction, and agency with regard to learning and literacy development in his work on social cognitive theory. He explained how and why students learn well in a group or setting and why a learner's agency is an important component of learning, cognition, and motivation. Bandura (2001) described agency as the intentionality of an agent, or person, and their involvement in a specific act. His work made a case for predicting human behavior through the use of a psychological framework that addresses sociocultural needs. When educators can employ social development and social cognitive theory in concert with one another, then they can increase their ability to understand how to build instruction that connects students to repositories of motivation through the social aspect of learning.

Vygotsky's and Bandura's work on social development theory and social cognitive theory, respectively, supports the notion that literacy is a social activity and that literacy development is socioculturally based. When educators use these theories as part of an overall framework that is designed to improve schools for African American students, they should not only seek to improve students' agency to engage in school, they should also seek to bring about change in the overall institution of school so that it responds to the cultural, language, and academic needs that are often unique to African American students (Johnson, 2016).

The connection between the sociocultural nature of literacy in Vygotsky's and Bandura's theories lies at the center of how these researchers assert that learning is constructed. Both Bandura and Vygotsky agree that learning is socially based and that learning is constructed through dialogue, human interaction, and reflection upon one's own ideas as new ideas are introduced (Vygotsky, 1978). As Lewis (2001) proved in her study with 5th-grade students who participated in a book club, and as Kucer (2009) posited in his model for literacy development, literacy is constructed in much the same way. Lewis's study documented the importance of positive interaction among peers, social power, and student dialogue about texts to help students develop literacy. She also documented that when social components were missing, students either rejected texts or chose not to actively participate (Lewis, 2001). Students' rejection of literature and literacy events in Lewis's study was directly linked to Bandura's (2001) thoughts on student agency and motivation.

In 2016, I used the work of Vygotsky, Bandura, and Lewis to design a study to engage teachers in professional development that immersed them in inquiry about their perceptions, their background knowledge of their students, and their feelings about the instructional practices that they used to build literacy. As a key component of the inquiry into teachers' instructional practices, participants were asked why they thought African American male students rejected school as an institution generally, and school-based literacy specifically. The literature review and the findings from the study documented that African American male students are more apt to engage in school and in school-expected literacy when they have connections to their teachers, school, and school-related texts; when their teachers have recent and relevant professional development aimed at understanding their students' literacy needs; when their teachers have expansive definitions of what literacy is; and when their teachers have engaged in dialogue and inquiry that improved their understanding of African American students' literacy practices.

These findings supported the notion that African American male students should be engaged in school-based literacy by educators who seek to understand their lives, their culture, and language, and who match texts to students' interests. The research also led to the development of the Black Male Literacy Paradigm and helped broader dialogue among the study participants to emerge about literacy and schooling for African American male students. What I also found in my research was that specific conceptual frameworks about how to engage African American males in school-based literacy were rare.

Studies documented in Kucer (2009), which included his model of literacy, and Lewis (2001), which asserted that literacy is a social act, examined the social aspects of literacy development by using theoretical perspectives. In Kucer's (2009) model, literacy events transcend the boundaries of the cognitive, linguistic, sociocultural, and developmental aspects of learning. Viewing literacy as transcending sociocultural parameters supports the idea that literacy development does not occur in a vacuum. Thus, when models emerge that account for social and cognitive interactions between human beings, they reflect the reality of this development. The research supports the notion that cognition is developed through experience, language is developed through mimicry, refinement of vocabulary is developed through observation, interaction with other human beings is ongoing, and development progresses with age, maturation, and experience (Bandura, 2001; Koffka, 1935; Kucer, 2009; Vygotsky, 1978).

When delving deeper into frameworks such as Bandura's social cognitive theory, we are able to juxtapose it with processes of how students develop literacy and engage in literacy events. When we use frameworks aimed at helping us understand how students develop literacy, we can also understand how to motivate students. When we examine motivation for its connection to sociocultural factors affecting the agency of a student, we may hypothesize that there is a direct or significant effect. Bandura (2001) stated that humans set personal goals, and if in the course of pursuing those goals, they feel that they are being "exploited, coerced, disrespected, or manipulated, they respond apathetically, oppositionally, or hostilely" (p. 5). Thus, students must feel that texts are relevant to their lives and that their home or primary culture is valued at school and in the classroom. If we believe in the idea that human beings must experience flow in order to be completely engaged in an activity, then the same belief should apply to students' participation in in-school and out-of-school literacy events, and educators should engage in inquiry about how we aid students in having those experiences.

Establishing literacy as a social act is especially salient for African American students. Literacy and literacy events are developed in sociocultural contexts—they require access to language, common experiences, and ways of knowing, and they must allow students to experience flow. Chapter 1 established that the denial of access to literacy for African Americans throughout American history has had contemporary implications. Along with the denial of access to literacy itself, African American people have faced the denial of access to many of the social experiences that make up the so-called American experience that is so often found in texts and that school institutions expect students to know and understand. Without foundational knowledge of the social allusions often made in texts that support the dominant cultural perspective, African American students (males in particular) find themselves unable to connect with texts that are introduced in school.

When students are engaged in evidence-based literacy instructional practices, literacy events have the potential to address their sociocultural needs. Evidence-based models that encourage the use of relevant and engaging texts, that provide the opportunities for students to engage with a more knowledgeable other, and that provide the opportunities for students to experience flow all help African American students, who frequently feel disenfranchised from school, connect to school-based literacy. Conversely, when students' literacy is not aligned with the expected school-based literacy it can adversely affect their academic progress. Teachers, schools, and districts need to understand that it is important for African American male students to feel success with material that is appropriately challenging while being appropriate for their age and skill level (Bandura, 2001; Smith & Wilhelm, 2002; Vygotsky, 1978).

Social cognitive theory, social learning theory, and the findings from Lewis (2001), Kucer (2009), and Johnson (2016) are inextricably connected to Maslow (1943), who outlined the concept of motivation in his hierarchy of needs and theorized that, in order for people to reach self-actualization, basic needs must first be met. Physiological needs and safety needs are at the bottom rung of the hierarchy that Maslow introduced. In order to meet African American male students' basic psychological needs, schools can commit to helping them feel valued, respected, and heard.

Maslow's hierarchy of needs and Bandura's social cognitive theory each discussed the need for internal motivation and a connection to the social aspect of learning and literacy development. As a rung on the hierarchical ladder, the need to socially belong corresponds to Bandura's thoughts on sociocultural factors influencing a student's motivation to succeed. These thoughts on motivation and sociocultural phenomena can be used to explain student behavior and motivation and how these affect cognition. If motivation, behavior, and cognition are negatively influenced, student participation in school-related literacy events may be limited, and students may reject school-based literacy or even the institution of school itself. Furthermore, we can account for African American male students' rejection of school-based texts by considering a number of factors. Some of the factors that influence African American students' rejection of school-based texts include a misalignment of students' primary or home discourse to the secondary or school discourses (to be discussed later in the text), use of texts that exist outside of students' contextual knowledge, and a lack of relevance of school materials to students' lives. When considering the aforementioned factors, educators may note that they contribute to a disconnect between lived experiences and the experiences documented in school curricula.

Learning theories such as those presented by Vygotsky and Bandura should be integrated with literacy theories such as the ones presented by Gee (2001) and Heath (1989) to encourage the use of instructional practices aimed at building students' self-efficacy to improve and connect with their literacy. Bandura (2001) stated, "Efficacy beliefs are the foundation of human agency" (p. 10). Efficacy can be defined as the capacity to produce a desired result or effect (Bandura, 2001). According to social cognitive theory, efficacy is most apparent during times of social interaction where members of a group work toward a common goal. Because a student's level of participation in literacy events depends heavily on his or her sense of agency and efficacy, it is necessary to show the link between agency, efficacy, and the theories that explain how students learn and how their learning is linked to their identities.

Along with social cognitive theory, two other theories support the notion that students' agency and efficacy are increased when given the opportunity to participate in learning in a social construct: social development theory and reflex theory. Social development theory posits that an individual's efficacy increases through the presence and participation of more knowledgeable others. Reflex theory suggests that efficacy increases in individuals when one masters one particular skill, and the mastery of that initial skill leads to the mastery of several other skills. Social development theory, social cognitive theory, and reflex theory all suggest that in order for learning to occur in human beings, there must be opportunities for socialization in order for people to learn from and with others, there must be personal and communal efficacy and agency, and there must be an external stimulus (such as a teacher) to guide learning. To provide the proper guidance to students, classroom teachers must have adequate and relevant professional development that includes knowledge of these theories.

Vygotsky (1978) argued that reflex theory and gestalt theory could be integrated, and therefore were not mutually exclusive. Reflex theory is the belief that improvement in skills in one area is transferable and can lead to the improvements in other areas. Vygotsky's understandings of the two theories led to his development of the zone of proximal development. As stated previously, the zone of proximal development, or ZPD, identifies the developmental stage between a student's actual, or developmental, age and the possible trajectory of acquirable knowledge that a student could achieve with help from a more knowledgeable other. For many students, particularly African American students whose literacy development may not be aligned with the expectations of school, the ZPD may be much more limited than that of students who have experiences that make the content in school texts more accessible to them. It is important to note that the work of Koffka, Bandura, and Vygotsky helps to define learning from agentic and sociocultural perspectives and their theories provide a foundation for developing solutions that meet African American male students' learning needs.

Another theory of learning and literacy development that is central to how African American students engage in school-based literacy was introduced by Rosenblatt (1978). Rosenblatt introduced the transactional theory of reading and writing, a model that built upon decades of research on literacy. The transactional theory of reading and writing contradicted learning theories that were grounded in behavioral models. Furthermore, Rosenblatt's theory counteracts the notion that poverty and race are responsible for skill deficits or a lack of connection to school-based literacy among African American students. As an educator, I often hear unresearched and undocumented perspectives about the link between poverty, race, and literacy development, particularly with regard to African American students. In fact, it is not poverty or race itself that is responsible for the disconnect between African American students and school and school-based literacy; rather, it is the pervasiveness and permanence of racism and the lack of access to social experiences that set the conditions for poverty. A very clear distinction needs to be made on this matter: As it relates to African American children, the cycle of generational poverty is racially and socially motivated, and this cycle has implications for literacy.

The transactional theory of reading and writing has several components but suggests that in all literacy events, there is an interconnectedness between the sociocultural experiences of the reader, the technical reading skills (e.g., morphemic and phonemic awareness) of the reader, the intended meaning of the writer, the multiple linguistic variations of particular words (e.g., puns, double entendres, words that have multiple meanings), and the type of text being read (Rosenblatt, 2004). Transactions—which can be defined within the context of this theory as exchanges between two parties—occur between the reader and the text. Rosenblatt (2004) stated, "the reader and text are involved in a complex, nonlinear, recursive, self-correcting transaction" (p. 1371). The reader generates meaning by accessing the contextual knowledge that he or she brings to the literacy event and connecting that knowledge to the signs, or words, on the page. This is an important point to address because as educators we seek solutions to address the literacy needs of African American male students by trying to fix the students rather than adjusting the learning environment to meet the students' needs.

AGENCY AND IDENTITY

Often, when students reject school or school-based literacy, they are rejecting the context within which school-based academic content exists. The school context often supports the views, language, and mores of the dominant culture, all aspects of the school environment that often run counter to the identities of many African American male students. In her theory, Rosenblatt spoke about the public and private meanings of language used within a text and how those meanings help students connect with texts or cause them to reject them. She compared the public and private meanings of texts to an iceberg. The tip of the iceberg is what we can see; however, underneath the water there is a larger, unseen portion of the iceberg that can only be accessed if one dives below the surface. The public meanings within language are the ostensible, direct meanings of language, which correlate to the tip of the iceberg, while the private meanings of language are the nuances, allusions, or references that are connected to ideas that are not readily apparent, like the part of the iceberg that is beneath the surface of the water.

Rosenblatt's thoughts on language variations are similar to the thoughts of Gee (1989,1999), Bakhtin (1986), and Cazden (1988) when they discuss the differences between home or primary discourses and school or secondary discourses and the connection that needs to be made between the two in order for students to generate meaning from texts. These discourses, which are both literal and figurative in nature, are inseparable from students' identities. When African American students' home discourses are rejected or devalued in school, students often see this as an affront to their identities, and they reject the secondary or school discourse as a result.

As educators, we have to assume that students will take different reading stances based on the type of text they are reading, that they will approach similar texts in different ways, and that they will do so despite our misconceptions about them having monolithic identities. Furthermore, when readers approach texts, they are actively connecting their identities, experiences, primary languages, assumptions, and beliefs to the text. So, when a reader is introduced to a text that does not align with their identities, they may approach the text differently than expected or reject the text altogether. African American male readers need teachers who understand their identities and that can help them connect those identities to school-based texts. As a result, we should approach literacy instruction and text selections for students with the understanding that different readers approach texts with different (or even multiple) identities.

As Rosenblatt (1978) stated in her theory, readers will approach a text taking one of two stances—an efferent stance or aesthetic stance—and they will connect their reading stance with their identity. Readers who take an efferent stance approach the literacy event with the intention of gaining information about a certain subject or range of subjects. Examples would include the reading of a newspaper, manual, or textbook. Readers who take an aesthetic stance approach the literacy event with the intention of being affected emotionally by the text. Examples would be the reading of a novel, poem, or letter. According to Rosenblatt, there are only two identified stances; however, no reader falls directly at one of the poles. The transactional theory of reading and writing asserts the notion that during a literacy event, a reader may exist somewhere along a continuum between the efferent and aesthetic stances. For example, a reader may take a stance that is largely efferent but that incorporates components of the aesthetic. The efferent and the aesthetic stances have implications for how the reader connects to and understands the text, particularly among African American male readers who may not have experience with the information, concepts, or language presented within a particular text and whose schema or background knowledge may differ from what the dominant culture supports.

As a result of this understanding about how readers approach texts and how their identities are linked to their understanding of texts, it is even more important that teachers' understandings of the linkage between students' identities, language, and contextual knowledge help them build students' academic agency. Identity also has a direct connection to agency, which is discussed in depth in Bandura (2001) and documented extensively in Lewis (2001). Literacy events, particularly for African American male students, are socially based; should provide opportunities for students to experience flow by connecting with texts that are relevant to their lives; are directly connected to student agency and efficacy; and do not occur in a vacuum.

Social cognitive theory not only established the three modes of agency (learning, cognition, and motivation) as a foundation for determining human action and interaction; it also addressed the environmental factors of overall culture, language, and the ability to interact socially with others, which serve as contributors. Bandura (2001) also pointed out that the environmental factors that contribute to personal agency relate directly to environments that people choose, those they do not choose, and those that they themselves construct.

Accordingly, agency, efficacy, and varying degrees of human social interaction help make up an individual's identity, and it is this identity that allows us to connect to literacy and literacy events. This sociocultural view has a direct connection to student learning and literacy; thus, viewing literacy through a sociocultural paradigm allows one to give credence to the cultural factors of language and social experiences as they relate to cognitive development and address student learning and learning behaviors using a holistic lens (Kucer, 2009; McMahon et al., 1997; Vygotsky, 1978). This sociocultural view of learning and literacy goes beyond the mere assertion that poverty is the main cause of student underachievement and cause for disconnect with school-based literacy.

Moreover, it is important that learning and literacy engagement be viewed not strictly as a process linked to cognition but rather as an interconnected set of processes that includes the developmental and maturation processes, the sociocultural paradigm, knowledge and mastery of linguistic elements, opportunities to connect one's identity to texts, and recognition of cognitive elements. Viewing literacy in this manner gives human beings the ability to gain exposure to previously unavailable thoughts, constructs, contexts, language, and experiences. The understanding of the interconnectedness of the work of Vygotsky, Bandura, Rosenblatt, Kucer, and Maslow, along with my own research on improving literacy instruction for African American male students, helped me to develop the Black Male Literacy Paradigm.

CHAPTER 3

Black Boy Fly

The Black Male Literacy Paradigm as an Instructional Framework

The ability to read awoke inside of me some long dormant craving to be mentally alive.

—Malcolm X

THE BLACK MALE LITERACY PARADIGM

The Black Male Literacy Paradigm is a research-based instructional framework that is composed of the several areas that make up literacy development for Black male students. Although the paradigm has the express intent of improving literacy development for Black male students, it can be employed to improve literacy for all students. The BMLP was born out of theoretical and practical research, actual teaching experiences, data collected from teachers and administrators, and conversations with students about what they need in order to connect to school and school-based literacy. The paradigm operates with a few key assumptions:

- Literacy development is a key factor in academic achievement.
- Literacy is socially constructed (Kucer, 2009; Lewis, 2001; Tatum, 2005).
- There should be a firm connection between the practice of educators, the literacy development of African American males, and student socialization.
- Literacy opens up a world to students to which they might not otherwise be privy.

With these key assumptions, Figure 3.1 presents a visual representation of the paradigm and the factors that have a global influence on the literacy of Black male students. In the text following the figure, an

43

Figure 3.1. Black Male Literacy Paradigm

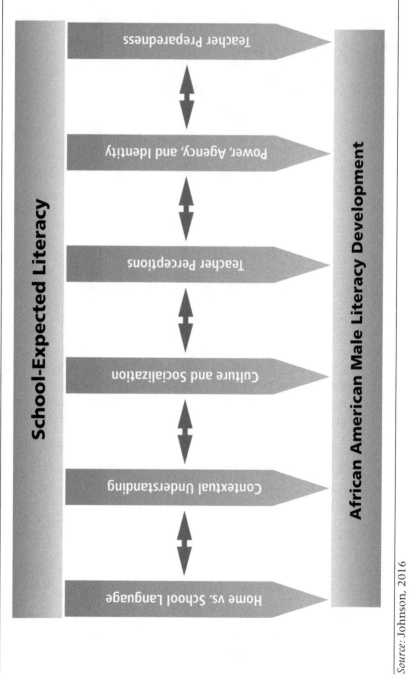

School-Expected Literacy

Teacher Preparedness

Power, Agency, and Identity

Teacher Perceptions

Culture and Socialization

Contextual Understanding

Home vs. School Language

African American Male Literacy Development

Source: Johnson, 2016

explanation of each of the components will provide more specificity as to how Black male students connect to expected in-school literacy and how each component can be applied in classroom settings.

The Black Male Literacy Paradigm represents an extensive review of the literature regarding how African American male students connect to literacy and how they are socialized, the implications of their schooling experience, and the psychology and physiology of learning. The components are interdependent and include ideas about social justice, culturally relevant teaching, and the historical implications of the schooling of African American children.

HOME VERSUS SCHOOL LANGUAGE

In order to be able to access the full scope of human interactions, including language, literacy, and literary content, human beings must be able to rely on their schemas to connect them to multiple discourses and identities, and they must be able to do this concurrently, separately, and selectively. Because the term *discourse* has both literal and abstract definitions, it is necessary to define discourse for our current context. Gee (1999) described discourse (or language) in the following manner:

> Language has a magical property: when we speak or write we craft what we have to say to fit the situation or context in which we are communicating. But, at the same time, how we speak or write creates that very situation or context. It seems, then, that we fit our language to a situation or context that our language, in turn, helped to create in the first place. (p. 11)

Simply put, a discourse can be a spoken language or vernacular, a code of ethics, or a set of meanings derived from surface-level or underlying meanings in language or behaviors (Gee, 1999; Kucer, 2009).

Human language, particularly the English language, is nuanced and contains words that have multiple meanings. It is also highly contextual and relies on background knowledge and experiences for the individual to generate meaning. When we approach the topic of Black male literacy with this understanding of how nuanced the English language is, American understandings about how language is formed and should be used, with its multiple variances, is thus dependent on one's ability to seamlessly navigate in and out of schemas to apply meaning to new learning and new situations. As a result, students have to rely on the cultural schemas and knowledge that they have prior to the literacy event, and they must use those to make meaning from language found in texts that are introduced in school, which often support the dominant cultural and linguistic narratives. In order for students to build their reading stamina, they also must develop the ability to engage in this sort of meaning-making, whether a more knowledgeable other is present or not. It is commonly assumed (foolishly) that there is a monolithic human, cultural, social, and socioeconomic experience, and this myth has to be dispelled in order to help African American children develop schemas necessary to understand the allusions often found in texts assigned in school. Many learning institutions support the belief in a monolithic human cultural experience and require students to interact only with content that supports that belief. Here is where the problem lies when trying to connect African American students to the institution of school and school-related content. Built into the structure of school is the idea that every student who enters into the doors of a school either has had similar experiences, uses the same schemas, or both. Accordingly, schools are the vehicles to affirm, support, and reify the ideals of the dominant social and language structure.

As humans, we all use multiple discourses to make meaning of experiences with different or conflicting environments. The primary discourse, or home language, is the language we speak that is aligned to our personal cultural meanings, mores, and vernacular, and it represents the language that we use in our most comfortable environment(s). Our home languages might be highly cultural and inextricably linked to our identities.

The secondary discourse, or school language, is the language that represents subtler variations in language sometimes connected to experiences of the dominant culture. Gee (1999) refers to the secondary discourse as the surface structure of language. Reminiscent of the iceberg analogy used earlier, the secondary discourse is akin to the tip of the iceberg. Because school is a microcosm of the larger dominant society and supports its values and language, African American students often find themselves unable to connect with school since its frequent adherence to the secondary language structure does not align to their home or primary languages. Conversely, African American students' White peers often enter the school discourse environment experiencing an alignment between their primary or home discourse and the discourse of school.

I believe that this particular component of African American male students' connection to literacy, particularly with regard to expected in-school literacy, is the most important. If African American students' identities and language are devalued in school environments, and if the school's cultural mores conflict with their own, they will reject the school environment to preserve a sense of self. As a means to assuage this conflict between students' language and the language of school, Guerra (2007) spoke about the notion that students should be taught how to move through transcultural spaces and morph their identities to fit the environments in which they find themselves. When a student morphs his identity, he accesses the different language patterns, out-of-school experiences, and funds of knowledge that align with the standards for participation for the current environment.

School texts often represent and support the dominant cultural worldview; additionally, school-related texts use language and rely on students' schemas to which many African American students may not be privy. As a result, misaligned expectations of cultural experiences, language used in school and in texts, and inappropriate and unaligned policies and instructional practices cause many students to reject school as an institution, even though they may understand the importance of school specifically, and education in general. It is important for teachers and schools to understand this point and design instructional practices, choose texts, and develop relationships that seek to value and understand the language practices and seek ways to value the identities of African American male students.

CONTEXTUAL UNDERSTANDING

The English language is filled with words that have underlying meanings, words that can be used in multiple contexts, and words that have particular implications depending on the receiver and the sender. Because language can either help or serve as a barrier to access to school content (especially when it is used by and for African American students in the school environment), educational institutions need to help African American students understand the intertextual and historical nature of competence created through the understanding of word meanings and their subtexts (both explicit and implicit). Students who do not develop such competencies are excluded from other socially related events that involve literacy in academic settings (Bloome & Bailey, 1992).

Helping African American male students understand the intertextual nature of language refers not just to texts themselves but to the broader use of language and how language is connected to the prior experiences of the user and receiver. In order to connect African American male students to school language and expected school texts, teachers need to help them develop what is called intertextuality. Kristeva (Kristeva & Moi, 1986) first used the term *intertextuality* to explain the nature of language as it exists in its various forms and environments, referring to intertextuality as "an intersection of textual surfaces rather than a point (a fixed meaning), as a dialogue among several writings" (Kristeva, 1980, as quoted in Alfaro, 1996, p. 268).

Alfaro (1996) explained that outcomes related to intertextuality are multifaceted. In order for students to gain meaning from language and text, they need to understand the core of what intertextuality is in order to utilize it during literacy events. Alfaro defined intertexuality as "the relation of co-presence between two or more texts—that is, the effective presence of one text in another which takes place by means of plagiarism, quotation, or allusion"(pp. 280–281).

The idea of intertextuality supports the assertion that literacy is sociocultural in nature and that educators need to understand how literacy and language is developed for African American students, and for African American male students specifically. The aspects of literacy development and connection to in-school literacy for African American male students that have been mentioned thus far, which include the concept of flow, the understanding of culture and socialization, student identity, and the historical implications of schooling for African American students, all hinge upon the type of language that is available to them and the types of language to which they are exposed either through discourse, texts, or experiences. The convergence of all of these components of language helps develop intertextuality for students. Students have to understand multiple contexts, allusions, texts, and situations, and have to be able to apply this knowledge quickly and seamlessly. In order to understand what students need, educators should engage in activities to get to know and understand their students and fill in gaps in experiences where they see a disconnect.

CULTURE AND SOCIALIZATION

Chapter 3 of this text will go in-depth about the importance of the socialization of African American male students and what it means for their connection to literacy; however, it is necessary to briefly delve into the topic here. In Newkirk's (2002) *Misreading Masculinity: Boys, Literacy, and Popular Culture*, he talked extensively about how the socialization of male students plays a major role in how they are perceived and how they connect to literacy and language. Ideas about African American male students are formed, reinforced, and held by those in the dominant culture (including teachers), and their perception of these students is influenced by how and to what extent they interact with them. As a result of these ideas about African American maleness in a field dominated by middle-class, White women, the socialization and perceptions of African American male students are impacted by the access granted to them based on others' preconceived notions. If one also adds the perceptions of Black males held by those in the dominant culture, it becomes evident that African American male students have to overcome several obstacles before being granted access to school-related discourses and their accompanying texts. The perceptions that others have of African American male students confines their existence to a doom loop: The lack of access to certain social situations reinforces perceptions of them, and those perceptions serve as a barrier to access certain social experiences. If social situations provide access to language for students, and if those experiences often exist outside the school setting but at the same time are aligned to the discourse of school, African American students find themselves existing as noncitizens in classrooms that should be built around serving their literacy needs.

Words and language are directly aligned to how students are socialized and should be viewed as vehicles to allow access to the discourse of school as they support one another. This notion supports the premise that the number of words to which a child is exposed is directly correlated with his ability to access the language of the dominant language structure that is also taught, supported, and reinforced in school-based literacy (Hirsch, 2003). Teachers and schools must then attend to designing instruction that has to address the problem identified by Luke (2003):

> The problem, then, is this. The selection, codification, and differential transmission of a dominant set of literate and linguistic practices via institutions like schooling must contend with unprecedented and increasing diversity of background knowledge and competence, linguistic and cultural resources, available discourses and textual practices brought to and through classrooms and schools. (p. 137)

I am often confronted with questions from educators such as "How do we address the issues that occur at home when we have no control?" or "What do you expect me to do when students don't come to my classroom already reading?" What many educators (whether they are African American or Caucasian) often fail to realize is that sociopolitical and economic contexts informed by the dominant cultural perspective undergird the roadblock to accessing literacy for many African

American students. When confronted with questions about students' home lives and reading abilities (which many believe are connected), a few interrelated thoughts arise for me: (1) There is a difference between reading and literacy, (2) literacy is situated in multiple contexts, and (3) there is more depth to the sociocultural nature of literacy, which includes teachers' agency and efficacy. When we reduce literacy to its technical parts, such as the ability to read, we ignore the multifaceted nature of literacy and the several contexts in which it exists (e.g., sociopolitical, sociocultural, economic) and the implications of each. Using a mindset where we ask questions about students' reading abilities rather than about their literate lives as a whole, we ignore cultures that use oral traditions and storytelling, poetry and rap music, and call-and-response traditions often found in different religious services. Our ideas about what literacy is need to be expanded.

With regard to the sociopolitical barriers to literacy development for African American male students within the school context, politicians and lawmakers have weighed in on the conversation. In fact, in 2018 in the case *Gary v. Snyder*, a federal judge in Detroit ruled against the idea that literacy should be guaranteed as part of a students' participation in school. The plaintiff in the case (a group of African American students and their parents) asserted that the children of Detroit had not been given an adequate education, citing a lack of supplies and unskilled and unmotivated teachers, and because of these things, students in the Detroit Community School District (formerly Detroit Public Schools) were denied access to literacy. Richard Snyder was listed as the main defendant as he was the governor of Michigan at the time and had used his power as governor to take over Detroit Public Schools for a period of 10 years. The judge in the case sided with the defendant's claim that ". . . access to literacy is not a constitutionally protected right, so the failure to provide such access cannot constitute a valid claim under 28 U.S.C. § 1983" (*Gary v. Snyder*, p. 3). Judge Murphy, who presided over the case, stated, "The Court is left to conclude that the Supreme Court has neither confirmed nor denied that access to literacy [is] a fundamental right" (p. 29). The contradictory nature of Governor Snyder's position becomes evident when one considers that in 2017, the State of Michigan enacted a law requiring that every 3rd-grade student be proficient in reading according to the state-administered assessment. As educators, we must rebel against notions such as these, which punish students and schools for their lack of reading achievement while denying that the state has an obligation to provide adequate access to literacy, and support literacy development for our children, particularly

African American children, even if our state governments and the federal government will not.

As a result of expanding our understanding about what literacy is, we can affirm that literacy development encompasses more than students' skill levels. While reading skills are extremely important, as educators we cannot focus solely on that and stop there. We must help students build literacy by exposing them to a wide variety of texts and using their lived experiences to connect with texts. Moreover, we can build students' reading skills while simultaneously encouraging them to connect to out-of-school and in-school texts.

Earlier, I made the connection between the early history of African Americans in this country and the institution of school. While it may be easy for one to recognize the historical plight of African American children in education by pointing to the institution of slavery, the Black Codes, and Jim Crow laws and blaming those past misdeeds for current inequities, it becomes much more difficult to explain and accept that the cultural forces that shaped those historical events are still at work in the present-day academic, economic, and social oppression of African American students. To do this, we need to set the context and show how the socialization of African American students today is tied to the political movements and ideologies that have shaped schools.

In 2001, the federal government passed the largest and most sweeping education reform initiative in our nation's history: No Child Left Behind. Among the mandates that were the staples of the legislation were the following:

- One hundred percent of students were expected to reach proficiency in reading and math by the year 2013.
- Each school and district was to meet adequate yearly progress (AYP; the metrics for meeting AYP were determined by each state's department of education).
- Schools that were the lowest performing in the state would face restrictions and fall under scrutiny by their state department of education and the federal government, up to and including facing closure and reopening as a charter school.
- Each state was tasked to disaggregate its student performance data into subgroups by race, gender, special education status, English language learner status, and socioeconomic status.

The aforementioned are just some of the mandates to which states and school districts were subject under *No Child Left Behind* legislation.

On its surface, one may contend that the mandates of No Child Left Behind were sound policy that had the goal of improving and reforming public schools, particularly those that existed in urban centers. But the implications for urban schools and suburban schools with significant African American populations were damaging. Not only were the physical environments of their schools impacted through school closures, but African Americans' overall schooling experiences were negatively impacted.

As schools were forced to examine their disaggregated student data, they were able to quantify what they already knew: that African American students scored lower, on average, on standardized assessments than their White counterparts. In response, schools began intervention programs and after-school tutoring, and districts began identifying African American students (males in particular) in disproportionate numbers for special education programs (Johnson, 2016). While after-school intervention programs are not necessarily bad, there is not sufficient evidence to support their wide-scale use for improving the achievement of African American students, and individual and widely varying solutions that were not part of a systemic plan to improve the literacy outcomes for African American students should not have been looked at as the answer. Another implication of the No Child Left Behind legislation was how it fed the history of social and academic repudiation of adequate schooling, as documented in the complaint brought forth in the *Gary v. Snyder* case, a 2018 complaint against the Detroit Public Schools, the new Detroit Public Schools Community District, and the state of Michigan.

During the same time period, as zero-tolerance policies were being implemented simultaneously and many times in concert with NCLB policies, African American students in particular were disproportionately singled out for suspension and expulsion. For example, a study conducted by the Department of Education (Porowski, O'Conner, & Passa, 2014) using school discipline data from the state of Maryland for the years 2009–2012 found that although overall rates of suspension and expulsion fell by .6%, the following was also true:

- Of students suspended or expelled for the same type of infraction, Black students were more likely to receive out-of-school suspensions or expulsion than were Hispanic or White students.
- Because rates of out-of-school suspension and expulsion decreased more rapidly for White students than for Black students, disproportionality between Black and White rates

increased in 2011–12, the most recent year examined, even though suspension rates for African American students had decreased.

- Black students received out-of-school suspensions or expulsion at more than twice the rate of White students (Porowski, O'Conner, & Passa, 2014).

Additionally, the study found that students who received special education services were suspended at twice the rate of non–special education students and that Black students in special education had the highest rates of out-of-school suspension and expulsion and the longest average removal time. The inequity in discipline administered to African American students compared to other groups was not an anomaly found only in Maryland; districts across the nation show a disparity in discipline between African American and White and Asian students. So, not only are African American students and families seeing themselves as nonparticipants in the schooling process because of the disconnect between themselves and the content and school environment, they were disproportionately being removed from schools altogether.

Subversive tactics like disproportionate discipline have the effect of furthering racist agendas and solidifying African American disenfranchisement from school. Moreover, they are directly connected to tactics deployed by opponents of integration during the time of desegregation. At the height of the integration movement, African American students were escorted into school buildings by armed guards, and the Supreme Court forced school districts to comply with federal desegregation orders; however, persistent racial bias meant that African American students were never given full access to the social constructs (e.g., extracurricular clubs, activities, and events) required to understand and connect with school-related content. Furthermore, as many African American families chose to leave school districts that were resource poor and did not serve their children's academic needs, they were confronted by school districts that relied on disciplinary practices that kept many African American students from being full participants in the school environment. One of the ways that schools and districts reified the notion that African American students did not belong in school environments, particularly suburban schools that had historically restricted physical access, was to establish zero-tolerance discipline policies whereby African American students were disproportionately suspended and expelled.

Zero-tolerance policies in schools were a way for schools to assuage the fears of policymakers and parents about school violence (Skiba &

Rausch, 2006). Moreover, as schools were under increased pressure to meet strict academic demands from the federal government per NCLB, they used suspension and expulsion in the following ways: as a means to deter other students from behaving in the same manner as those being suspended, to make schools safe for learning, and to send a message about school safety (Skiba & Rausch, 2006, pp. 1064–1065). School officials thought that by giving the appearance of safety and eliminating students with high incidence of bad behaviors, they would be able to achieve the academic outcomes for which they were being held responsible. Even though schools had begun enacting zero-tolerance policies in the late 1980s and early 1990s, they began to see it as an effective means to rid schools of undesirable students in order to help meet the academic requirements of NCLB. However, zero-tolerance policies all had one main problem in common: They were often used to suspend or expel students for even minor offenses, along racial lines. Since schools began using discipline as an intervention, they exacerbated the decline of achievement for Black students. Skiba & Rausch (2006) stated, "One of the most important findings of educational psychology of the last 30 years is the positive relationship between the amount and quality of engaged time in academic learning and student achievement" (p. 1067). Zero-tolerance policies, coupled with NCLB mandates, created a viscous cycle for Black children. Black children were suspended at disproportionate rates, and the so-called achievement gap increased. As the achievement gap increased, schools and school districts felt pressure to close the gaps so they suspended more of the undesirable students. As students spent more time out of school because of suspensions and expulsions, their disconnect from the school environment increased and their school achievement decreased.

In addition to exacerbating disproportionate school discipline rates for African American children, NCLB legislation forced schools in urban and rural areas to use the same assessments that schools in wealthy areas used, and the resulting scores were used to compare schools to determine their effectiveness. Schools faced the threat of closure if they were not able to significantly raise test scores within a 4- to 5-year time frame. The result was that districts with larger populations of African Americans, economically disadvantaged students, and students with special needs were disproportionately burdened by NCLB requirements compared to districts with few or no students who fit into these categories.

In the Detroit area, the schools that faced the threat of closure or reorganization were mostly in depressed urban areas or communities with large African American populations. The NCLB legislation sparked questions about whether or not the mandates were specifically

targeted at schools and districts with high African American populations, thus targeting African American students. Moreover, predominantly White districts that had sizeable African American populations
had to grapple with how to provide supports for their African American
students while maintaining the social and academic structures required
of them by their communities. After several years of districts making
attempts to prepare 100% of their students to be proficient in reading
and math, the federal government allowed each state to apply for a
waiver from the original mandates. Michigan was one of the states that
applied for a waiver. In a subsequent measure to try to address failing
schools, Governor Rick Snyder instituted the Education Achievement
Authority (EAA), which was initially designed to take over each school
that performed in the bottom 5% based on the state-designed and
-implemented standardized test. After much political backlash and pos-
turing by policymakers, the new EAA decided to only take over schools
in the majority–African American city of Detroit, leaving schools in
other suburban and urban areas in the bottom 5% untouched. Thus,
it is easy to surmise that the goal of the EAA was to gain control of the
majority–African American schools within the city of Detroit, as no
other schools in the state were taken over by the entity. As a result of
this change and others, schools that could not meet the demands of the
imposed mandates were forced to close, hire entirely new staffs, and
reopen as charter schools. In many of the schools that were absorbed
by the EAA, classes were taught by teachers who were trained by private organizations, and not the traditional colleges of education where
most teachers learn their craft.

As an unfunded mandate of the federal government, NCLB did not
provide financial resources to individual states to make academic accommodations for students. Although financial resources were never
given to meet the unreal demands of the legislation (some may argue
that states were given these resources through the federal aid that they
were already receiving) and many schools and communities struggled to meet the demands of the law, arguably the most disappointing
outcome was the negative impact that NCLB had on the schooling of
already-underserved African American students. The several requirements for measurement, accountability, and assessment did not account
for students' disconnect with school, the chasm between the out-of-
school literacy practices of African American students and the expected
in-school literacy, and the barriers to accessing social institutions that
African American students face. Moreover, the process of disaggrega-
tion of data by race and socioeconomic status never forced states, districts, and schools to acknowledge the historical implications of race

and schooling for African Americans in this country; thus, schools continued to ignore the connection between the socialization and culture of students and the school environment and school-expected literacy.

TEACHER PERCEPTIONS

With the study that I conducted and highlighted in my dissertation, *Understanding the In-School Literacies of African American Males Through a Sociocultural Paradigm: Implications for Teacher Professional Development* (documented in Johnson, 2016), I sought to gauge teachers' understandings of how African American male students adapted their identities, language, and out-of-school literacy practices to school environments and expected in-school literacy. The data collected from the study helped me identify strategies that teachers believed helped students connect to school. Teachers with whom I engaged believed the following essential components were necessary to effectively engage African American students in school, and in school-expected literacy specifically:

1. Teachers need to help students make connections to the school, the teacher(s), and the text(s).
2. Teachers should reconceptualize their current definitions or develop expansive definitions of literacy.
3. Educators need to engage in inquiry to improve their understandings about how students develop literacy.
4. Schools and districts should research and implement evidence-based instructional strategies for literacy.

Each one of these components will be explained in depth in Chapter 5; however, as a part of the Black Male Literacy Paradigm, acknowledgment of the impact of teachers' perceptions on their students must be an immediate, ongoing discussion and must exist in multiple contexts. Hattie (2012, 2016) supported the notion that teachers' beliefs in their students' abilities to engage in complex tasks, analysis, and discussion have a significant impact on students' academic achievement. Hattie (2012) conducted a meta-analysis of 1,200 meta-analyses and isolated the 150 most effective teaching practices (the meta-analysis was updated in Hattie, 2016). After taking the data from the studies and calculating the effect size of each practice, he found that "teacher estimates of achievement" (or teachers' perceptions of student abilities) had the highest effect size (1.62) of all 150 teaching practices (Hattie, 2012, 2016).

The sentiments of teachers in my study mirrored Hattie's conclusion. The data collected from teacher conversations and inquiry into their practices showed that when teachers believed that students could achieve at high levels, the students met those expectations. Conversely, the data collected from teachers also supported the notion that when teachers had negative perceptions of their students, students did not perform well. The teachers felt that when they or their colleagues did not exhibit high expectations of their students, the students felt disconnected from school altogether. Accordingly, teachers documented that many of their students recounted to them that when teachers did not believe in them or had low perceptions of them and their abilities, the students rejected the school and school-related content.

POWER, AGENCY, AND IDENTITY

The research of Bakhtin (1981, 1986), Gee, (2001), Lewis (2001), and Lewis and colleagues (2007) all support the notion that students link their identities to the texts to which they are exposed. This is especially relevant for African American students in general, and African American males specifically, because of the way in which race, class, and socialization intersect with the institution of school. If texts or other school content supported by the school is representative of school values and mores, and if those values in some way devalue, make defunct, or disregard African American students' identities, the students will reject that content. Moreover, Lewis (2001) provided evidence that identity, agency, and the connection to school are also linked to social power. When students reject school and school-related content, they lose social power among their peers and teachers and are looked upon as social and academic outcasts.

Guerra (2007) explored the idea of teaching students how to morph their identities to move in and out of transcultural spaces. In order for students to connect with texts in new environments, they have to adopt new and multiple identities to relate to the values inherent within those texts. For example, an African American student must know the rules and behaviors of his community and act appropriately there while adjusting his identity (not foregoing it) to act accordingly in other environments.

TEACHER PREPAREDNESS

The question that I face most often from educators when addressing this topic is: "How do I help African American male students with their literacy?" This question is multilayered and has to be addressed with a multilayered approach. The Black Male Literacy Paradigm is designed to be one such approach, giving schools and educational institutions the foundational framework to begin to answer that question. Many teachers that I have encountered feel a sense of efficacy with regard to their overall ability to reach most students, but nonetheless feel powerless to help their African American students. Said another way, teachers know how to reach their Caucasian or Asian students, but do not know how to reach their African American students. The multi-layered response to the question of how to help African male students with their literacy has to be rooted in an understanding of how African American students develop literacy that is associated with their cultural backgrounds and affiliations and the racial, sociopolitical, and sociocul-tural histories in which their identities exist.

Teachers who participated in this study indicated they had not been exposed to recent and relevant professional learning opportunities that helped them understand how African American students connected to school-based literacy. They also believed that many of their colleagues had not been exposed to those learning opportunities, either. My study (Johnson, 2016) engaged teachers in a 5-day professional develop-ment series to meet this need for participant teachers. The themes that emerged from this study helped the participating teachers, and they can serve to help a broader number of educators in the field under-stand their African American male students.

The study helped to address two interrelated purposes. The first purpose was to engage teachers in a book club model of profession-al development that was designed to generate thoughtful discussion and opportunities for critical reflection about their perceptions and be-liefs (those of which they are cognizant as well as those of which they are unaware) of African American males' in-school and out-of-school literacy practices. The second purpose was to assist teachers in mak-ing connections between their perceptions and beliefs about African American male students and the critical role these perceptions play in curricular and pedagogical decision making, including instructional planning, classroom instructional strategies, text selection, and assess-ments (Johnson, 2016).

The study also documented that teachers believed that if they were properly prepared, they could help their African American male students connect to school-based literacy. If educators continue to believe the prevailing idea that students are the ones who need to be fixed, and that historically marginalized students simply do not want to be successful in school, then efforts to close the opportunity and achievement gaps will fail. To provide academic equity for students, professional learning for educators must prepare them to engage African American youth in literacy and must be grounded in sociocultural research and socioculturally based solutions as well as social justice theories and practices.

SUMMARY OF THE BLACK MALE LITERACY PARADIGM

Each one of the components of the Black Male Literacy Paradigm is designed to help educators understand the sociocultural factors that influence African American male students' connection to school-expected literacy. While understanding each one of the components does not guarantee the connection between African American students and their identities to school-based literacy, each component, as it is used interdependently with the others, provides a beginning framework for teachers and schools to intentionally address the literacy needs of African American male students. To improve schools and school environments, and to facilitate African American male students' connection to school-expected literacy, educators should engage in a few essential behaviors:

- Schools must build into their school cultures practices where principals and teachers gather information about who students are and use that information to develop culturally appropriate instruction around students' identities.
- Schools must identify texts, or allow students to choose texts for themselves, that are relevant to their lives and their experiences.
- Students must be given opportunities to experience flow.
- Teachers must be engaged in ongoing professional development with the expressed intent of helping them understand African American male students' literacy behaviors and how to align those behaviors to expected school behaviors and literacy.

If schools and teachers commit to embedding practices such as these in their core literacy instruction for African American students, they will begin to generate the capacity to address these students' needs.

LITERACY ASSESSMENT INSTRUMENTS
AND LITERACY DEVELOPMENT

When considering how to help educators understand the components that help African American male students connect to expected school literacy (socialization, relevant texts, historical implications of African Americans and schooling, and identities that students bring to literacy events), it is becomes readily apparent that although there is a disconnect between African American male students' identities and school, their literacy is assessed in the same ways as that of their White counterparts. The most commonly used standardized assessments for literacy assumes a White-dominant cultural narrative. Furthermore, standardized assessments do not take into account the variation in language patterns between African American students' multiple literacies (home and school). As a result, African American students are not connecting to school as an institution and to the expected school-based literacy, which assume a familiarity with the language of the dominant culture, but they are assessed based on their knowledge and understanding of those same school constructs.

The assessments that are used to determine literacy proficiency should be examined more closely (Tatum, 2005). If we assume that student literacy data collected by standardized assessments are valid, we would also agree with the notion that literacy skill proficiency and the connection between out-of-school literacy and school-based literacy among African American male students is not congruent with that of their White counterparts. If we look at literacy through the sociocultural paradigm, we might further agree with Smith and Wilhelm (2002) and Tatum (2005), who attribute the continuing gap in literacy proficiency for African American males to the irrelevancy of texts to the lives of the students who are expected to read them. Therefore, we should use assessments that take into account the sociocultural nature of literacy rather than just the technical skills. African American male students, just like all other students, need to utilize contextual knowledge, cultural experiences, academic language, and social codes to make connections to texts, and standardized assessments only test for students' assimilation to or understanding of the school context.

One of the ways to address the literacy needs of African American male students is to view literacy through the sociocultural paradigm (Kucer, 2009; Lewis, 2001; Smith & Wilhelm, 2002; Tatum, 2005). Learning and literacy are socially constructed practices, which makes it necessary to view literacy through a sociocultural paradigm that allows for students' lives to be linked to literature and literate behaviors. As a result of viewing literacy and learning as socially constructed practices, teachers may find it necessary to establish a definition of literacy using a sociocultural framework before they plan instruction and assessments for their African American male students.

A few of the aspects of students' lives that may affect their literate behaviors are their cultural mores and values, the language used in their home and community, the economic statuses of their families, and their access to multiple sources of literature. The current standardized testing landscape does not examine students' literate behaviors using a sociocultural framework, nor do standardized tests and their developers subscribe to a definition of literacy that is multifaceted. As teachers learn to use evidence-based strategies and assessments that are constructed to view literacy as a social practice, they should also seek to learn how to help their students move between transcultural spaces and morph their identities to make connections to texts. Although teachers have little control over the standardized literacy assessments that are used, they have a fair amount of autonomy with regard to the types of texts to which students are exposed and how students are assessed on their understanding of those texts.

Franzak (2006) supports the notion that literacy assessments are geared more toward categorizing students and placing them into a reading hierarchy rather than developing assessments that truly assess students' reading capabilities. The categorization of students into reading ability groups has led to the belief that it is the schools' responsibility to narrow the gap between students' reading scores rather than alter the assessment itself. The categorizations of students according to ability documented by scores achieved on standardized tests are used as data to support the claims of Herrnstein and Murray (1994) and other "medical model" supporters. The medical model asserts that intelligence and achievement are primarily linked to genetic and biological factors rather than environmental or social factors.

At this point, it is important to digress briefly to make a connection between standardized testing in general and how students' literacy is assessed, as a means to further support the use of a sociocultural paradigm in instruction and assessment practices and to view literacy development from a growth mindset. Herrnstein and Murray (1994) supported the notion that the difference between the scores of African American students on standardized and cognitive tests (mainly documented by IQ tests) are attributable to a number of factors, including ethnicity. Herrnstein and Murray's assertions were based on data collected from several psychometric-based assessments. They compared the statistical patterns generated by these exams by ethnicity, socioeconomic status, and perceived cognitive ability. They concluded that (1) there are differences in cognitive ability according to ethnicity; (2) test bias should not be considered a factor that produces the gap in scores between African American students and White students; (3) there is a correlation between socioeconomic status and cognitive ability; and (4) there is a correlation between genetics, race, and cognitive ability (pp. 269–315). Furthermore, they concluded that tests such as the SAT are an accurate predictor of college success based on student performance and that if tests such as these were biased against African American students, then colleges and universities would underpredict the actual performance by African American students on these tests rather than overpredict.

Tests such as the SAT were derived from the work of French psychologist Alfred Binet, who began to develop psychometric tests, such as the Binet-Simon Scale (1916), that were aimed at assessing the mental acuity of children. Binet's tests led to the labeling of many children during his time period as "stupid," "retarded," "idiots," and "imbeciles." The work of Binet and Simon (1916) was among the first to test students' IQs and was a precursor to more contemporary intelligence tests. One of the more recent iterations of Binet & Simon's IQ test is the Scholastic Aptitude Test, or SAT, developed by the College Board. The SAT is one of the more commonly used tests to determine whether students should be admitted to institutions of higher learning. Although on its surface, the SAT's ostensible purpose is not to assess students' literacy development, one could argue that the exam does test students' literacy capabilities and assimilation with the language and experiences of the dominant culture. Nevertheless, as a derivative of the Binet-Simon scale, the SAT ultimately assesses students' aptitude and uses literacy as the vehicle.

The SAT as a measurement tool, as supported by Herrnstein and Murray in their study, does test for reading comprehension and students' verbal skills, particularly the sections dedicated to analogic analysis. The data collected from psychometric assessments such as IQ tests have led researchers such as Tatum (2005) to assert that such instruments are flawed because they usually measure basic reading skills and comprehension of the dominant culture rather than students' aptitude to understand materials related to their life experiences.

The confidence in and dependency on psychometric exams to accurately measure intelligence and literacy development, which Herrnstein and Murray and others support, has led to negative educational consequences for African American students (Johnson, 2016; Tatum, 2005). Even the data on literacy proficiency collected from assessments administered by the National Assessment of Educational Progress (NAEP) and the U.S. Department of Education do not provide the full scope of the engagement with literacy of African American students. Franzak (2006) and Lewis (2001) supported the notion that many assessments that make attempts to assess students' literacy skills do not account for "the sociocultural construction of textual interpretation and evaluation" (Lewis, 2001, p. 121). The use of psychometric and other skills-based assessments cannot account for a broad definition of literacy and all the components that lead to literacy proficiency and the overall participation in high-quality literacy events.

To aid in this conversation, Heath (1989) made reference to the issue of literacy development in African American students and student contextual knowledge as it related to the connection of students to texts. She asserted that schools and teachers often view the development of literacy skills with a finite lens, framing literacy as a set of technical skills. However, Heath called for educators to consider multiple definitions of literacy. She asserted that expansive definitions of literacy include conceptions of literacy as having a connection to context, language, and identity. Schools and districts that position themselves as viewing literacy only as a set of technical skills do not make allowances for considering sociocultural frameworks to assess students' literacy. Schools' positions on literacy assessments, text selections, and teacher professional development may result in a lack of attention being paid to the content of the literature presented to students, with the technical aspects and the mastery of the mechanistic elements of literacy development receiving far more attention (Johnson, 2016).

The research of Smith and Wilhelm (2002) and Tatum (2005) found some common ground with the research of Heath (1989) on what conceptions of literacy should include. Because literacy is often defined by the context of school and academic reading, and because the sociocultural aspects of literacy are often ignored, when educators recognize the varied forms of literacy, they can set the stage for the reconceptualization of the definition of literacy and help other teachers and schools change their perceptions of their students' efficacy. As a result of teachers across schools and communities reconceptualizing their definitions of literacy, a movement would have to ensue to assess students based on a sociocultural paradigm rather than a fixed one.

Assessment of literacy and literacy-related skills should be viewed using a sociocultural lens and by using qualitative measures (Johnson, 2016; Kucer, 2009; Lewis, 2001; Smith & Wilhelm, 2002; Tatum, 2005). Such measures could include allowing students to write creatively about their understanding of a text, accepting videos or other multimedia responses, allowing students to design graphic novels, and encouraging students to write and act out skits. The relationship between students' connections with texts and the assessments that measure students' reading proficiency has a direct impact on how literacy development is viewed by the teacher and the student. Educators must understand that in order for students to connect with texts, they need available engaging texts (both out-of-school texts and in-school texts) that allow them to experience flow. Educators also need to understand that failure to promote students' connections between themselves and texts may have a negative effect on students' proficiency scores on standardized tests. Moreover, the use of assessments that do not measure literacy in a qualitative way has led to African American students' underperformance on standardized tests.

If those same assessments are not aligned to literacy practices that build students' agency and efficacy, then they further serve in devaluing African American students' literate identities. These assessments reflect a deficit model of thinking by educators, and Heath (1989) discounts the notion of deficit thinking as it relates to the literacy development of African American males specifically. Deficit thinking can be defined as the beliefs, actions, thoughts, and language associated with negative suppositions about a group of people's abilities and aptitude. Although some assessments and practices may present as possible solutions to the issues regarding literacy development of Black students, many still perpetuate the idea that African American males are incapable of achieving because of their circumstances or lack of skills or intelligence. If educators continue to assess African American male students on literacy and modes of thought and variations of language that are foreign to them, then any interventions that we try would be aligned to deficit models of thinking that suppose that students cannot handle rigorous content and texts.

Heath (1989) also pointed out that cultural anthropologists have documented the rich verbal forms and literary history of African American people, and within that rich literary history there are stories of triumph, happiness, and perseverance. The connections that African American students create with literary forms within their cultural communities are sometimes disconnected from the types of literacy expected in school. If we use Heath's thoughts about the other facets of literacy (e.g., oral), then we would be compelled to develop alternate or progressive definitions of literacy and what it means to participate in literate practices. The notion of African American students feeling devalued in school is a by-product of the lack of support and use of texts that are relevant to their lives (Fisher 2005; Ogbu, 1991; Smith & Wilhelm, 2002; Tatum, 2005).

Along with phonemic and morphemic awareness, fluency, and word recognition, literacy development also includes student recognition of social codes, socialization of students, the use of academic language, and pedagogical practices used by the teacher. The data collected from studies like Johnson (2016), Lewis (2001), and Smith and Wilhelm (2002) showed that students connected to literacy in nontraditional ways that did not include how they mastered the technical skills of reading. The data showed that students indicated that school-based literacy did not match their real-world interests, but they documented that they participated in out-of-school literate behaviors that included reading magazines, science-fiction novels, and websites.

The reconceptualization of the definition of literacy should include the components of literacy that are often devalued by schools but what Heath (1989) documented as integral in helping students connect their interests to the literacy expected in schools. She listed the often-forgotten components of literacy, such as storytelling, writing, music, and poetry writing. The question that educators should pose for themselves is: How do we engage students to connect with literacy in ways that interest them, and how do we assess student literacy development? The findings on student literate behaviors inside and outside of school are important to note because they have implications for assessment, text selection, and teacher perceptions. Teachers' text selection should align with a more expansive definition of literacy, allowing assessment practices and the results gleaned from assessments to reflect students' true literacy proficiency.

Although the research on African American male literacy shows why African American students often have a difficult time connecting to in-school literacies, the fact remains that the data from the assessments that schools and districts use place African American males students at the bottom of the literacy proficiency continuum when compared to their White and Asian peers. A problematic practice within the field of education is that we continue to use those same standardized, criterion-referenced assessments to measure students' literacy proficiency. Literacy proficiency cannot be properly measured using one-dimensional assessments that assume that each student has identical cultural experiences and understanding of the content. Nonetheless, schools, politicians, and educational statistical agencies continue to use standardized tests as a measure for student literacy progress. Policymakers, state boards of education, schools, and teachers should commit to using more qualitative and authentic, nonbiased assessments to measure students' literacy development. In addition to the types of qualitative assessments listed earlier, other authentic, qualitative, and nonbiased assessments can include surveys of student literate interests and how their out-of-school literacy compares to what they learn in class, allowing students to compose their own texts (such as graphic novels), and allowing students to speak verbally about their literate journeys. Encouraging students to see themselves as readers and writers, rather than a number or a letter grade, helps improve students' self-esteem and efficacy. Teachers can explore multiple ways to assess students' reading development, but it must be done in concert with an expansion of their definitions of literacy.

Subscribing to the type of deficit thinking that places sole emphasis on standardized assessments to determine students' literacy achievement has led to the belief that African American students have reading deficits and that they are devoid of literacy skills that can be transferable to the school setting. Expectations about the ability of Black students to successfully participate in literacy events are often formed without examining the full scope of what can be deemed as literacy or literate behaviors (Heath, 1989). All educators have the responsibility to value the varied forms of literacy and help readers generate meaning by encouraging them to immerse themselves in texts that are rich and meaningful to them. Furthermore, schools can help students develop agency and self-efficacy by allowing them to choose texts that are relevant to their lives. If schools can make the connection between literacy development and the other factors that influence literacy, such as the role that teachers' perceptions play, text and assessment selections, and teacher professional development, then literacy instructional practices and interventions become more effective and meaningful.

WHAT CAN TEACHERS DO RIGHT NOW?

- Schedule time during class to allow students to participate in activities that promote flow.
- Build dialogue sessions into regular planning that encourage students to share the different ways they experience literacy.
- Read to kids using books that have characters to whom they can relate.
- Talk about what you/they are reading and ask for their opinions about the text and characters.
- Encourage student choice of texts using a variety of different genres (not all students of color are engaged by books about sports).
- Help students build social power in the classroom by paying close attention to the ways that they socialize.
- Build assessments that are inclusive of newly formed expanded definitions of literacy (assessments should not just be skill-based).

WHAT CAN ADMINISTRATORS DO RIGHT NOW?

- Build schoolwide interventions that are grounded in research and evidence-based practices.
- Structure professional development using frameworks like the Black Male Literacy Paradigm.
- Provide funding to teachers to help them build their classroom libraries (K–12).
- Have open dialogue with teachers about the "code words" we use to refer to Black kids (such as *tough group, students in poverty, diverse students*).
- Plan activities during Black History Month and beyond that include a variety of the contributions of African Americans.

CHAPTER 4

We've Got the Power
Culture and Socialization

> Mainstream middle class children often look like they are learning
> literacy (of various sorts) in school. But, in fact, I believe much research
> shows they are acquiring these literacies through experiences in the
> home both before and during school. . . .

> —James Paul Gee

POWER AND CONTEXTUAL UNDERSTANDING AND THE
RELATIONSHIP TO LITERACY

Another component that allows researchers to use literacy development as a means to improve overall academic achievement is related to
acknowledging that learning, and thus literacy development, is a social
process that is connected to social power (Kucer, 2009; Lewis, 2001;
Tatum, 2005; Vygotsky, 1978). To view literacy development as a social
process means to acknowledge the sociocultural factors that influence
literacy, which encourages teachers and schools to address those factors. Some of the factors that account for students' disconnect from
in-school literacy development, include, but are not limited to, lack of
understanding of academic vocabulary, lack of understanding of context, the difference between the home discourse (of African American
students) and school discourse, and the positioning of social power and
comprehension of social codes by African American students within
the classroom.

With regard to student vocabulary, academic language, and the impact of the connection to expected school literacy, students are often
exposed to vocabulary and academic language that is decontextualized
from the content being studied and the relevance to their lives (Bloome
& Bailey, 1992; Tatum, 2005; Vygotsky, 1978). For African American
students, whose primary or home vocabularies sometimes differ from
school discourse, a decontextualized use of vocabulary terms external-
izes the content. Students who are able to use vocabulary in context

have access to materials that are relevant to their lives, and students whose home literacies are given credence in the classroom and linked to classroom content have a better chance at developing literacy and language that are congruent with the expectations of the school.

The lack of social power also impedes the connection to school-expected literacy. In the book *Literacy Practices as Social Acts*, Lewis (2001) conducted a study and noted that students who did not make connections between their home discourse and school discourse also lacked social power in the classroom. She noted that social power and socialization in the classroom were the most important factors in students' literacy development. In her study, she observed a 5th-grade class for a whole school year, and the classroom teacher used the book club model as an instructional practice. As a part of the book club, students were grouped with their peers according to teacher selection. Students were required to read passages from texts that they chose and were asked to write their thoughts on those passages by connecting them to their lives, to other texts that they had read, and to other class discussions. Students were then asked to participate in discussions with their reading groups that were related to the texts and their reading logs.

As educational researchers like Vygotsky and Bandura have suggested, students learn when they are allowed to express their contextual understanding and are given the space to dialogue about their comprehension with more knowledgeable others (which can include other students, teachers, or other adults). When students engage in learning as a social process, their understandings change based on the different information and vantage points presented by others and the challenging of their perspectives. Lewis (2001) documented that when students lacked the social power and social codes needed to obtain that power among their peer group, they also lacked access to the dialogue that allowed them to change their perspectives; thus, their access to learning was limited.

To connect their literacy practices to expected school-based literacy, African American students must be given the space to learn appropriate social codes within the classroom. Social codes are the behaviors, mores, or adaptations to an environment that would be acceptable to most members of that environment. I recognize some teachers may find it difficult to teach students the social codes that would be acceptable in school and that would grant them access to opportunities for socialization with other students; however, if teachers understand the backgrounds from which their students come, they can structure their classrooms in such a way that allows for the linkage of student experiences to the context of the school. By helping students participate and build the processes that allow them to link their contextual understanding to that of the school or the classroom, teachers can help students build the social capital needed to participate in the learning process.

Contextual knowledge plays a prominent role in student literacy development. When students begin any literacy event, whether it is at home or school, they bring with them a repository of information that allows them to access the content. Students' contextual knowledge is linked to their identities, and their identities are linked to their culture and language. All of those entities affect how they view the world (Bakhtin, 1986). By understanding the role that contextual knowledge plays, we can help students make connections to reading and help them learn multiple social codes. Helping students make connections to their lives also helps them understand academic vocabulary and contextual references within the texts they read. Furthermore, as Lewis (2001) highlighted in her study, and as Kristeva (Kristeva & Moi, 1986) and Alfaro (1996) documented, intertextual understanding helps students make meaning. Helping African American male students understand the underlying, or secondary, discourses present in much of in-school reading, and adding those understandings to their cultural and academic ethos, will aid their understanding of school-based literacy.

THE ACADEMIC ACHIEVEMENT GAP
VERSUS THE EDUCATION DEBT

Educators have been spending time, money, and resources to address a phenomenon known as the academic achievement gap. As it is commonly defined, the achievement gap is the difference in the scores on standardized assessments and in the graduation rates of African American students as compared to the achievement of White and Asian students using those same measures (Franzak, 2006; Morgan & Mehta, 2004). The academic achievement gap is documented in local, state, and nationally standardized assessments, and there is a distinct and noticeable disconnect between how students actually connect to literacy in practical situations (e.g., classrooms) versus how they are assessed on standardized tests.

One of the most commonly cited factors for the difference in achievement between African American students and White students is socioeconomic level. Many believe in the notion that there is a direct correlation between poverty and intelligence or achievement.

Herrnstein and Murray (1994) proposed that there are direct links between race, socioeconomics, and achievement. They also intimated that African American students and other students of color were less intelligent because their test scores indicated it. As a result of Herrnstein and Murray's racist claims about the intelligence and achievement of people of color, their book was met with much criticism from politicians, educators, and scientists.

While there are less-controversial perspectives than the ones presented by Herrnstein and Murray (1994) that propose direct links between poverty and achievement, the idea is still problematic. Authors like Payne (1995), for instance, asserted that poverty could be understood by using a framework and that the understanding of that framework could be used for improving learning outcomes for students. The problem with notions such as these is that they rarely address the sociocultural and sociopolitical factors that contribute to poverty and underachievement. Moreover, there is minimal evidence that a student's economic status is a primary determinant for his or her achievement, although there are a preponderance of students who fall in both low economic status and low achievement categories. The belief that the economic level of the student is the main factor contributing to underachievement in African American students is countered by Morgan and Mehta (2004), who point to the fact that the academic achievement of African American students cannot be solely attributed to income, as the children of African American parents who have comparable incomes to their White counterparts oftentimes experience different levels of success.

The fact that there is still a gap in observable achievement between African American students and White students with comparable income levels is a phenomenon that should have educators, researchers, and politicians scrambling to look for answers and solutions to address it. However, school reform is mostly centered on using data from culturally biased assessments to continue to drive home the point that African American students don't fare as well and that it is due to their family's income level. In a meta-analysis conducted by Hattie (2016), he found that socioeconomic status had an overall .54 effect size on student achievement. While, according to Hattie (2012), socioeconomic status may yield a statistically significant impact (an effect size of .4 or above was considered significant), there were roughly 100 other variables (instructional in nature) that had a more significant impact on student achievement than socioeconomic status. Thus, the notion that poverty has a significant impact on student achievement, as it specifically pertains to African American students, needs to be examined further.

In their 2006 report *Leaving Boys Behind: Public High School Graduation Rates*, Greene and Winters cited a correlation between underachievement and the dropout rates of African American students. According to Greene and Winters's data, African American students on average performed about 20–30 percentage points lower on standardized exams than their White and Asian peers. The assessments measured their achievement in reading and math proficiency. Additionally, African American students had overall graduation rates that were about 20–30 percentage points lower than their White counterparts. Similarly, the 2013 *Condition of Education* report by the National Center for Education Statistics (NCES) documented that between the years of 2009 and 2010, the average national graduation rate was 78%, while the graduation rate of White students was 83% and the graduation rate of African American students was 66% (NCES, 2013). In Michigan in 2013, the average graduation rate of all students was 75%, the graduation rate of White students was 81%, and the graduation rate for African American students was 59% (NCES, 2013). In previous decades, there was no evidence that concern was given to the achievement gap that existed between African American students and their White peers, and empirical studies conducted to address the issue were nonexistent (Morgan & Mehta, 2004). After examining hundreds of studies that addressed academic underachievement, Morgan and Mehta (2004) found that very few studies addressed the issues surrounding the underachievement of African American students specifically.

The data that highlight the achievement gap also identify a gap in reading proficiency scores. The annual NCES *Condition of Education* reports document the findings of the reading scale scores of students as they are measured by the National Assessment of Educational Progress (NAEP). The data have consistently reported a gap in reading scale scores between African American students and White students since the early 1990s. The average differential in reading scale scores between African American students and White students has ranged between 27 and 35 points (NCES, 2011, 2013). Although data like these help illuminate that there is in fact a gap between the reading proficiency of African American students and their White counterparts as measured by standardized assessments, researchers like Morgan and Mehta (2004) have contended that not enough studies exist with empirical findings that present viable solutions to addressing the discrepancy in graduation rates and reading proficiency between African American students and White students. Furthermore, studies have not provided districts and schools with the type of authentic data needed to delve deep into the reasons why African American students perform lower on these assessments.

In my experience as an educator, when data are provided to the educators in a system, very little instruction changes on a systemic level, even when educators are made aware of the academic discrepancies. When interventions are implemented, they are usually programmatic in nature and rarely seek to change the core instruction of the classroom, the culture of the school, or the social practices enacted by the staff that support the larger dominant cultural context.

Although standardized assessments do not accurately depict African American males' proficiency and connection with literacy, what they do is highlight the lack of emphasis that schools have placed on the problem of using equitable assessment and instruction methods that meet the literacy needs of African American students. One can access the assessment data in any school in the United States and predict that African American students will fall at the bottom of the literacy continuum. The NCES's *Condition of Education* also reported that there was a roughly 27-point negative differential when the reading scale scores of 8th-grade African American students were compared to those of White students (NCES, 2011, 2013). Furthermore, other data show that 12th-grade African American students also have roughly a 27-point negative differential when compared to the reading scale scores of White students. Scale scores were used to calculate reading proficiency on a 0- to 500-point scale.

The NCES also reported that between the years 2000 and 2010, approximately 33% of all 4th-grade students (all races) read below basic reading level, approximately 25% of all 8th-grade students read below basic reading level, and approximately 26% of the total population of 12th-grade students read below basic reading level (NCES, 2011). Basic reading proficiency is defined as partial mastery of fundamental reading skills as measured by the NAEP. Assessments administered by NAEP test for skills that students should know or be able to do with respect to their grade level (Lindo, 2006; NCES, 2011, 2013). In other words, assessments like the NAEP and other standardized assessments test for students' ability to comprehend text and language that aligns with the context of school. As a result of that understanding, the problem with the disconnect between African American males' in-school and out-of-school literacy can be properly identified. If African American students (particularly males) disconnect or reject texts that exist within the school context, and if most standardized tests assess their understanding of those same texts and their assimilation with the dominant culture, then data from those same assessments will tell us that African American males cannot and do not read. The 2016 version of the NCES *Condition of Education* does not show achievement scores that are much improved from the 2011 and 2013 reports. Thus, according to the NCES and the NAEP, reading proficiency scores have remained flat within the past 7 to 10 years.

Ladson-Billings (2006) presented a different view of the achievement gap. In her article "From the Achievement Gap to the Education Debt: Understanding Achievement in U.S. Schools," she asserted that the achievement gap is not a gap at all; rather, it is an educational debt that is owed to African American children. Ladson-Billings made the apt comparison between the achievement gap and the American deficit and debt. A deficit is established when expenditures exceed revenue, while a debt represents what is owed but never paid. As Ladson-Billings pointed out, many presidential administrations have bragged about eliminating the national deficit while the national debt continued to grow. While many presidential administrations may have temporarily eliminated the deficit, the national debt has been growing for quite some time (Ladson-Billings, 2006). Thus, "our focus on the achievement gap is akin to a focus on the budget deficit, but what is actually happening to African American and Latina/o students is really more like the national debt. We do not have an achievement gap; we have an education debt" (p. 5).

To pay the educational debt, we need to acknowledge the unaddressed sociopolitical, economic, and psychological needs of African American children along with their academic and literacy needs. Any movement toward meeting these needs for African American children will have to include schools as central to the solution and will have to occur in tandem with national social and economic justice movements. Schools and districts must be courageous, unapologetic champions of social justice in order to improve schools for African American males.

One of the ways schools can start to pay back the educational debt owed to African American students is by seeking improved connections to school-related literacy. Improved connections to school-related literacy have proven to be the single most important factor for increased overall student achievement across subject areas (Lindo, 2006). Although researchers such as Lee (2002); Lindo (2006); and Schoenbach, Braunger, Greenleaf, and Litman (2003) have documented a positive correlation between student achievement and teacher engagement in subject-area work through increased classroom conversation, they have also indicated that educators do not frequently engage in discourse with one another about how to improve literacy. Conversely, for the most part, schools typically do not seek to understand the literacy practices of African American males from the students themselves; instead, students are exposed to and required to read texts that represent and support the dominant culture.

In light of schools needing to address the other sociocultural needs of African American male students, engagement with professional learning that is relevant for teachers and aimed at helping them improve the connection to literacy for their students, while important, is rare (Bryk & Driscoll, 1988; DuFour & Eaker, 1998; Lortie, 1975; Tatum, 2005). As a way to address this unmet need for teachers, embedded within the structure of the Black Male Literacy Paradigm is teacher professional learning specifically aimed at providing practical, evidence-based literacy interventions for teachers to use, opportunities for teachers to learn about the sociocultural factors that influence literacy for African American males, and recognition of the influence that home language, culture and socialization, and power, agency, and identity play in the lives of students.

The notion that America owes its African American students an education debt is rooted in the idea that education—and thus, literacy—is a civil right. History has proven that over the past few centuries African American people have been denied social, economic, and academic rights. If we can agree that literacy is a civil right, and if we use our quantitative assessment data to determine how we are securing those rights for our students, then we can further agree that we as a nation have failed to secure African American students their civil right to a free and appropriate education. If we do not believe that the standardized tests that we use are accurate measures of African American students' academic ability (which is the stance I promote in this book), we also have to agree that we do not provide access to appropriate literacy and we do not administer authentic assessments that measure their true relationship with literacy.

As the 13th Amendment to the Constitution made the institution of chattel slavery illegal, the Fourteenth Amendment (ratified by the states three years later) gave African American people the legal rights that were already given to every other naturalized American citizen. Even with the abolition of slavery, access to education was not open to African American children. Access to the social, economic, and political institutions were necessary then, and continue to be necessary, for successful engagement in academic and literacy endeavors. Those same institutions that were built into the nation's fabric were also built into the institution of school and within school content. As stated earlier, since the institution of public school was built as a means to teach core content (e.g., languages, mathematics, history, and reading), literacy was required for students to engage in these content areas, and it became the vehicle by which one could fully engage in American democracy.

The pull toward literacy has been strong for African American people since we arrived on these shores. Once here, we participated in the oral traditions of storytelling, heirlooms passed down to us from our African ancestors. We immersed ourselves in clandestine literacy activities by the warm, dim glow of lanterns. We prayed to God to send us a Moses to deliver us from the despotic tyranny of the modern-day pharaoh. We were the progeny of the continent that birthed one of the first literate societies on the planet, architects of an alphabet and written language. Our pull toward literacy was innate.

The debt owed to African American children began to accrue the moment the first shackles were placed on the wrists and ankles of the first human cargo. The education debt began to grow exponentially as the institution of slavery sunk its jagged claws into the supple flesh of the foundation of this nation. The debt increased exponentially with every lynched body that swung from poplar trees, during the very moment when Emmett Till and thousands of young Black boys like him were innocently massacred, with every bullet that pierced Black flesh, with every billy club, with each burning cross, every time a young boy or young girl was spat upon or kicked or attacked as they tried to enter a school. The debt is not a monetary one, but it is the spawn of the denial of the constitutional and human rights of life, liberty, and the pursuit of happiness. James Baldwin once said that unless America understands, acknowledges, and begins to repay its debt to Black people, the country will continue to go down this path toward destruction. African American students come to school knowing full well the history of this country and the absolute denigration that their ancestors faced. Not only have African American students inherited the pain of their forefathers, but they are heirs to the physical and psychological terrorism woven into the collective psyche of American society. They come to school angry about the fact that they know, even if they cannot articulate it, that the country, and by proxy, the institution of public schools, owes them a debt that is not acknowledged or paid.

What emerges as a result of viewing the academic performance of African American males as an education debt is the need to further examine the lack of access to content, language, and resources in schools and other cultural institutions in which African American students may engage. The lack of opportunities that African American students face and the devaluing of their culture and experiences are precursors to the gap in achievement between them and their White counterparts. Many school districts and education scholars have begun examining the impact of the education debt on students' literacy and overall achievement in school.

STUDENT SOCIALIZATION

Many have cited low literacy proficiency, poverty, the educational level of parents and other family members, the quality of the schools, the home and community environment, racist school structures, and the rigor of students' educational programs as causes for the disconnect between school content and the lives of African American students (Fisher, 2005; Franzak, 2006; Morgan & Mehta, 2004; Somers, Owens, & Piliawsky, 2008; Wood, Kaplan, & McLoyd, 2007). When we consider these variables, it is important to draw attention to the work of Noguera (2003), Kirkland and Jackson (2009), and Delpit (1996). These researchers have spoken directly to the importance of the sociocultural factors that influence the connection to literacy in African American male students.

Noguera (2003) made deep connections to the pervasiveness of school failure among African American male students and the home environments of these students. He stated, "scholars and researchers commonly understand that environmental and cultural factors have a profound influence on human behaviors, including academic performance" (p. 433). Environmental and cultural factors are rarely addressed in instructional planning in schools, and almost never accounted for on standardized assessments that measure for reading proficiency. Noguera also touched on an important theme commonly found in the literature about the literacy of African American male students. The literature supports the notion that there is a relationship between the environments from which many African American male students come, and their academic failure and literacy development. Even though researchers like Noguera have adequately made this connection, there are not enough studies that provide empirical evidence of the link between students' home environments, the cultural environments in schools, and the literacy and academic achievement of students.

Kirkland and Jackson (2009) found that students' socialization had a direct impact on their connection to literacy. The students in their study categorized themselves into subgroups based on their social connections with one another. What the researchers found was that students' language, reading preferences, clothing, and music all affected how they saw the world, and that their perceptions of the world helped them make connections to several different literacies. Many of the subcategories to which students belonged were socially institut- ed or self-proclaimed, which provided some insights about linkages between socialization, power, and literacy practices. Sometimes it is students' allegiances to these cultural connections that position them against school-expected literacy (Delpit, 1996; Kirkland & Jackson, 2009; Ogbu, 1991; Steele, 1992).

Thus, we can conclude that students' socialization and power is based on their self-identified cultural connections along with the ones that are placed upon them. Their cultural connections may be based on their neighborhood affiliation, ethnic background, music choice, or heritage. Therefore, if the status of "coolness" (the term *cool* was ex- plored in Kirkland and Jackson's research) does not align with what is deemed cool within their school texts, students may reject those texts. Conversely, when students are taught to develop multiple identities that may incorporate ideas outside the boundaries of what they originally might not deem as cool, they may be more apt to accept them.

Delpit (1996) presented a different perspective and approach to promoting student learning and literacy through connection to one's cultural environment. Delpit challenged Gee's (2001) assertions that secondary or dominant discourses are impossible to teach. The second- ary or dominant discourse is the surface language that many members of a group or society understand. It is often thought that marginalized students cannot learn the dominant discourse because they have very little contact and access to the cultural and economic institutions that provide the foundation on which it stands (Delpit, 1996). However, as Delpit documented, teachers who recognized the need for students' participation in the dominant discourse also provided the means for them to do so. Delpit recounted several stories in which students of color, who came from poor families, attended inferior schools, and had no access to institutions and activities that allowed them to participate in the larger dominant discourse, were able to transcend those obsta- cles by acquiring the language of the dominant discourse and using it to challenge cultural and economic oppression.

The core of Delpit's argument referenced the significant role that teachers play in helping students acquire the dominant discourse with regard to language and literacy development and understanding of the dominant culture. It is important to note, however, that Delpit (1996) did not call for the devaluing of students' home languages, discourses, and cultural practices. She encouraged educators and researchers to support the idea that "the point must not be to eliminate students' home languages but rather to add other voices and discourses to their repertoires" (p. 163). Delpit's stance on the role of teachers in helping students acquire the necessary discourse to aid in their connection to school-related literacy was similar to the position taken by Tatum (2005), wherein he argued that teachers should participate in a three-pronged approach (incorporating theoretical, instructional, and professional development strands) to improving the literacy development of African American males. When teachers have students whose voices are devalued and whose primary discourse differs greatly from the discourse of school, the teachers need to help students to navigate through permeable boundaries between discourses and form malleable identities (Delpit, 1996; Lewis, et al., 2007; Tatum, 2005).

Based on the research about the socialization of African American male students and the implications for helping them connect to school-expected literacy and content that exists within the school context, here are a few recommendations for educators:

- Embed school-related literacy events in the theories of Vygotsky and Bandura by designing instruction that allows students to participate in literacy that involves social processes.
- Conduct inquiry sessions about what learning and literacy are and view them from a sociocultural perspective that account for students' varying discourses.
- Position the learner at the center of instructional, classroom, and organizational decisions.
- Develop professional development around teachers' understandings of how students' identities are formed and about how students can form multiple identities that give them access to the larger secondary discourse through school-related texts.

When it comes to literacy, if educators can agree on some basic tenets—(1) that literacy is a social process, (2) that African American male students often disconnect from or reject the institution of school and school-related texts, and (3) that standardized assessments do not accurately measure African American male students' literacy proficiency—then it should not be surprising that data collected from the NCES show that African American students have consistently scored significantly lower on assessments such as the NAEP (see NCES, 2011, pp. 42–44; NCES, 2016, pp. 144–146). The Black Male Literacy Paradigm provides an alternate view of how literacy is developed by seeking to help teachers and other educators to reconceptualize the idea of what literacy proficiency is and use alternate assessments to measure it.

It is common for schools and districts to use data from assessments like the NAEP or other state- and locally sponsored standardized assessments, but it is the use of these data that has contributed to high instances of school dropout among African American students and continued low achievement on standardized tests. Teachers, administrators, parents, and students review the data that position African American students at the bottom of the achievement continuum, and support without scrutiny the internalizing of this data that destroys the academic self-esteem, agency, and efficacy of African American children. As mentioned earlier, without agency (the motivation to complete a task), and efficacy (the belief that one can successfully complete a task), African American students will not be successful in school, and this type of data is detrimental to building both agency and efficacy. Moreover, this type of data is used to disproportionately track (many times without the type of inquiry needed to determine appropriate placement) African American students into remedial math, science, and English classes, and countless others are steered into special education programs. All too often, African American students, particularly African American boys, find themselves unable to get out of these tracks and shed these designations.

If we take a deeper look at what is said about student performance data, researchers like Ernst-Slavit and Mason (2011) documented the effect of academic language on the literacy development of students. They stated that data about literacy proficiency of African American students showed that "many students perform poorly because they cannot handle the unique linguistic demands of each academic content area" (p. 430). When students lack the language specific to a content area, they fail to make connections to the context of the text. Contextual knowledge (which is connected to socialization and social experiences) is needed to help students connect to texts. It refers to the background knowledge students bring to a literacy event to make connections to meanings and promote comprehension.

Since we have already established that the connection to school-based texts is paramount in the move toward improved academic outcomes for African American male students, we should delve deeper into how gestalt theory (Koffka, 1935), social development theory (Vygotsky, 1978), treating literacy practices as social acts (Lewis, 2001), and exploring the literacy lives of African American males (Tatum, 2005) all coalesce. Additionally, while theoretical foundations are important, educators need to understand how they can be practically applied. Educators need to have an exhaustive study of the ways that

African American male students develop literacy habits. We need to take the advice of researchers like Lindo (2006) who support the idea of expanding the number of research studies related to literacy that include African American students and their experiences as a focus. Although studies such as the ones that Delpit, Kirkland and Jackson, and Noguera conducted can help add to the body of research that specifically addresses the needs of African American male students, more are needed. When the findings of multiple research studies are explored, applied, and reinstituted after application, we move closer to a solution for remaking the institution of school as a vehicle to improve literacy development for African American male students.

Lindo (2006) examined 971 articles related to reading intervention experiments. She found that none of the articles disaggregated findings according to race, with no listed implications for African American students. Furthermore, Lindo found that only 14 of the 971 documented studies she reviewed had 50% or more African American students as central figures of the studies and only 79 of the total number of articles used school-age children in kindergarten through 12th grade. Moreover, she found that no studies focused on the professional development of teachers. Given the documented data on the achievement of African American students on standardized assessments, particularly in the area of reading, both quantitative and qualitative studies and data are needed.

We know that African American males fully participate in the classroom environment and in school-related literacy events when they know and are able to use the academic language of the school or classroom and when they socialize within the environment with other student academicians. Moreover, when African American male students are able to understand and use social codes that are appropriate for the classroom, they are able to gain the social power necessary to participate in social learning processes. As a result, when students make connections socially, they are able to make connections to texts and they develop the ability to make references to other texts and information pursuant to the content being discussed (Bloome & Bailey, 1992; Cazden, 1988). The understanding of context plays an important role in literacy development and has a direct connection to students' background knowledge via academic vocabulary, cultural experiences, and socialization within and outside of the classroom environment. Thus, it is extremely important to give teachers the basis to understand how students access school-related literacy through the sociocultural paradigm.

The most commonly cited factors affecting the achievement of African American male students are not the only existing factors. Some may argue that the aforementioned factors are most consistent with academic underachievement in African American males; however, they only speak to student and family behaviors and other non-school-related activities. The negative sociocultural factors that are most often mentioned do not implicate the core instruction of the classroom (see Elmore, 2003), school policies and processes, the barriers to obtaining content knowledge, and teacher preparedness. Students' experiences in school have a direct connection to how they view school and access academic content. For many African American males, school environments have a direct correlation with their academic outcomes. A sociocultural approach to addressing students' learning needs can help teachers understand the factors that affect students' in-school literacy connection and how the impact of these factors have historically contributed to school failure for African American students.

WHAT CAN TEACHERS DO RIGHT NOW?

- Make sure school and classroom celebrations are inclusive of African American students regardless of their economic or social standing in the school.
- Plan lessons that speak to the cultural history of African American students.
- Align your curriculum to the necessary skills while incorporating content that reflects the cultural experiences of African American students.
- Multiple texts should be made available for students, not just the ones that teachers love or those that are a part of the "canon." The research shows that students connect with books when they choose them. Make an effort to include student selections in your curriculum.
- Build a list of the ways that you can begin to pay back the education debt at the classroom level.
- Help students understand the dominant discourse by connecting their home language to the language of school.
- Put African American males in leadership positions in the classroom and encourage them to run for positions like president of student council.

WHAT CAN ADMINISTRATORS DO RIGHT NOW?

- Work with teachers to identify the components of the education debt and discuss strategies that schools can use to pay back the debt.
- Build a co-teaching model where teachers can collaborate on designing classrooms founded on equity.
- Organize in-district bus trips where staff can visit the communities that feed into the school.
- Give students of color a voice by promoting regular whole-school dialogue days where students can talk about their school experiences and provide feedback to staff.
- Hold schoolwide literacy events that include students' favorite characters from what they are reading.
- Give students the ability to participate in recess time or other times when they can play and/or be creative.
- Partner with the closest public library and take groups of students there to familiarize them with the space.

CHAPTER 5

You Mean I Can't Even Be Black in the Hallway?!?

Discourse Communities and the Relationship Between Power, Agency, and Identity

> None of us—black, white, Latino, or Asian—is immune to the stereotypes that our culture continues to feed us, especially the stereotypes about Black criminality, Black intelligence, or the Black work ethic. In general, members of every minority group continue to be measured largely by the degree of our assimilation—how closely speech patterns, dress, or demeanor conform to the dominant White culture—and the more that a minority strays from these external markers, the more he or she is subject to negative assumptions.
>
> —President Barack Obama

STUDENT IDENTITIES

The intersectionality of culture, race, gender, pedagogy, and literacy is well documented and either leads to connection or disconnection between African American students and school content, resulting in either the immersion in or rejection of the institution of school. The intersectionality of these themes speak not only to the nature of how literacy is developed for African American students but also to the misguided expectation that African American students should automatically connect to school-related literacy. Additionally, these themes highlight the need for educators to understand the multiple literacies that African American male students bring to the school environment and how those literacies connect to their identities. Although the impact of each of these themes is situated theoretically in research studies, data support the importance of the discourse of home and community and its connection (or lack thereof) to the discourse of school. Understanding of the impact of these themes and how they intersect to shape literacy can be pragmatically applied to the real-world context of schools and classrooms to improve literacy instruction.

As discussed in Chapter 2, agency and efficacy are essential components in the making of a person's identity. Gee (2001) defined research in literacy using sociocultural means as focusing more on the identity of the research subject, rather than on strategy development. If we proceed with the notion that learning and literacy are socially constructed, according to Gee, one's cultural identity is central to the understanding of a text. Simply put, if a student's identity does not match, or runs counter to, the ideas presented in a particular text, that student will either reject or fail to comprehend that text. Conversely, if a student is given the proper tools to effectively develop literacy in the school context (e.g., a highly skilled and prepared teacher, culturally relevant texts, instruction that values their out-of-school identities, and skill development where needed), there is an increased likelihood that a student will connect their identities and out-of-school literacy activities to the school environment. We must understand that perceptions about African American students' identities are tied to how well they assimilate (or do not assimilate) to the dominant cultural narrative, and the perceptions of their literacy development are tied to the literacy assessments that we give to them. As we established previously, school-expected literacy supports a dominant cultural worldview, so it is only natural that the assessments that follow are also aligned to this worldview. With this understanding, the case can be made that the assessments that we give to African American students test more for their identity alignment to texts or their knowledge of the dominant cultural worldview rather than for the different repositories of knowledge that they possess that represent their lived experiences.

It is important that teachers' choices for texts, assessments, and their perceptions about students and their abilities are aligned to their students' cultural experiences and identities. When teachers approach teaching their students with these commitments, they help increase their efficacy and agency. While students need the opportunity to assert their identities and talk about how their identities either restrict or give them access to texts, teachers also need opportunities to speak about how their own efficacy, agency, and identities connect to those of their students. The Black Male Literacy Paradigm makes the space for teachers to speak about their own perceptions and beliefs about students' identities and how those perceptions can aid students in the connection to in-school literacy, adding to the larger conversation about literacy as it is viewed through the sociocultural paradigm.

As Bakhtin (1986) pointed out, identity is also linked to contextual knowledge, and contextual knowledge is linked to how texts and content are perceived. So, student language and discourse are linked to identity and how students comprehend content within and outside of their contextual framework (Bakhtin, 1981, 1986). Consequently, it became especially important that the discussions that I led in my own study (Johnson, 2016) were framed to help teachers understand student identity and the role it plays in students' connection to school-expected literacy. In order to understand how to connect students' identities to the texts and the secondary discourses inherent in school, we must establish a common way to approach this idea of what an identity is.

Gee (2001) defined and framed the concept of identity in the following way:

> When any human being acts and interacts in a given context, others recognize that person as acting and interacting as a certain "kind of person" or even as several different "kinds" at once. . . . A person might be recognized as being a certain kind of radical feminist, homeless person, overly macho male, "yuppie," street gang member, community activist, academic, kindergarten teacher, "at risk" student, and so on and so forth, through countless possibilities. The "kind of person" one is recognized as "being," at a given time and place, can change from moment to moment in the interacting, can change from context to context, and, of course, can be ambiguous or unstable. Being recognized as a certain "kind of person," in a given context, is what I mean here by "identity." (p. 99)

Guerra (2007) documented his ideas about the existence of student identity within the context of school, home environment, and literacy development, and discussed learning and identity as interrelated entities. Learning is situated in participation, while participation is situated in one's ability to access a particular discourse community (Guerra, 2007). Discourse communities are groups of people who make up a culture, speak a particular language or vernacular, subscribe to a code of ethics, or believe in a cause. The discourse communities to which students belong help shape their identities.

Learning is made more difficult when an individual's identity exists, or is expected to exist, in multiple discourse communities. If students are denied access to a discourse community because they lack the knowledge necessary to participate, particularly in regard to contextual references in texts, they essentially lack power to access the content (Lewis, 2001; Lewis et al., 2007). A precise strategy for helping students master the art of accessing content, particularly for African American males whose primary discourse community is often different from that presented in school-based texts, is to teach them how to move between transcultural spaces (Guerra, 2007). The idea of moving in and between transcultural spaces means that individuals should be taught to morph their identities to fit the needs of a particular rhetorical environment, whether it be cultural, academic, or social. To help teachers understand African American males' literacies, it is necessary to guide teachers through conversations about how to help students navigate cultural spaces at different times and junctures.

DISIDENTIFICATION WITH SCHOOL

Researchers like Steele (1992) have written about the idea that African American male students struggle with moving between transcultural spaces because they have the fear of "acting White." Theories about stereotype threat (Steele's [1992] stereotype threat theory) and opposition to the dominant culture (Ogbu's [1991] oppositional culture model) are linked to students' identities and how students connect to school environments and school-related content. The theories posited by Steele and Ogbu highlight the fact that the devaluing of the lives of African American males (in and out of school) often leaves them feeling marginalized in school. With regard to school, underachievement among marginalized groups is often defined by factors produced by the problem rather than the problem itself (Campano & Vasudevan, 2009). In other words, many times the negative experiences of marginalized groups such as African American males are looked upon as the problem (e.g. underachievement, overidentification for discipline, low reading scores) rather than the factors or environment that created those outcomes. The fact that the problem of underachievement and literacy proficiency in African American males has not been addressed with workable and sustainable solutions further marginalizes students.

Theories such as the oppositional culture model and stereotype threat theory have sought to provide alternative explanations for underachievement of African American students. Referencing Ogbu's and Steele's work about stereotype threat and African American students' disidentification with school, Fisher (2005) conducted a study to test the validity of these theories. Her work centered on explaining why students rejected school. She asked questions about whether students actually disidentified with school as an institution, or whether there were other factors that led to underachievement in African American students. Disidentification refers to the intentional rejection of school as an institution because of the historical and sociocultural factors that have prevented African Americans from being successful in this country. Interestingly, Fisher posited a view counter to Ogbu's. She hypothesized that African American students reject school rather than show opposition toward it. Many may view this difference as negligible; however, the difference between rejection and opposition speaks to the question of value.

Fisher's hypothesis was in line with the research of Smith and Wilhelm (2002), whose study of boys' literacy practices documented that boys rejected school because much of the curricula were not relevant to their lives, even though they still understood the value of school as an institution. Disidentification with school would suggest that students do not find an alignment of their own cultures, mores, and values, with the cultures, mores, and values supported by school; thus, they find it difficult to identify with school as a structure and an institution. However, Fisher's study found that underachieving students' attitudes toward school were generally positive. The African American students in her study documented that they respected and admired students who performed well in school. Furthermore, students in both Smith and Wilhelm's and Fisher's studies cited that personality differences between teachers and students and differences in teaching styles served as a barrier to learning.

Fisher further discounted Ogbu's theory by challenging his notions of African Americans' cultural and social experiences in the United States. Ogbu's (1991) oppositional culture model postulated that because African Americans' ability to achieve economic, social, and educational success has been hindered throughout history, African American students have developed an opposition to the system of schooling, don't see value in it, and believe it will continue to perpetuate the ideas of the larger dominant culture while devaluing theirs. While the oppositional culture model has some validity, it fails to examine the full spectrum of African American students' abilities and does not delve deeply enough into schools' and teachers' impact on student learning and literacy development. By only examining the issue of academic underachievement in African American students through a historical lens, Ogbu's theory ignores significant contemporary cultural, pedagogical, and structural factors that contribute to the disconnect and rejection of school by African American males.

The stereotype threat theory, postulated by Steele (1992), made the assertion that when controlled for environmental factors, economic factors, and the skill levels of the students, African American students do not achieve at the same levels of their White and Asian counterparts because they have disidentified with educational success as a result of low self-worth. Again, students in the studies conducted by Smith and Wilhelm (2002), Lewis (2001), and Tatum (2005) did not indicate that they disidentified with the institution of school itself; rather, they did not connect with their teachers' pedagogical practices and school content.

Students' self-worth has been considered as a factor contributing to academic underachievement documented in the studies of Fisher (2005) and Chavous and colleagues (2003). Self-worth can be defined as an individual's perception of one's abilities, accomplishments, and contributions to the functioning of the larger society. Both Fisher and Chavous and colleagues used survey instruments to measure students' self-perceptions. They found that students generally had high perceptions of themselves, even when academic data showed that they were unsuccessful in school. Findings that document high self-worth in the face of academic underachievement run counter to Ogbu's and Steele's notion that self-worth contributes to underachievement or that students are oppositional to the idea of school.

Chavous and colleagues (2003) further documented that students in their study seemed to protect their self-concept and self-worth in academic environments because of the strong affiliation that they had with those African Americans throughout history who had experienced academic success. They also found that African American students' academic achievement did not have a correlation with their global self-esteem, a term used to describe the general feelings that one has about oneself as a person and an academic being. Thus, Chavous and colleagues concluded that African American youths had strong self-beliefs about who they were in affiliation with their race, culture, and history, and those self-beliefs had nothing to do with negative data and assumptions about academic achievement.

The concept of school disidentification was further explained by Morgan and Mehta (2004), who defined a student's disidentification as the refusal to accept the mores, cultural norms, and values that are accepted and reinforced by the dominant culture and the school institution. Within the sociocultural construct of the dominant culture, racial and cultural subgroups often become marginalized because they either have not adopted the ideas of the dominant culture; are unaware of the expectations of the ideas within the dominant culture; are not presented with opportunities to learn the ideas of the dominant culture because of a lack of resources, socialization, or power; or reject them altogether because the ideas run counter to their own cultural identities.

Thus, marginalized groups become disassociated with the cultural ideals of the dominant culture, which are often supported and reinforced in schools and in the type of literacy expected in school.

Steele's stereotype threat theory defined a threatening stereotype as an assumption having the potential to interfere with an African American student's everyday educational performance in school, particularly on important tests. Steele further stated that students try too hard to avoid the low performance that makes the stereotype more plausible as a characterization in the eyes of others, and even in themselves. Steele's theory contained a number of assumptions that were not based on the type of empirical data presented by Fisher (2005) and Chavous and colleagues (2003). Qualitative data presented in studies like Fisher's (2005) contested the ideas of Ogbu and Steele and documented that there was no correlation between self-esteem and academic achievement on tests or otherwise. The conversation and debate around stereotype threat theory and the oppositional culture model speaks to the need to explore how agency, motivation, and efficacy impacts student learning and literacy development.

The scholarship around agency, on the other hand, has some relevance to Steele's assertions. When speaking about human agency, Bandura (2001) contended, "people have to make good judgments about their capabilities, size up sociocultural opportunities and constraints, and regulate their behavior accordingly" (p. 3). Viewing stereotype threat theory from the perspective of student agency as described by Bandura, and comparing that to the data collected by Fisher (2005) and Chavous and colleagues (2003) on positive global self-perceptions held by African American students, one could conclude that students' performance on tests is marred for reasons other than feelings of fear of performing at a low level because they feel that low performance is what is expected of them.

To solidify the point that educators and researchers should search for more causation between self-esteem and underperformance on standardized assessments and other measures of student achievement, it is important to briefly delve deeper into the concepts of behavior and motivation. The work of Maslow (1943) can help us with this conversation. It is necessary to analyze why African American students might feel some sort of performance anxiety (or stereotype threat) when asked to perform on assessments that measure for their academic achievement. The antithesis of stereotype threat theory, the ideological notions that African American students have a "fear of acting White," asserted by Fordham and Ogbu (1986), also has roots in the practice and belief that the many constructions of African American students' identities are not valued in school. If we were to briefly assume that there is some validity to stereotype threat theory (or some aspect of it), then it can be attributed to African American students' academic and cultural identities not being valued within the school context. If some aspect of stereotype threat theory is plausible, then it can be constituted as a behavior, and we can support the contention by Maslow (1943), that "behavior is almost always, biologically, culturally, and situationally determined" (p. 371). Maslow's statement sets the stage for an examination of the factors leading to the rejection of school literacy by African American males as more of a symbiotic relationship between several factors rather than a stance originating in students' perceptions of self, based on their history and their racial identity, as asserted by Ogbu (1991) and Steele (1992). The theoretical work of Maslow (1943) and Bandura (2001) reifies the relationship between the socioculturalist point of view and student literacies.

However, Ogbu's and Steele's theories should not be totally discounted. There is evidence of school and school-based literacy disidentification among some African American male students, but that disidentification is related to several factors. Based on assumptions gathered from stereotype threat theory and school disidentification, or the opposition to school as an institution, Morgan and Mehta's (2004) study tested three implications to determine the relationship between global self-esteem and student achievement. If proven true, these would support stereotype threat theory and the oppositional culture model through empirical data:

Implication 1: The relationship between academic self-concept and academic achievement should be weaker for Blacks than for Whites.
Implication 2: The relationship between global self-esteem and academic self-concept should be weaker for Blacks than for Whites.
Implication 3: The relationship between global self-esteem and academic achievement should be weaker for Blacks than for Whites, and if disidentification mounts throughout high school, the relationship should weaken over time. (pp. 84–85)

Morgan and Mehta's study only found evidence to support the first implication. They believe this reflected that Black students discount the importance and validity of performance evaluations as measures of their academic competence relative to Whites (Morgan & Mehta, 2004). Furthermore, they found that "when black students select levels of global self-esteem, they are as likely as are white students to rely on their own evaluations of their academic competence" and that "when black students select levels of global self-esteem, they are as likely as whites to rely on their own academic performance" (p. 95). In other words, aside from their lack of faith in school assessments, Black students were found to be just as identified with schooling in general as their White peers.

So while one might assume that since there is a significant variation in how Black and White students perform on standardized assessments that there would be a significant variation between how Black and White students perceived themselves, Morgan & Mehta (2004) did not find this to be the case. However, they did note, as Fisher (2005) did, that although African American students did not totally reject school as a concept, they still disidentified with it on some level, particularly in relation to performance assessments.

Although researchers have developed plausible theories as to why African American male students reject school and school-related content, there are other perspectives to examine. As educators continue to attempt to get students to conform to school environments, consideration should be given to the voices of students as we try to understand why they reject the idea of school and its values. An important part of African American students' identities is their language, music, experiences outside of the school environment, family, and socialization with friends. Schools have consistently devalued African American students' identities while attempting to connect them to the values and mores of the school environment. Because schools espouse and uphold the views and values of the larger dominant culture, when students reject or disidentify with school, they are also rejecting society's attempt to dominate their identities and define who they are.

STUDENT SOCIAL POWER AND VALUING STUDENTS' IDENTITIES IN SCHOOL

To understand teachers' perspectives about how African American male students' identities connect to literacy, I conducted a study (Johnson, 2016) where I facilitated several activities to elicit conversations with teachers and analyzed the data collected. The study also served as professional learning for the teachers. The teachers documented their understandings that the identities students bring to the school environment are essential in helping them connect to school-expected content. The teachers' qualitative data further showed that it is particularly necessary for the identities of African American males to be valued in school, as they felt that school environments where they worked did not promote (and in some cases worked actively against) connecting African American male students to school.

During the same time period that I was conducting this study, I was in the hallway of one of the schools that I supervised as I was leaving a meeting. The school is located in one of the most affluent school districts in the state of Michigan (and nation)—a district with a long history of racism, discrimination, and overt exclusionary housing and schooling practices directed at African American people. The school is predominantly White, with African Americans comprising about 10% of the student population. While walking in the hallway, I overheard a conversation between a group of young African American males and a White female, a person I presumed to be a teacher in the school. The young men were in front of their lockers and were using vernacular with one another. The teacher walked up to the group and began to correct their grammar. After she walked away, one of the young men replied, "Damn, I can't even be Black in the hallway?!?" The exchange indicated the extent to which students feel their home or primary language is not valued in school, and thus, their identities are not valued.

The data collected from the teachers in the study captured their understandings of the importance of valuing students' identities as a means to connect them to teachers, and to the school as an institution. Acknowledging African American male students' cultural identities is essential to helping them link to in-school texts and in-school contexts. As Gee (2001) asserted, if students' identities run counter to understandings of ideas presented in a school-based text, and there is no space in the classroom to deconstruct representations of identity present in texts, they will reject the text. Similarly, if students' identities are not valued at school or in a classroom, they will reject relationships with teachers and reject the school environment.

As part of the study, participants read Tatum's *Teaching Reading to Black Adolescent Males: Closing the Achievement Gap* (2005). I engaged 25 teachers in discussions and activities about their experiences with teaching African American male students, specific to their literacy instruction. Valuable data was collected as teachers who taught in urban and suburban areas discussed instructional practices, historical implications for schooling for African American males, and their own efficacy as teachers. As we explored Tatum's text, we focused much of our conversation around his Nesting Ground Framework, which consists of three strands: (1) Theoretical Strand, (2) Instructional Strand, and

(3) Professional Development Strand. Our participants explored the strands and talked about their experiences with each.

During our time together, the teachers and I discussed the idea of teachers reconceptualizing their definitions of literacy and the role that literacy played in the lives of their African American male students. At one point, the teachers split into table groups to discuss this topic and their conversations were recorded. Lynn (one of the teachers in the study; note that only pseudonyms are used here) talked about the need for teachers to listen to the voices of students when choosing appropriate texts. Lynn also advocated that texts be linked to students' experiences and identities. In her advocacy for giving students a voice, Lynn stated, "You know, like giving them permission to be 16 and Black, and have an opinion, right?" She understood that teachers have to understand that young Black men have a unique perspective that aligns closely with their identities, and they should be allowed to express their perspectives without fear of retribution.

Lynn's language and actions were deliberate in that she chose to advocate for and value students' identities, and she understood that their ethnic culture was central to this idea. She also addressed a point that I have heard many teachers highlight with regard to getting to know African American male students: She believed that teachers should give their students a voice and abandon the fear of being thought of as racist when students speak their truths. This idea is germane to the point about valuing students' identities. The nature of the comments of the young man in the hallway is symptomatic of a disconnected relationship between students and teachers, and students and the school.

The idea that schools and teachers should develop and maintain student connections as they value students' identities is a complex subject. In my study, it was a foundational belief held by the participant teachers that students' identities are and should be connected to school-based literacy. The study participants' beliefs about this notion helped a few themes emerge, one of which was the idea that in order to connect students' identities and out-of-school literacy practices to the literacy practices expected in school, there needed to be connections between the student and text, the student and the school, and the student and the teacher. This conversation about student identities and social power and how the two influenced literacy practices continued throughout the study.

At the end of the study, I conducted a focus group interview with the teachers who wanted to participate. As a part of a larger conversation about student power and identity in the classroom, I asked the participants the following question:

. . . [W]hen we talk about identity, when we talk about social power, and when we talk about how students may or may not feel connected to the activities of the classroom. . . . Do you see that in your classroom? Do you see that play out? Even if we took out race as one of the factors, do you see students' ability to participate in activities in your class relate to how they're perceived by their peers?

Jane responded by discussing why she believed students disconnected with school:

There's a whole thing that goes on. And then you have the fringe people. And the fringe people, from my view, tend to be the kids who are the minority students, who are the kids in the lower socioeconomic groups. And you know, what happens—what starts to happen at the beginning of the year, is these kids who are in play groups together—who are in those private preschools together—who were—who do all the neighborhood club activities together—tend to bond and want to run your classroom together.

Jane spoke to the idea that students need to experience power in the classroom to connect with school and school literacy. Lewis (2001) found in her study that when students did not experience social power in the classroom among their peers and with the teacher, they found it harder to connect with texts; thus, these students found it more difficult to access content. It is the job of the teacher and administrator(s) to build classroom and school environments that are inclusive of students who come from different cultural, economic, and social backgrounds through relationships. These relationships help students experience social power in the classroom and in the school as a whole. Jane's experiences with students in her class exemplified the fact that the students who have access to and understand the cultural mores of the dominant culture find it easier to connect with school-related content.

As Jane spoke about how she made connections with her students to help them connect to the institution of school, she also spoke about the need to help students connect to in-school texts. She understood that the relationships teachers develop with students and those students' connections to texts are not mutually exclusive. Other evidence that supported Jane's understanding of the connection between African American male students' need to link their cultural experiences to the texts was recorded in the group discussion when I asked participants to discuss a word, phrase, or sentence that resonated with them. It was clear that Jane's understandings of the importance of connections for students developed as a result of her participation in the professional development series.

In the same activity where Jane's responses provided data about how students' identities allowed them access to school content, I asked for participants to talk about how the professional development series changed them. Jane started a conversation with her group members by asking her group: "Where do we have this strong Black male in our literature or [t]hat we talk about in class?" Jane actually connected to one of the notions proposed by Tatum (2005), our guiding text, echoing his call for African American male readers to be exposed to texts that have strong African American protagonists with a positive life trajectory. Another teacher answered Jane's question this way:

> We need to find texts that reach all students. And as our presenter [has] talked about, you know, it's helpful for all students to have strong male—African American male role models in their texts, just as it is to have everything else that we carry every day. So, we need to maybe find bridge texts and things we can bring into our classroom that allow us to make those leaps, even if we're doing a novel that doesn't have that, like maybe we can find something that relates directly to that—hits their culture, their feelings.

As a part of the facilitation of the study, I presented instructional strategies that teachers could use that were connected to the idea that teachers' perceptions and beliefs about literacy should be addressed. Hence, the participants' discussion of possible instructional strategies was not done in isolation of their understanding of the sociocultural nature of literacy.

The aforementioned participant's response to Jane's question about the lack of Black male protagonists in the literature was apt in the fact that, even though some of the main school-related text selections might not include Black male characters, it is incumbent upon teachers to provide supplementary texts that meet the cultural needs of their students. She also mentioned the need to place the same type of importance on finding Black male role models in texts as that placed on "everything else that we carry." The designation of "everything else we carry" can include anything from skill development for students to the way classrooms are set up. As the participant suggested, when teachers do things such as finding bridge texts, their understanding of student literacy further solidifies the connection of the student to the text, particularly if teachers use out-of-school texts with which students are familiar.

Without a pathway to help students make connections to the text, the school, and the teacher, it becomes impossible for teachers to get to know their students, to develop and implement meaningful activities for students, and to understand the need to reconceptualize their ideas and perspectives about how students engage in literacy events in the classroom. Furthermore, with these understandings about student socialization, the importance of social power, and the idea that students need to be able to connect their cultural identities to texts, it is important that teachers engage in activities that allow them to get to know their students.

WHAT CAN TEACHERS DO RIGHT NOW?

- Plan lessons that allow students to engage in alternate literacies (the oral tradition, poetry and spoken word, performances, and so forth).
- Build trust with African American males by engaging in dialogue protocols where the teacher and student have equal voice.
- Allow students to design theme groups and teach the standards through those themes.
- Allow students to do lesson planning and teach lessons.

WHAT CAN ADMINISTRATORS DO RIGHT NOW?

- Dedicate space in the building that fosters cultural awareness and participation in literacy events, where students can be creative.
- Require all office staff, custodians, and cafeteria workers to engage in conversations about how to value the identities of Black male students.
- Create coalitions between all school/district personnel and families where they engage in discourse about Black maleness.
- Participate in whole-staff inquiry about evidence-based literacy practices:
  - » Book club
  - » Student choice
  - » Teacher collaboration around literacy interventions
- Use dedicated time to build restorative teams as models to build culturally relevant instruction, classroom, and discipline practices, and assign African American males to the most effective teams.
- Use human resources in effective ways—teachers should loop with groups of students (where possible) to build long-lasting, positive relationships with students and families.

Part II

NOTES ON THE STATE OF

. . . BLACK BOYS

educator's oath

I swear to fulfill, to the best of my ability and judgment, this covenant:

I will respect the hard-won gains in labor practices, pedagogical practice, and research with regard to student learning, of those educators in whose footsteps I walk, and will willingly share such knowledge with the brave souls who are to follow that enter our noble profession.

I will apply, for the benefit of all learners, all measures that are required, working diligently to avoid the common practices of apathy and educational malpractice.

I will remember that educating children involves art as well as science, and that student learning should be my ultimate goal, outweighing the philosophy that learning can be measured only by standardized tests and other quantitative measures.

I will seek help from my colleagues when the answers to problems elude me.

I will take the responsibility to seek professional development opportunities intended to enhance my skill level with regard to my instructional and leadership practices.

I will respect the individuality of my students, recognizing that they may come from various and differing walks of life. With that understanding comes the fact that all students learn differently and that learning is socioculturally based. However, I must understand that one's education is of utmost importance and I have been entrusted with the responsibility to inspire and influence a student's life trajectory. It is in my power to change the lives of the students whom I serve, and this responsibility must be met with humility and awareness of the preceding fact. With this trust, I must understand that it is a great debt that I owe to society.

I will remember that I do not raise test scores, but I provide an education to a living, breathing human being, whose education and growth as a student and member of society will have a direct effect on his or her quality of life. If I am to provide an adequate education, I must remember that I must also address the sociocultural needs of my students.

I will inspire student learning whenever I can, as learning is preferable to standardized testing.

I will remember that I am a member of society, with special obligations to all of my students, those who succeed academically as well as those who struggle.

If I do not violate this oath, may I enjoy life and art, and the fruitfulness that students experience in their lives as a result of my fulfillment to them. May I be respected while I live and be remembered with affection thereafter. I pledge to act so as to preserve the finest traditions of my calling, while I seek creativity and innovation. Through these things, I will experience the joy of learning of those whom I serve.

—aaron m. johnson, 2013,
educator . . . student,
@i2_sing_america

CHAPTER 6

Where I'm From

Teacher Identities and the Impact on African American Male Students

"You know, this— this data makes me think that it's clear as day that there's an issue. You know? When you can put pages of data together to show that there's an issue. And when prison projects and construction are based on 3rd- and 4th-grade reading levels, then clearly the connection has been made between literacy and our African American males and future time in prison. If we know all of those things, why do we just keep doing what we do? Where is the systemic change that needs to take place? And I think that—that to me is the most alarming part of it all, is we know. And time, effort, and dollars don't necessarily go into changing it."

—Michael, middle school teacher

UNDERSTANDING LITERACY
THROUGH A SOCIOCULTURAL PARADIGM

In the quote above, Michael, a participant in my study, spoke eloquent-ly about his beginning understandings of the state of literacy and lit-eracy instruction for African American male students. He opened up the space to have a dialogue about the sociopolitical and sociocultural issues that impact the student literacy connection. He asked important questions that began to acknowledge that the issue has to do with a so-cial system that may resist or even construct barriers to positive change. In further dialogue, Michael posed questions to his colleagues that led his group to have the following conversation:

Susan: I think systemic change can happen when you have diversity in the voices that are heard that are pushing forward that systemic change. We keep having the same players play the same games and then keep getting the same thing. So, I think, you know, some of those people who are leaders need to tell

you where to begin . . . diverse perspectives and having more—
you know . . .

Michael: But you know what? They—in some ways, they may
just be going with the flow. Like we're all educators, and in
some ways, this has been our experience. I mean, you know
[collectively]—probably got more than a thousand years of
experience in this one room, but here we are going, "What?
Really?" And that's what we do. So—so people are—who are
[*sic*] to have power or in a position to make change—they just
may not be aware.

Susan: Yeah.

Kathy: They really may not be aware.

Michael: And they may not be interested.

Kathy: Right.

Michael: Because you look at this data and you're stuck with two
conclusions: One, Black people aren't capable, or two, there's
institutional racism. And if it's institutional racism, then the
institutions have to look at themselves.

This conversation is an important one because it helps establish
a few teachers' thinking and perceptions about the educational landscape for their students. This conversation occurred early in the study
and is a good example of how the teachers' discussions helped them
engage in an inquiry about their own thinking.

The teachers in this dialogue mentioned various sociocultural barriers, social constructs and practices, and ideas, all of which influence
how African American male students connect to school-related literacy with the accompanying implications. For instance, Michael spoke
about how the rate of prison construction is determined by the reading
proficiency of 3rd- and 4th-grade students. There seems to be some
controversy around that claim; however, if one examined the reading
proficiency of the students in most school districts (particularly urban
and suburban school districts), it would be easy to conclude that if the
claim that prisons are built based on 3rd- and 4th-grade reading scores
is true, one could predict that prisons would be populated disproportionately by African American males.

When one studies the implications of such a phenomenon, one
could argue that the school-to-prison pipeline also has connections to
school discipline and instructional practices. Moreover, the comments
made about whether administrators, policymakers, or other teachers understand or care about what is going on in schools, classrooms,
and in the policy realm spoke to the purpose of engaging teachers in

dialogue about how new understandings of African American male student literacy can influence classroom practices and institutional practices as a whole.

As Michael stated, if one believes that African American students are less intelligent, there is no more work to be done and schools can continue to look for strategies to fix the students who enter America's classrooms rather than address perceptions about students and pedagogical practices. However, his comment indicates that he believes that if school institutions and people within them addressed their oppressive practices, policies, and instruction, doing self-reflection and evaluation could change the institution. Studies such as this helped teachers engage in conversations to address their perceptions and develop appropriate instructional practices to take steps to change the structure of school to fit the needs of our most vulnerable learners.

MEET THE TEACHER PARTICIPANTS

In the study that I conducted, I collected data from several subsets of groups as well as the group of teachers as a whole. I collected and analyzed data in the following manner: (1) large- or whole-group data, (2) small subgroups of teachers who were split up into groups of five during specific activities, and (3) a group of teachers identified as focus participants. Focus participants were identified using a range of criteria that included their total number of years in the profession of teaching, their experience teaching African American male readers, their own ethnicity, the uniqueness of the pre-data collected from them, and their feelings about the effectiveness of professional development in which they had previously been involved. I used the data I collected from the focus participants (recordings of their conversations, participation in activities, and writings they submitted) to do case studies.

I gathered the group of focus participants at the conclusion of the workshop series and had a conversation with them similar to the one described in the previous section. When presented with the data about the literacy proficiency of African American students in the region, state, and the nation, participants were asked to respond to the data and consider their own students' data and their instructional and institutional responses to their students' literacy. A dialogue ensued:

Jane: That's where I think a lot of things need to be addressed, where obviously the statistics are in the end. You know, we got this many kids in prison, and some of them I was pretty surprised at. You know, I've seen some statistics before, but these were pretty profound. Even federal—where's the initiative starting? I mean, this start[s] [at] 3 years old, get these kids in schools, set up programs in schools. Instead of dealing with building more prisons, there should be more pre-preschool, schools for parents and kids. I mean, even if it means dropping the 2- or 3-year-old off for a structured program, get him immersed in reading, get him immersed in education, and just—you know what I mean? And that—I'm bringing more people of different ethnicities [*sic*] and race into the teaching profession.

Lynn: I mean, I—I've seen all of this. I've been shocked and—you know, I was horrified by it already. Seeing [it] all together at once is kind of a new shock to the system. But when you look at who these kids see at school every day, right—who the teachers are, who the support staff is, what kind of role models, what kind of leaders they have every day—and you do back up and you see that 83% of elementary teachers are White women—that's where it's happening. It's that these kids do not have somebody who looks like them being successful in a building that they are trying to be successful in. And that—that does something to a kid. They kind of disconnect, and they— they pull back a little bit. And you know, by the time they get to us, we have to do some kind of radical things to change it. I think too, the—the special education versus advanced, and gifted and talented, is really what I've been struggling with. Especially when it comes to not being placed solely in a special education program. But what classes are these kids being led to? Right? What classes are our African American males being kind of corralled to? Are they being encouraged into taking these higher-level classes—taking these AP classes? Or, are they being kind of—you know, for lack of a better word—dumped into these lower-level classes, cause that's where we think they can achieve? So that's what I've been struggling with.

Julia: What's systemic, I think—and you know, as a language arts teacher in middle school—I think that there's not a big focus right now. Like, in our special education department and some of the other things we do—and I'm not trying to be critical of one area—but there isn't a big focus on literacy. And I don't understand why that's not the biggest thing they're doing. All we spend our time on—in my experience—is math. Like, the kids just get a—second math class. With their math teacher even in there now in our grade level, helping them out with math skills. But they can't read and write. They can't be successful in science, social studies, language arts, a foreign language—

Lynn: Life.

Jackie: Anything.

Lynn: Yeah.

Jackie: Even some of the math questions on the ACT are so language-based—

Julia: And no one's doing reading literacy for them. No one's doing that. And we have kids that are in special ed that are two or three grade levels below what they should be reading, and there's nowhere to reach them, 'cause there's no class in the day to do that.

The conversation among these teachers clearly documented that they have a good understanding about the importance of literacy in the lives of their students. They grappled with the reality of African American students' disconnection from school and the kinds of literacies expected of them, as well as what the teachers believed was contributing to the problem from an instructional and structural perspective. In this piece of dialogue, what was particularly striking was the teachers' understanding and articulation of the implications and the access that exists when a student has a life filled with literacy and the turmoil that may exist when a student's life is devoid of the promise that may be found in literacy.

As I read through and listened to the audio from all of the teachers' conversations, I thought about the young man who attempted to steal my shoes when I was a child. I thought about my friend who lived across the street from me when I was growing up who was lured into drug trafficking. Were these teachers making an attempt to walk in the shoes of their students and other African American male learners? If the teachers of my friend and the young man who tried to rob me had made attempts to understand their lives and found the types of texts that would engage them, would those African American males still have pursued paths that deviated from school and other appropriate societal behaviors? Were they just products of their environments? The teachers in my study engaged in conversations about opening up opportunities for African American male students by using literacy, and they answered some of these questions for me. Their beginning ideas and conversations set the stage for their ongoing thinking about the ways in which literacy could be used to deter African American male students from prison and other negative outcomes.

This study and my subsequent analysis of teachers' dialogue helped me understand their perceptions of African American male students and the impact of those perceptions on their students' literacy. The study was designed as a professional development series using a book club model and Tatum's (2005) book as the guiding text. Teachers voluntarily signed up for the study and agreed to have their data used for analysis. Three essential questions that drove the data collection and analysis:

1. What is the progression and evolution of teachers' knowledge of and accompanying perceptions of the African American male students they teach?
2. In what ways might teachers' developing understandings about the in-school and out-of-school literacies of African American males contribute to their decisions about pedagogy and curriculum in ways that are culturally relevant and meaningful to the African American male students they teach?
3. How does the book club model of professional development encourage teachers to implement the book club model with their students, build a structure of sustainable instructional literacy practices within their classrooms, and provide opportunities for meaningful inquiry about their pedagogy?

Book club is an instructional practice that represents an alternative view on how to use group structures to facilitate the idea that literacy is a social act. In book clubs, students become members of a discourse community and are exposed to language that is varied in structure and complexity as well as ideas that represent diverse points of view. Additionally, students are provided equity in the ability to access the teacher. As the teachers in the study engaged in the type of discourse that helped answer these three questions, other questions emerged about classroom practices, societal expectations, and teachers' perceptions of African American students. The teachers also talked about schools' ability to build environments that would honor students' identities and engage them in literacy.

It is my belief that a deeper understanding of the literacies of African American males will contribute to improved strategies for teaching reading and literature for them. At the beginning of the study, many teachers asked that I provide strategies for them to take back to their classrooms; many of them admitted that the reason they initially signed up for the study was to learn new strategies. However, I designed the study and operated with the philosophy that teachers would best be able to help African American males connect to school-based literacy by understanding how literacy is developed for them and by fostering a sense of efficacy to help them do so. I did not, however, discount the notion that strategies are important. In fact, strategy development is essential, though Tatum (2005) encouraged educators to go beyond strategy development:

> Skills and strategies are only working tools; they have little utility for advancing students' literacy. They are similar to providing a student with a hammer and nails: simply giving someone a hammer and nails does not mean that the person will come up with the idea of building a house. (p. 85)

Strategy development, integrated with opportunities for teachers to consider the role of literacy in the lives of African American male adolescents, gave teachers the tools to address the literacy needs of their students. The opportunity to participate in professional development also gave them the tools to develop student-centered classroom environments. Furthermore, documenting and acknowledging teachers' perceptions and understandings of their students' literacy behaviors helped them gain a deeper understanding of their beliefs about the in-school and out-of-school literacies of African American males. Recognizing that perceptions drive teachers' decisions about curriculum and instruction planning, pedagogy, text selection, and assessment, this study sought to understand the connection between teacher professional development and the literacies of African American males through a sociocultural paradigm. I believe the teachers who participated in the study gained a deeper understanding of students' literate lives within a broader social context.

Within the context of this study, quantitative data underscoring African American students' literacy proficiency were used only to guide the conversations for teachers and to set the stage for them. The conversations generated from this study have the potential to improve the overall achievement of African American male students and led to the development of the Black Male Literacy Paradigm, a collection of conceptions, behaviors, and practices emanating from an exhaustive review of the literature on developing literacy for Black male students (including data from my own study) that teachers are encouraged to use to help build literacy for their students. The components that comprise the Black Male Literacy Paradigm—home vs. school language; contextual understanding; culture and socialization; teacher perceptions; power, agency, and identity; and teacher preparedness—are interdependent and should be used to build classroom instructional practices, design professional learning for teachers and administrators, and plan and construct school environments that meet the social needs of African American male students.

In order to use the Black Male Literacy Paradigm to its full extent, there are a few key steps that educators should take. First, educators should build and engage in the authentic assessment of content knowledge based on students' overall literacy experiences and real-world experiences. Second, educators should participate in ongoing inquiry, dialogue, and self-reflection about their perceptions of students. Third, educators should seek to expand and/or reconceptualize their understandings of the literacies of their African American male students. Their reconceptualized understandings should include multifaceted definitions of literacy and include thoughts about academic vocabulary that is related to the content (Marzano & Pickering, 2005; Marzano, Waters, & McNulty, 2005; Tatum, 2005, 2008). When teachers use academic language that is aligned to the content area, students gain a deeper understanding of the meaning in context. The teaching of reading is often thought to be the job of English language arts teachers; however, students must be able to access the content and understand the standards of participation in all of their classroom environments and across all subject areas (Cazden, 1988). Lastly, educators should engage in professional learning activities that help them understand the importance of socialization, identity, and contextual understanding for their students and that give them strategies to help students access school-related texts.

TEACHER IDENTITIES AND THE ROLES THEY PLAY IN BUILDING STUDENT LITERACY

Although I collected data from every teacher who participated in the study, I used the data from a smaller group of focus participants for deeper analysis. In doing this, I had the ability to focus on the expertise of participant educators and extract common themes. Also, focusing on a smaller focus group of teachers allowed me to gather data and isolate themes across all of the teacher demographic groups that were represented among the 25 study participants.

Before introducing the data collected from the focus participants and the other teachers who participated in this study, it is necessary to spend some time discussing the generalizability of the results and the legitimacy of using results from ethnographic studies to make conclusions. Ethnographic studies should be designed in such a way that there are multiple means of collecting data to lend validity to the study (Lincoln & Guba, 1985; Thurmond, 2001). In this study, I established the validity of the results by ensuring that they were generalizable, that the design of the study was aligned to research-based study designs, and that the participant sample was large enough and representative of the larger population. Furthermore, this study was valid because, if replicated using the same study design and data collection methodology, it can be reasonably assumed that it would produce similar results. In order to add to the validity of this study, I initially determined that I would not need a large number of study participants for the case study. However, I later determined that based on the potential variation within the data (e.g., number of years of experience, experience with teaching African American students, and personal data), I would need a larger subset for the case study. The case study consisted of doing deeper analysis of the focus participants' individual data and the data collected from their conversations as a group. I had a total of 25 participants whose conversations were available to me.

Another way that research studies such as this one achieve validity is through the triangulation of the data. Triangulation is the use of multiple sources, multiple methods of data collection, multiple investigators, and multiple theories (LeCompte & Schensul, 1999). I chose to triangulate the data collection methods for this study. Participants' conversations were recorded as they responded to prompts about their instruction and their students, their participation in activities was recorded, I collected writing samples from them, they responded to two separate surveys, and they participated in a focus group interview. This study involved engaging teachers in a series of different meetings; thus, the triangulation of data collection through the multiple methods allowed me to collect information across time, experiences, and events. Using the data collection method of triangulation added to the trustworthiness of the overall findings.

Finally, I engaged in conversations with teachers who had varying experiences. Those experiences were important to consider because I wanted to ensure that teachers who taught African American male students in homogenous and heterogeneous populations were represented; I also wanted there to be a variance in the number of years of teaching to provide a comparison of beginning, mid-career, and veteran teachers; and I wanted to see if certain patterns or commonalities emerged in the conversations that I had with them. Thus, it was important to know information about the lives and identities of the teachers who participated in the study to draw conclusions about how those identities connected to how they instructed their African American male students. The following descriptions are of the focus participant teachers. The descriptions help us to understand their racial, socioeconomic, and professional identities.

Lynn: The Optimist

In table group discussions and in the focus group interview, Lynn indicated that she had African American male students enrolled in both her standard and advanced-level English classes. Lynn identified herself as a Caucasian woman on her initial survey, and later during the focus group interview, she specifically identified herself as Jewish. She indicated that she was born and raised in the district where she taught and stated that she learned her values of providing an equitable education to all children from her father. She did not expand on how her father specifically influenced her with regard to her outlook on how to educate students.

At the time of this study, Lynn was teaching high school English in a predominantly White, wealthy school district in a suburb of Detroit. When I examined the performance data found on the MI School Data website for the district where Lynn taught, I discovered that students in the district outperformed the average for the state and the county in the subject of reading. The website MI School Data (mischooldata.org) is a database developed and monitored by the Michigan Department of Education. It keeps the educational statistics of each of the schools and school districts in the state. When compared to other districts, the district where Lynn taught was frequently ranked as one of the top-performing districts in the state. Lynn's experience is unique because she indicated that during the same time period that this study was conducted, she taught both advanced-level and standard-level 11th-grade English classes.

I characterized Lynn as an optimist because she held the belief that she could help meet African American male students' literacy needs despite the turmoil that they may have faced in and out of school. Furthermore, Lynn used her ability to form relationships with her students as a means to engage them and increase their efficacy to relate to expected school-based literacy. Lynn showed that she believed in her students' abilities to connect with rigorous school-related content, regardless of whether or not her students had previously struggled with literacy.

Jackie: The Nurturer

Jackie self-identified as an African American woman. Jackie was a teacher in an alternative school and had a wide range of experiences in her 14 years of teaching. She taught students with varying abilities, in urban and suburban areas. I characterized Jackie as a nurturer because she had an undying belief in her students' ability to succeed, she built strong relationships with them that helped her understand their lives and find appropriate school-related content for them, and she differentiated her instructional strategies to meet the needs of all her learners. Jackie indicated that many of her students experienced a tremendous amount of turmoil in their lives. The participant teachers in this study frequently identified the adversity in students' lives as a barrier to their success in school and with literacy. Jackie was adept at recognizing the tumultuous lives that her students endured and adjusted her instruction accordingly. This was one of her strengths as a teacher.

At the time the study was conducted, Jackie was teaching in a district that was a suburb of Detroit where African American students made up 94% of the student population. In the initial survey, Jackie indicated that she had taught in the same district for the past 13 years at the middle school level, high school level, and at the district's alternative high school. During her tenure, she had taught English language arts, Economics, civics, government, African American history, and world history. During the study, she was teaching Advanced Placement Government at the alternative high school to 12th-grade students who had an average 8th-grade reading level.

Although I am a veteran educator, as an educator and researcher, I made an incorrect assumption about alternative schools. I made the assumption that students like Jackie's, who attend alternative schools, did so because they did not thrive in their comprehensive high school environments. Alternative schools are frequently structured to provide environments for students who have experienced school failure or who struggle meeting the standards of behavior that comprehensive high schools expect. However, I learned through Jackie that students attended her school for varying reasons, including credit recovery, a desire for a smaller school and class size, proximity to major lines of transportation, and a flexible schedule that helped to promote after-school employment.

To support why I made this incorrect assumption about what types of students attend alternative schools, I think it is prudent to provide a few pieces of data about Jackie's school and district. According to the MI School Data website, the school where Jackie was teaching was 98% African American, and 61% of the students received free or reduced-price lunch.

Information about families' financial statuses is collected every year from parents, and it helps districts determine how to provide services for students. The purpose for documenting students' free and reduced-price lunch status is to make an attempt to determine whether or not there is a relationship between students' socioeconomic status and academic performance. Frequently, the *economically disadvantaged* (a term used by the state of Michigan) group is largely made up of African American students. Districts have often made declarative statements that link school failure among African American students to their economic statuses. However, the importance of studies such as this one was that it controlled for many of the external sociocultural factors, including socioeconomic status, to help to engage in inquiry about why students fail. The incorrect assumption that I made about the types of students who attend alternative schools is indicative of the narrative that achievement data tell about who a student is and what they are capable of.

In the whole-group and table group discussions, Jackie spoke about meeting the needs of her students, regardless of their academic or behavioral history. Jackie indicated that before students arrived at the alternative school, many did not succeed academically (not just because of their lack of ability) at their respective comprehensive high schools. Throughout the study, she documented the need to use different instructional strategies to help students connect their out-of-school literacies to in-school literacy.

Jane: The Passionate Teacher

Jane indicated that she had been teaching for 32 years. She had spent her first couple of years teaching in a predominantly African American school in the Detroit public school system. The school district where she taught at the time of the study was a suburb of Detroit bordering the city on its southeastern side. When one crosses from the city of Detroit into the school district where Jane taught, it is easy to see the stark contrast in the physical environment and in the racial and socioeconomic makeup of the people who live there.

Jane's experiences with teaching students from varying backgrounds and academic abilities was invaluable. Jane showed a progression in her thinking and an understanding of the need to accept, validate, and promote out-of-school literacy to help students connect with in-school literacy.

In the focus group interview, Jane said, "As an idealistic, White, female teacher who was right out of college, I didn't understand the varying issues with which African American students had to contend." I interpreted her statement to mean that, in her initial foray into the world of educating African American students, she was not prepared to teach students who dealt with trauma in their home lives that directly affected their access and connection to the school environment. Jane articulated what many young, White teachers have experienced when they have African American students in their classrooms. When students have trouble connecting to the school environment and experience school failure, many teachers do not know what to do to help their students.

Jane indicated that when she first started teaching, she suspected that her principal and other administrators served as barriers to students' learning; however, she felt that the administrators thought they were helping students. For example, she said that in her first years of teaching, the school administration would alter students' answers on state tests and would monitor her teaching for the purpose of making sure that students' classroom experiences were geared toward performing well on state assessments rather than on learning the content. When I asked her about her early experiences with the administration at the school where she began and how she approached learning with her African American students, Jane became quite emotional. She expressed some regret about leaving Detroit Public Schools after 2 years to teach in her current school district: "When I was there, I did good things; I felt like I just sold out."

Jane was the most veteran of all the teachers in the study, and her experiences with teaching students at both ends of the socioeconomic scale gave her a unique perspective. Also, I believe Jane's experience and years within the field of education helped her see the need to help African American male students be successful in school by improving their connection to school-related literacy.

Julia: The Analyst

Julia self-identified as a White female in her initial survey. She also indicated that she felt confident in her abilities as a teacher "most of the time," but that she could only "somewhat" help her African American male students perform at high levels. Interestingly, when a conversation

ensued in one of her small-group activities about the role that stereotypes of African American males play in how teachers instruct them,
she had this to say:

> You know what, I was actually kind of thinking as I was looking
> to you guys, you know, how can we get past some of the
> stereotypes that they think, but when they come in my classroom,
> aren't they stereotyping us? You know, and does that impact how
> they . . . how they take in what it is we have to offer, or how they
> don't take in what we have to offer based on, you know, the way
> they think they know us?

Julia's response to the impact of stereotypes of African American
male students caused her to question the students' frame of mind
as they entered her class and classes like hers. If I were to surmise
her thinking with regard to this line of inquiry, I would speculate
that that she believed that the African American male students at
her level (middle school students, ages 11–13) shouldered part of
the responsibility of the disconnect from the classroom environment
and fractured relationships with teachers. Her question about whether African American male students stereotyped teachers when they
encounter them in classrooms spoke to the adultification of Black
boys that Wright and Counsell (2018) spoke about in their book, *The
Brilliance of Black Boys*. Adultification is a term used to describe the
assignment of adult qualities, feelings, and actions to Black boys, usually by White people.

Julia indicated that she taught in a suburb north of Detroit, and
that she had taught in her school district for the past 10 years. She has
taught English language arts and social studies, and all of her years in
her current district were at the middle school level. Julia's district had
been consistently rated among the top-performing school districts in
the state.

According to MI School Data, the district where Julia taught had
a 91% aggregate graduation rate. Because Julia taught middle school,
I used student assessment data in the reading category, which records
performance at the middle school level, from the Michigan state assessment to get a snapshot of her school; however, it was also important to
highlight data pertaining to high school–age students to set the context
for how students performed on the middle school to high school continuum. Furthermore, high school assessment data are often viewed to
be a representation of how well a district can effectively educate all of
its students.

Assessments like the SAT and ACT set standards for districts that deem students college ready based on how they perform on them. At the time of this study, the ACT was used as the state assessment for high school students. The ACT organization set the mean score of 22 to denote whether a student is college ready (the College Board, owner of the SAT, set a relative score to deem students college ready). In Michigan, the statewide mean ACT score for reading was 19, while the mean ACT score for students in Julia's district for reading was 21. Based on the data collected from MI School Data, 50% of all the students in Julia's district were deemed college ready using ACT's metrics. When the data were disaggregated, using the composite score of 22 as a benchmark to determine college readiness, 50% of White students were deemed college ready, while only 29% of African American students were deemed college ready. The mean ACT score in the area of reading was 21 for White students and 18.5 for African American students. Furthermore, as measured by the ACT, 72% of all students were proficient in the area of reading, 82% of White students were proficient in reading, and 50% of African American students were proficient in reading.

Julia's identity as a teacher showed strongly in her qualitative data. Although she did not share a lot about her personal beliefs, I believe conclusions can be made about her beliefs based on what she did reveal. She asked lots of probing questions that helped to bring forth conversations among her colleagues for further analysis.

The themes in the following chapters give insight as to how teachers feel about their efficacy (connected to their identities) and the impact of their instruction on the African American male students that they teach.

WHAT CAN TEACHERS DO RIGHT NOW?

- Understand teacher identity (personal and professional) and participate in inquiry with other teachers about how teacher identities influence instruction for African American male students.
- Clarify and articulate your purpose for wanting to improve the literacy development of African American males specifically (to colleagues, students, parents, and administrators).
- Participate in professional learning aimed at mitigating teacher bias (e.g., workshops on educating for social justice and equity, antiracism institutes, and literacy instruction with the focus on Black males).
- Define and articulate the differences in purpose of the use of instructional strategies vs. addressing teacher perceptions of Black males.

WHAT CAN ADMINISTRATORS DO RIGHT NOW?

- Provide time and space for teachers to participate in ongoing inquiry about their identities.
- Provide resources to teachers (e.g., texts, access to professional development).
- Collaborate with teachers to build professional learning around the Black Male Literacy Paradigm.
- Give ongoing, direct, and specific feedback to teachers about their behaviors and instructional practices regarding how they help Black males connect to the school environment and build literacy for them.

CHAPTER 7

A Walk in Their Kicks

Understanding the Literacies of African American Males

Fires can't be made with dead embers, nor can enthusiasm be stirred by spiritless men. Enthusiasm in our daily work lightens effort and turns even labor into pleasant tasks.

—James Baldwin

ENGAGING AFRICAN AMERICAN MALES IN LITERACY

Dialogue between teachers in my study was recorded and analyzed using a framework developed by Gee (1999) called discourse analysis. Although Gee may not have intended for his discourse analysis framework to be used as a coding framework, it was integral in helping the themes from the teacher dialogues to emerge. As explained in Chapter 2, Gee described discourse (or language) as highly contextual and as having a "magical property." It was necessary to use discourse analysis to extrapolate the themes from the teachers' conversations because of the contextual and fluid nature of language and thought.

As the teachers in this study participated in several discourses about their perceptions and understandings of the literacies of African American male students, meanings were derived from their dialogues. My analysis of the teacher dialogues helped me identify recurring themes based on Gee's methods and theory on discourse analysis. Within a discourse community, participants engage in an exchange of verbal and written signs, codes, and modes of behavior based on accepted norms that they share. Gee's (1999) work on discourse analysis provided the foundation for the initial coding. Discourse analysis involved coding data as being connected to one or more of the six building tasks:

- semiotic building
- world building

- activity building
- socioculturally situated identity and relationship building
- political building
- connection building

In the case of the teacher dialogues that I conducted, the six building tasks acted in concert with one another to formulate the discourse community. The study participants acted in ways similar to how students act during school-based literacy events: They often raised questions about the text, they agreed with some of the assertions and disagreed with others, and they grappled with content as it related to, or misaligned with, their social experiences. Gee (1999) posited that the six building tasks used in discourse analysis "use language as a means to construct or construe a situation in certain ways and not others" (p. 86). Therefore, the building tasks served as the foundation of the construction of knowledge by classifying language I collected through the various methods. Within this particular discourse community, the construction of knowledge helped me answer the guiding research questions that I identified earlier.

After I applied discourse analysis to the teachers' conversations, four distinct and identifiable themes emerged: (1) teachers' recognition of the importance of and relationship to students' connections to teachers, school, and texts; (2) teachers' expansion of their definitions of literacy; (3) teachers' improved understandings of students' literacy practices; and (4) the necessity of teachers' use of evidence-based instructional strategies. The following section will highlight the dialogues between teachers and provide critical analysis about why African American male students do not connect to in-school literacy, why they disidentify with or reject school, and how they assert their identities amid school cultures that seek to devalue them. This chapter will focus on the first theme that emerged, as it had several facets that need to be explored in detail. The other themes of teachers' expansion of their definitions of literacy, improved understanding of students' literacy practices, and necessity of the use of evidence-based instructional strategies will be explained in further detail in Chapter 8.

TEACHERS' RECOGNITION OF THE IMPORTANCE OF STUDENTS' CONNECTIONS TO TEACHERS, SCHOOL, AND TEXTS

The themes that emerged from the teachers' dialogues showed that they understood how sociocultural factors in the lives of their African

American male students sometimes serve as barriers to making connections between in- and out-of-school literacy practices. During the course activities and focus group interviews, several teachers spoke about either their unawareness of, or their failure to make the connection to, African American male students' lives and their disconnect from school, the school culture, and school-related content. However, several of the teachers, such as Lynn, had very clear ideas about the ways in which school fails African American male students.

To understand the teachers' thoughts about how students connect to school, teachers, and text, it was necessary to first understand their beginning perceptions about why African American students failed at school. In a whole-group discussion on the first day of the series, teachers were asked why they felt it was necessary for them to attend a professional development series that sought to address the needs of African American male students. The notion that some of the teachers believed that student failure was the sole fault of the students or their families was supported by what they told me in their initial surveys. In those initial surveys, which were administered prior to the first day of the series, I asked participants to respond to the following prompt: "List the three top reasons why you believe your African American male students do not do well in school." There were certain common themes among 22 of the 25 teacher-participants who answered the question about the school failure of African American males. The most common reasons cited for school failure were

- low motivation among students,
- students and families not knowing the importance of school, and
- limited vocabulary.

I noticed that many of the participants had predetermined that failure for African American students fell squarely on the students' shoulders and it felt as though they wanted to stake their claim about this notion prior to the beginning of the study.

In my experience as an educator, I often find educators blaming student failure on their families, particularly African American families. What educators are really witnessing are African American students' disconnection from school and its culture, but what gets blamed are students' socioeconomic backgrounds and the environments from which the students come. In an effort to gather data on the beginning perceptions that teachers in this study had of their students, I found it necessary to ask certain questions. Some of the questions that I asked were the following:

- What would you like to gain from this class?
- Briefly explain how the professional development that you have received has helped you with your African American students.
- Would you say that you strongly agree, somewhat agree, somewhat disagree, or strongly disagree with the following statement: I believe that I can help my African American male students perform at high levels.
- I have used the following strategies to improve the literacy development of my African American male students (please list).
- Please briefly describe your feelings about in-school literacy and out-of-school literacy.
- List the three top reasons (and explain) why you believe your African American male students do not do well in school.
- I feel like the following sociocultural factors influence my African American students' literacy development (please list).
- Please list the ways that you believe students can display literate behaviors.
- Briefly explain what you do when student interests and experiences do not match your expectations for reading practices.

While analyzing the data elicited from questions from the two surveys that I administered, conversations that I recorded from teachers' participation in activities, and the focus group interview, I found that teachers' perceptions emerged. I also found that there was a link between the biases of teachers and the perceptions that accompanied those biases. It is important to briefly discuss teacher bias, as those biases have a direct impact on the instruction of African American male students.

Connections to the Teacher: Teacher Perceptions and Bias

In my research journal, I documented that teachers believed that they did *not* have personal biases when it came to their students. I noted:

We continued with discussions about disproportionality in discipline among African American students, power in the classroom, and teacher perceptions. Many teachers indicated that they did not have personal biases against students and that their perceptions were not harmful but that they believed that students and families did not value literacy, therefore, students did not perform well in school.

In the hours of audio recordings that I collected from discussions (I listened to much of it and read the transcriptions of all the data), the recorded responses of activities that I facilitated, and the data from the two surveys, I found that some of the teachers did, in fact, have biases that were linked to negative preconceptions about students with regard to their abilities in the classroom as well as their lives outside of the classroom. This was particularly the case for teachers who spoke about their students of color. Furthermore, I found in subsequent discussions and activities that the teachers freely discussed their biases about students, whether the discussion of those biases was conscious or not. For example, one of the activities we did was called "Chalk Talk." In this activity, we first watched a video entitled *You Don't Even Know Me*, a promotional video for the novel by the same name by Sharon Flake (2010).

The video featured four different young African American male students who performed poetry about how society and their teachers don't take the time to get to know them. They spoke about being regarded as thugs or criminals, and being perceived using negative perceptions even when they frequently participated in academic, creative, and prosocial endeavors such as music, poetry, art, and literature. The purpose of using the video was to allow teachers to hear the authentic voices of African American male students who felt as though their teachers did not make an effort to get to know them. To elicit dialogue from classroom teachers about how they answered the call of the video to get to know their students better, I asked teacher participants to provide information about which activities they engaged in to get to know their students.

Each table group of teachers was then asked to respond to the following prompt: "What do you know about your African American students?" Participants had the opportunity to respond to the prompt only by writing their responses down; as part of the protocol for this activity, they were instructed not to provide a verbal response. If individual participants wished to respond to the writing of another member of their group, they could only do so by writing. I did not ask participants to identify themselves because the activity called for anonymity, which allowed participants to respond to the written comments of others in their group and the comments of participants from other groups. Participants had to have the space to feel safe and provide authentic answers. In my journal, I noted the following as I observed the activity:

All of the participants seemed to be engaged in this activity, but it was interesting to read their responses and read their body language while engaging in the activity. After the activity, the participants engaged in a whole-group conversation. I gathered that many of the participants did not do very much to get to know their students. According to the literature, this is particularly important for African American students.

As one reads the comments from the teachers in the "Chalk Talk" activity documented in Figure 7.1, although they were seemingly over-all positive, many of the comments used language or had an under-tone that either devalued students' experiences or did not speak to how teachers could better help students connect to the school cultural environment as they attempted to get to know them. For instance, one participant indicated that African American students are connected to music. As a response to that statement, another participant responded that students keep their headphones on to tune others out, even when

Figure 7.1. The "Chalk Talk" Activity Representing Teachers' Thoughts About How They Connect to Their African American Students

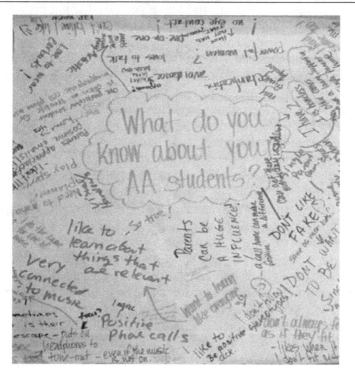

the music is not on. Without context, from this statement one might believe that African American students are generally disengaged from school if they choose to have headphones on. Other participants wrote about students being from single-parent homes, being homeless, or not making eye contact.

While teachers may have listed some of the behaviors or attributes of some of their African American students, absent from their characterizations was how they used what they knew about their students to help them connect to in-school literacy. Furthermore, many of the comments indicated that teachers' perceptions of their students may have served as barriers to how the teachers instructed their students. As I surveyed the charts, I noticed that none of the teachers spoke about what they knew about their students' in-school or out-of-school literacy activities.

In the video *You Don't Even Know Me*, each of the young men mentioned how they participated in literacy activities and explained that their teachers did not know about their participation in those activities. Similarly, the teachers in the study did not document the literacy activities of their students because they did not really know them. They spoke about the surface-level attributes of their students, which could have easily been determined without deep and meaningful relationships.

I had anticipated that the "Chalk Talk" activity would provide evidence of the numerous activities that teachers used to get to know their students and how they used that knowledge to connect students to in-school literacy. Instead, the activity helped me understand the preconceptions that teachers had of their students and the level of disconnection that those perceptions may have had from their students' actual lives and literate behaviors. Furthermore, this activity helped establish the progression of thought that teachers experienced as a result of participating in the study.

During the course of the professional development series, as teachers continued to talk and write about their understandings and beliefs regarding their students, it became more apparent that there was a disconnect between how teachers *said* they perceived their students and what their actual perceptions *were*. It is important to point out that I do not believe the teachers were intentionally being misleading. Rather, as the data will show, I believe that teachers were not aware of the disconnect between what they said regarding their beliefs and perceptions and their actual classroom practice. My intent, in part, was to engage teachers in the kind of inquiry that would enable them to better recognize, understand, and identify their perceptions of their students. The data led me to pinpoint that some of the teachers' perceptions were rooted in their biases and had the potential to influence other teachers to engage in instruction and choose texts that were irrelevant to students' cultures and experiences.

Another example where teacher bias was inherent in the perception of students was when I asked participants to respond to a guiding question while they indicated which strands of Tatum's (2005) Nesting Ground Framework they engaged in. As teachers reviewed the framework, I asked them to consider the following question: "What texts do you read that demonstrate strong African American males with a positive life trajectory?" The following is a quote from one of the participants as she answered the question. She was explaining to her colleagues that she thought students should learn how to connect with historical texts and that it was difficult for her to help African American students connect to these texts, such as a speech from one of the Virginia Conventions. She stated:

> When I teach that speech in the Virginia Convention, it's like they don't—they're not concerned about what the war was all about, or what was going on. They don't care. All they want is some barbeque on the Fourth of July [laughter]. You know. They want to hang out, turn up, or whatever. But when they get it, they understand that whole concept.

There were other comments such as this one where teachers' biases influenced their perceptions of their students. Furthermore, this teacher's group members laughed at her comment about her students as she mocked them with the type of vernacular that students may have used (e.g., "turn up"), which indicated that either they agreed with her characterization of African American students or they lacked the ability to voice an objection to the type of bias she displayed. This teacher continued to speak about her students' connection to their preferred genre of music and how she thought that the music the students listened to had very little artistic value, although it sometimes contained the themes that are found in school content.

Conversations such as these led me to develop subsequent activities and lines of inquiry to show how important it is to contextualize how teachers' biases influenced their perceptions. The argument can be made that specific biases can lead to negative perceptions of students, thus causing teachers to believe that the content that they select for their students is rejected, not because it is irrelevant to their lives, but because there is some flaw present in the student's thinking. Furthermore, as the teacher pointed out in her quote above, the students in her class(es) were not interested in reading about the Virginia Conventions; thus, they indicated that it was irrelevant to them.

A few assumptions can be made about the teacher's observation that her students were uninterested: (1) Students were uninterested in the Virginia Convention speech because it was not relevant to their lives or their experiences; (2) students did not understand the content or the context; or (3) the teacher's instructional methodology did not make it conducive for students to learn the concepts she was trying to teach. Based on the line of conversation about teacher biases, a fourth, but somewhat unaligned, point arises: If this teacher felt the way she did about the cultural experiences of her students, which was evident in how she spoke about them, what role did her conscious and sub-conscious biases and perceptions play in her students' rejection of the school text? Although I was not able to answer this question through the dialogue that I recorded, I believe questions like this one should be posed for further research to fully understand teachers' biases and accompanying perceptions as a means of understanding why students may reject school and school texts.

As the major themes of the study emerged during the application of the coding framework (discourse analysis) after the teachers' participation, it became more and more evident that the relationship between the teacher and the student was one of the most important connections in the learning process and in the process of helping African American male students connect to school content. As my analysis of the study data progressed, it occurred to me that this relationship is not unlike the connection between me as the participant-observer, the learners (teachers), and the text, and how essential it was for this study and the goals of this professional development series to have a constructive integration among these components. Moreover, this connection modeled the connection that teachers and the students should have, one that is essential in the learning process.

As I facilitated the activities of the professional development series, I needed to work to learn about and understand the experiences of the participants, particularly the teachers whose data I selected for deeper analysis. For me, this was a way to connect with the learners in this learning environment. In a short conversation during one of the sessions, I asked the participants to talk in their groups about how they believed African American male students are perceived in their schools. I sat at the table, interacted with them, and recorded their reactions to the prompt in my journal:

I noticed that the people in the group understood and accounted for the fact that they may have had negative perceptions of African American students. Also, participants talked about how those perceptions of students have had an impact on how they are treated in school.

During the table group discussion, Lynn's comment made the perfect connection to teachers' perceptions of their students and the sometimes uncommunicated expectations for behavior by which schools judge African American male students:

> But I think it goes back to, again, teacher perception. Because especially for us high school teachers, we assume because they've been in school for so long, that they have the understanding of the rules. So, when they walk into our classroom, we have these expectations that are already, again, unspoken. . . . And maybe this kid doesn't. Maybe they do need a more personal connection. Or maybe they do need a little bit more direction of all these assumptions that we put on them. And then they don't play the game the way we assume them to play. And then it creates a further disconnect.

Lynn's quote brings to the forefront the assumptions that many teachers have about their students, particularly their African American male students, who frequently find themselves in environments (like school) that have unspoken cultural and academic expectations and unspoken and unstated rules that students are expected to follow. The assumption that Lynn points out—that all students have knowledge of the rules of participation in classrooms—is similar to the assumption that students will automatically connect with school-based literacy just because that is what we expect of them. In my career, I have often heard educators make the claim that students should connect to school content because doing so will help them be successful in life.

There are two problems with assumptions like these, as I believe Lynn makes apparent. First, students are not often made aware of what is expected of them when they enter classrooms. They are often expected to read school content for the sake of reading school content, and they are often not made aware of the prospect of connecting with the content. It is the responsibility of the teacher to provide the connection for students. Second, the assumption is often made that students actually care (or should care) about the content and that learning it is somehow connected to their current or future interests. Furthermore, students are sometimes told that content is important but not told *why* it is important. Students sometimes reject the content because their teachers or school did not successfully make it seem relevant for them. The assumptions that Lynn brings to light are important to dispel because each one leads to negative perceptions about students who reject school content.

As one of the more outspoken participants in the study, Lynn explained that students sometimes experienced turmoil at the hands of their teachers, their school environment, the communities from which they came, or a combination of all three. In a survey that I distributed to all of the participants, I asked them to list three factors that they believed contributed to African American male students not doing well in school. Lynn replied this way:

> [Students] lack connection to the material; [they experience] cultural exhaustion—going through the day without seeing anyone in a position of authority who looks like you has to be exhausting—and, similarly, consistently having to code-switch or harness part of who you are is tiresome as well. [There is a] lack of understanding or compassion from teachers/administrators. I find that many of my students, particularly my African American males, are written off the second they do something seen as "wrong" or "inappropriate." Rather than trying to help students understand how to better navigate the rules of school, students are dismissed as being problem students too early.

Lynn's response was particularly relevant to the second research question, which asked how teachers develop their understanding of student literacy and its relationship to their cultural efficacy, leading to effective pedagogy and text selections for those students.

Lynn stated that she believed that the lack of connection students have with the texts, with their teacher, and with the cultural and social construct of school leads to school failure. She further documented the need for a connection between students' cultural experiences and expected cultural experiences in school and how students connect to school-related content. As Lynn talked about students' needs to connect with school and school culture, she also commented about the need for students to connect with their teachers and other adults at the school with whom they can identify.

Lynn's comments about African American students being "written off the moment they do something wrong" speaks to the larger issue of the perception of African American male students in public schools and in society at large. The fact that African American students are disciplined at higher rates manifests itself in higher rates of suspensions and expulsions for them, thus leading to an increased disconnect from school and its mores and values, and from school-related content. In Michigan, many districts have been cited by the Michigan Department of Education (2016) as having significant disproportionality with regard to the overidentification of African American students to special education programs and the disproportionate disciplining (e.g., suspension and expulsion) of those same students. These actions begin students down the path of the school-to-prison pipeline.

The analysis of the teacher data also revealed that several teachers took up this notion that teacher perceptions of their African American male students was important. One of the most notable pieces of dialogue to emerge in the study was when Julia spoke about how students develop literacy and how teachers have historically not valued the ways in which African American male students participate in literacy events. At one point during the study, I asked participants to respond to the following questions: (1) How do you choose texts?; (2) How important is contextual understanding to literacy?; and (3) Should you reconceptualize your idea of literacy? Julia responded in the following manner:

> Well, there was—there was a passage—this was one of the last things that I got to reading—on page 48—and they were talking about the movie *Finding Forrester*—and I think—I'm not going to read the whole thing. It was something to the effect of—this kid's writing this journal, and what he's writing is completely benign. It's just like, blah. And the guy who's his mentor says, "You're 16 and you're Black." Like, that's—and the kid right away is like, "What does that have to do with anything?" But writing about life through that lens—looking at what it is that makes your lens different than everyone else's lens—then kind of gives you an angle in which to see the world. And I wonder if, by pretending we don't have that lens—we don't see that lens—then we're also ignoring the fact that kids do have that lens. They are looking at our world. They are looking at our curriculum through their lens. If this is a really stupid book, if it has nothing to do with my life; if we are not thinking about the fact that they're thinking that way, we're not going to be able to make any sense of what we're teaching them.

Julia's commentary about seeking to understand literacy through the eyes of a 16-year-old Black male was key to being able to understand how her philosophy of literacy aligned to the instructional practices that she spoke about in this study.

Initially, I viewed Julia's thoughts through the lens educators should use to comprehend African American male literacy, using the notion that Julia was referring to how teachers should build semiotic, socioculturally situated relationships with their students. How African American students view the world, their schools, and literacy is shaped by their experiences, culture, mores, values, and language. Educators need to value African American males' lenses and the literacy practices that they bring to school literacy events. Moreover, Julia's points were similar to the sentiment expressed by Lynn, who suggested that teachers should be looking for the lens with which to understand the various contexts students bring to literacy events.

Lynn was the teacher who stated that students should be allowed to be "16 and Black and have an opinion." Because students are often disenfranchised from educational environments and school content by how their teachers treat them, being 16 and Black is sometimes a barrier between students' realities and their access to school-based literacy. Lynn suggested that oftentimes students feel disconnected from school and the content as a result of the treatment they receive from their teachers and how they are perceived. Through dialogue, Julia showed that she understood that the lens through which African American male students see the world is directly connected to how they view the literacy that is expected of them in school. She articulated that students may not find it easy to connect to themes in literacy of which they have little experience or understanding. As Julia showed, once a teacher notices a disconnection between students and their experiences and the school content, it becomes the teacher's responsibility to ensure that students are provided with contexts that they understand and can apply across texts and content areas.

To better establish how participants used the professional development series to allow their understandings to be positively influenced to understand the lives of their African American male students, in the focus group interview, I asked: "What role have you played in helping African American males connect to the literacy that's expected within your school or in your classroom?" Julia spoke about how she challenged her own thinking and perceptions to be able to help her students develop contextual understanding:

> I think, until this class, I was not doing enough to foster in-school literacy for my African American boys. This year the classes that I teach have changed. And because of that—and this is actually one

of the things I'm trying to fix in my school—because of the classes that I teach, I now have a much higher population of African American males. And I'm also—this has become my passion. This has become my mission in school, to improve school for these boys. In all ways. And I'm on—I don't know, 92 different groups dealing with that. But it's really—this has been my focus since the beginning of the year. And everything I do, and every book that I choose, and every activity that I, you know—it's with these boys in mind. And you know, some of the things that have really worked have been things like that language activity—helping them recognize, you know, that their language is valuable and is the way they speak, and there's nothing wrong with that.

Julia recognized her own growth in understanding African American male literacy. Furthermore, she articulated her commitment to viewing literacy through the lens of the African American male students that she taught.

Julia's thoughts and understandings about viewing literacy through the lens of her students addressed the first research question of this study: "What is the progression and evolution of teachers' knowledge and accompanying perceptions of the African American male students they teach when they voluntarily participate in a professional development series designed to enhance their understanding of both the in-school and out-of-school literacies of these students?" Julia's understanding of her own ideas and beliefs about literacy and how students connect to literacy confirmed the relationship between her instructional practices and her perceptions of students and their abilities. Through my analysis of conversations between Julia and her colleagues, I was able to assess how she called upon her instructional philosophy to help students connect to literacy. Analysis of Julia's understandings of literacy is directly related to the theme of connections and helped to illuminate the inextricable link between teachers' perceptions about their students' efficacy with literacy and their instructional response.

Furthermore, Julia's cognizance about what she learned from the professional development was significant. Her acknowledgment of how important it is for teachers to make connections to students so that the classroom becomes a comfortable learning space spoke directly to Rosenholz (1985) and Rowan (1990) and the notion of psychic rewards that teachers need to experience to be successful, with students' academic success being a major component. Some psychic rewards that might help teachers feel successful: witnessing student growth as a result of their instruction; access to opportunities that help them learn, fail, and be creative; and ongoing collaboration that help them influence the overall school environment (e.g., policies and curriculum).

Other teachers spoke about how important the connection to school as an institution is for African American male students. Accordingly, participant-teachers found that the idea of helping students connect to school and to teachers was the most important connection to be made, even before trying to help students connect to in-school content. Although dialogue among the focus participants demonstrated an emerging theme of the importance of connections to the teacher, school, and the text, my data analysis of two focus participants (Jackie and Jane) stood out as particularly important in helping to establish this claim. Jackie shared her feelings about the turmoil that students faced not only outside of school but also at the hands of their teachers and their school institutions. Furthermore, within the line of conversation about turmoil, Jackie spoke about teachers' roles in solidifying meaningful relationships with their students.

Jane also took up this theme in important ways in her comments about how the notion of student turmoil should be addressed through teacher–student connections. She spoke about her experiences with students' lack of efficacy with in-school content and how she helped them develop the self-efficacy to engage. Jane spoke extensively about how the idea of power and identity has played out in her classrooms over the years and how those concepts sometimes served as barriers for students to connect with the school as an institution and with in-school content.

Throughout the study, the topic of turmoil surfaced in multiple conversations. In Tatum's (2005) book, he talked about the turmoil that many African American male students experience in their everyday lives. Many of these experiences have served as barriers between students and school because their life experiences and contextual understanding do not connect to the context of school or the material found in their in-school texts. Among the participants in the focus group of my study, two chose the word *turmoil* and one chose the word *obstacles* as words that resonated with them from the Tatum text. The conversation about turmoil was important because Tatum talked about the impact of turmoil on African American male students' academic progress. He asserts that "the turmoil that Black males experience is deeply rooted in the history of America" (p. 26). He highlighted the period following the Civil War as particularly relevant to the turmoil African Americans face today. During this era, harmful depictions of African American people (e.g., the Black woman as "mammy"; the Black man as a marauder of some type) solidified a persona of the Black person into the American psyche. Tatum (2005) stated:

> The image of the Black male as a subhuman, unintelligent, sexually pro-miscuous, idle buffoon was everywhere—in stage shows, novels, adver-tisements, newspapers, and magazines—and it took hold of the American psyche. . . . These barriers, along with educational, economic, political, and social disenfranchisement made it nearly impossible for Black males as a group to climb above the bottom rung of the social ladder in jobs, ed-ucation, income, and political power. (p. 27)

Tatum refuted the notion that African American male turmoil exists only because of the current social, cultural, and economic positions in which African American people often find themselves; rather, he suggested that the turmoil of African American males began during the institution of slavery; continued through Reconstruction, the advent of the Black Codes, and Jim Crow; and continues today. According to Tatum, as a means to continue to discredit, dehumanize, and assert hegemonic dominance over African American people, the cultural and academic institutions of this country have served as the foundation of turmoil for African American male students. While the effects of these actions have manifested as problems within the African American community, they have deeply-rooted connections to American histor-ical actions and values.

The perceptions of African American males by the larger dominant cultural context have impacted (and continue to impact) the way school institutions view them and their ability to succeed. Tatum's analysis resonates with the words from Obama (2006) that opened Chapter 5, as they both establish that perceptions of African American males have served as barriers to academic success. If one views another as subhu-man, animalistic, and unintelligent, as propaganda and media images of African American males have reified for millions of Americans, the worth of Black lives is questioned and racist ideas continue to be sup-ported as they become interwoven into the cultural psyche of both in-dividuals and institutions. And negative images, thoughts, perceptions, expectations, and feelings about the abilities of African American males are also part of the culture that exists in the institution of school (and among school staff and students), as school is a microcosm of the larger American societal culture.

The idea that race, historical events, and perceptions of African American males have a connection to how students connect to texts and how teachers connect to them is something that the participants explored throughout the study. Perceptions about African American males are relevant to how teachers instruct them, and the fact that many teachers were raised in middle-class families and represent middle-class values may support the marginalization of African American male students through how teachers perceive them in school and which texts they choose for these students.

Because many teachers represent the dominant cultural values that many African American male students often reject, it is imperative that they understand the link between students' cultural experiences in their personal environments, the experiences of their parents and other family members, and the treatment that they face from the White dominant power structure. All of these things often support students being further marginalized and disenfranchised. Tatum's analysis of students' experiences with the popular culture and the media captures how many Black male students feel when they walk into classrooms, although they may not be able to articulate their feelings appropriately. The social power that African American male students lack in the larger society is the same type of social power they lack when they enter schools and classrooms.

Jackie's responses to two activities were especially relevant in helping to surface conversations about the impact of turmoil on the academic lives of students. Moreover, they provided data regarding her thoughts about students' connections to the teacher, the school, and the text. The first of the two activities was called "What's the Problem?, What's Not the Problem?" In it, teacher-participants were given the following prompt: "African American male students do not connect well with in-school texts." Participants were instructed to make a list of all of the things that they felt did and did not contribute to the statement. Afterward, they discussed their answers in their groups as I recorded their conversations on iPads. Jackie indicated in her response that, although many of her students struggled with the content of school-related texts, they struggled mostly to make connections within their school environments, primarily with their teachers. She stated:

> I teach at an alternative school in [District X]. And so our
> population is primarily African American. And so I wasn't really
> aware of what I was seeing and how that really relates to our
> nation as a whole. But I am aware, you know, that my classroom
> is primarily boys. I was aware of that. I always kind of wondered
> why. And I—I oftentimes have asked my students, "Well, why
> are you here?" You know? We started our class with "Why are
> you here?" And there've been a variety of reasons, some of

which have actually been experiences with their teachers. Which surprised me. And then they say that they don't feel empowered. That's what it comes down to. So, they've kind of felt victimized, in some cases, with experiences that they've had with their teachers.

Jackie spoke directly to what researchers Bryk and Driscoll (1988), Newkirk (2002), Ogbu (1991), Smith and Wilhelm (2002), Tatum (2005), and Vygotsky (1978) talked about in their research with regard to students needing to connect with both the school content and the school environment.

Just like teachers, students also need to experience psychic rewards by having a sense of agency in completing the work expected in school, and they need to understand the standards of participation to complete a specific task, all of which can happen if students develop relationships with their teachers and have a connection with the school as an institution. Jackie's comments about students feeling disconnected from school and the content as a result of how their teachers have treated them is indicative of the notion that teachers' perceptions of their students and their abilities and their understanding of their students' cultural backgrounds directly relate to how students connect to literacy.

Jackie's comments on students' experiences with their teachers were connected to the socioculturally situated relationship and identity building and connection building tasks from the discourse analysis coding framework. Her feelings about her students' experiences related to how students are perceived by their teachers and how students perceive their teachers. Furthermore, Jackie talked about how students cannot connect when they feel "victimized" by teachers.

The second activity that elicited important data from Jackie was called "Here's What, So What? Now What?" In this activity, teachers were asked to process local and national achievement and literacy data for African American students ("here's what"). They were then asked to discuss and record what the data meant for them and their instruction ("so what?") and develop potential solutions to fix the problem ("now what?").

To further emphasize the need for teachers to connect with their students, Jackie spoke about how she developed close relationships with her students to lessen their feelings of victimization:

I got tons of boys all the time. I laugh but it's—you know, if you're honest with them, they see care—they—sometimes they're so down because they're like—my son—"I don't know what to do." "Let's talk about it. Look at this and really dig in deep. Let's forget about everything else and let's talk about you. Because right now you're in control. You're 15, you're 16. You're in control of this. This is what you want to do. Let's not worry about what other people are telling you right now. What do you want to do?"

Jackie's relationships with her students enabled her to set the foundation to help them connect with the text and with school. Her thoughts about student connections showed the interconnectedness of her thoughts and feelings about student–teacher relationships and literacy, and her understanding about how to connect students to school and school-related texts. As Rosenblatt (1978, 2004) suggested, there is a recursive process involved in reading that occurs between the reader and the text, with the reader being involved in a relationship with the author or creator of the text. Jackie and the other focus participants suggested that, in order to help African American male readers begin relationships with authors and texts, there first need to be relationships between the reader and the teacher, and the reader and the school.

As I analyzed the dialogue of all of the participants, I was able to establish a more direct alignment between the relationships students have with their teachers and the relationships schools intend for students to have with texts. The two relationships are not disconnected, and educators need to understand this. The recursive process referenced by Rosenblatt (1978) and other researchers between reader, text, and author does not begin when the reader enters the literacy event and accesses a text; rather, it begins as a relationship between the reader and his or her environment and when readers engage in an ongoing process of self-awareness in which they formulate and continuously morph their identity and begin to feel that their contextual understanding and background knowledge is valued by the teacher.

Readers' connection to the teacher and learning environment must also include texts that are relevant to their past and ongoing experiences. Viewing the recursive process of literacy through this lens allows the reader to access and engage with the text. To further support this point, I used the data from an interview that was aimed at gathering teachers' thoughts about how they believe students connect to texts. Jackie did not participate in the focus group interview, but she provided her responses electronically. I asked her the question, "How important is it for students to see representations of themselves in the texts that they read?" Jackie responded:

It is extremely important for students to see themselves represented in the texts in which they read. The text allows students to feel validated, drawing a link between school and life. The text should also include African Americans who have "made it" despite the odds to help encourage the students that read the text.

I believe that because Jackie first develops a relationship with her students before introducing texts to them, she understands the types of texts that will interest them and the kind of texts that allow them to connect to the themes she wants them to understand. Jackie's thoughts about the need for students to engage in texts that are relevant to them spoke directly to Tatum's (2005) assertion that African American male students should have the opportunity to experience African American male protagonists in narrative texts that have a positive life trajectory. Jackie's view about students' connections to their teachers reveals that, in her experience, students experience school failure because they lack the connection to the teacher, which leads to a disconnect from the school and from the in-school content or texts.

To illuminate her feelings about the importance of students connecting with school as an institution, Jackie talked about some of the things her students conveyed to her about why they don't believe they connect with school. In one of the concluding activities, I asked participants to write down and discuss a word or phrase from the Tatum (2005) text that resonated with them.

Jackie indicated that Tatum's views on the turmoil of African American male students resonated most with her, as she supported the notion that turmoil has a negative effect on students when they try to connect with school. Jackie stated:

> To me, a lot of that turmoil has to be—has to deal with the multitude of ways that we—we tell or show or represent ways that Black males don't belong in school. And that is—it's kind of constant in a lot of ways. . . . There's a turmoil there—here. "If this is a place that I don't belong, that doesn't accept me for who I am, why should I engage in a way—Why should I follow those particular rules, or you know, whatever that is?" So I think that's a really, really big factor. So, for instance, Hamlet. There's a lot of ways as being a human being, they could engage. But the fact that this is White European culture, is that we don't help bridge with kids, is one more way of showing them that this isn't really about you. And it doesn't have to be that way.

The interesting and ironic element of Jackie's commentary is the way she implicates schools as entities that contribute to the turmoil of African American students. Unlike Jackie, many educators assume that the turmoil African American students experience occurs at home or outside the school environment. Jackie also made a direct link between negative perceptions and maltreatment by teachers toward students and the expectations that schools have for students to connect to the curriculum and texts selected for them, regardless of how they are treated by their teachers.

Often, teachers' negative perceptions or low expectations for their African American students lead them to select curriculum and texts that do not represent the students (Braunger, Greenleaf, Litman, Schoenbach et al., 2003; Heath, 1989; Newkirk, 2002; Tatum, 2005, 2006). Jackie's comment indicated that, as she recognized the need for schools and teachers to be inclusive of students' culture and experiences, she also understood that students have to become a part of the discourse of school and adapt to the broader school and societal context. Hence, Jackie believed African American males should become skilled at navigating multiple identities, multiple environments, and understanding multiple contexts.

Jane also provided significant insights that contributed to the theme of teachers' recognition of the importance of connections to school, teachers, and texts to emerge. Jane relayed experiences that spoke directly to ideas found in Lewis (2001), which emphasize students' need to feel social power, to connect to texts, and to be able to accomplish reading tasks put before them. Jane asserted that her Black male students had difficulty connecting with the school itself and school-related content because they lacked social power; thus, their self-efficacy was negatively affected.

Jane spoke about a young man in her class she tried to connect to in-school content. She described him as being up front and articulate about his own efficacy. Although the following quote from Jane is not specifically about her students' efficacy with literacy, it spoke to how Jane connected with her students and helped them see their own value as they attempted to connect with content. In the focus group interview, I asked the participants to respond to the following question: "What role have you played in fostering the in-school literacy practices of African American male students?" Participants spoke about their efficacy as teachers and how they influenced their students' efficacy and the relationships between themselves and their students. Jane responded to the question in the following manner:

When they walked in the door, the first thing these kids said to me—one little boy, he just—very articulate—he just said, "I want you to know, I don't do math." And I said, "I beg your pardon?" He said, "I don't do math. I don't get it, I don't like it, I don't do it." I said, "Oh. Okay." And I said, "Well, we have some room to grow." And they just sort of—and they sat, and all of these kids articulated to me, "I'm stupid. I can't do it. I don't get it. I hate school. My teachers get mad at me. This sucks." And so I told them all—I said, "You know what? I'm not even going to attempt to work on reading skills and math skills." I said, "I'm not even doing that. All we're going to work on is self-esteem." So that's all we did, community building and self-esteem.

Similar to the stories and experiences Jackie talked about, Jane's assertion that some of her students had experienced school failure because they had not connected with their teachers and that the students believed their teachers held negative perceptions of them helped establish that there was a link between students' connection to school-based literacy and the relationships they had with their teacher(s). Jane's experience and the experiences of her students were reminiscent of Maslow's (1943) hierarchy of needs: She sought to meet students' needs at the lower levels of safety, belonging, and esteem by connecting with them on a human level before attempting to meet their needs to reach self-actualization. To help a student reach self-actualization as it relates to literacy is parallel to students having the ability to connect to, contextualize, and apply concepts and themes found in expected school-related literacy. Jane's analysis of her students' efficacy influenced her decision about how she should approach the instruction for them.

Connection to School

Steele (1992), Ogbu (1991), and Morgan and Mehta (2004) defined student disconnect from school as a disidentification from the mores, values, and cultural norms of school because of schools' alignment with the larger dominant cultural structure, which often devalues African American students' home or personal identities. Whether African American students are characterized as disidentifying with or rejecting school, the fact remains that there is a fractured relationship. The findings from my study support the intertwined relationships among students' connections to the text, to the teacher, and to the school. The teachers in this study confirmed students' view of in-school literacy as irrelevant to their lives (Csikszentmihalyi, 1990; Heath, 1989; Kirkland & Jackson, 2009; Newkirk, 2002; Smith & Wilhelm, 2002; Tatum, 2005) and further suggested that if students lack connections and relationships with their teachers, they will not connect with school as an institution.

One of the activities in my study called for teachers to analyze Tatum's (2005) nesting ground framework. As a guiding question to the conversation, participants were asked to discuss their ideas about culturally responsive teaching and what it means for literacy. They were asked to engage in conversation about the nesting ground framework because of its relevance to the purpose of this study. It was important for participants to understand how the objectives of the study were directly related to the structure of the nesting ground framework. To understand the nature of teaching literacy to African American male students, one has to have the foundation to participate in conversations and inquiry about the theoretical, instructional, and professional development strands that combine to support student engagement.

To set the context for the conversation that emerged around the nesting ground framework, it is necessary to clarify and identify participants' thinking before and after the conversation. Participants read an analogy introduced by Tatum that asked them to compare the teaching of reading of African American male students to the preparation of a dinner for those of a different culture from their own. Tatum stated that in the preparation of the dinner, we would ask our guests about allergies or aversions to spices, likes or dislikes, and portion size. The analogy of the preparation of a dinner for those of a different cultural background speaks to teachers' need to understand and participate in culturally responsive teaching for students whose cultural backgrounds are not represented in the texts that they are expected to read.

Participant conversation related to the understanding and relevancy of the nesting ground framework and its connection to culturally responsive teaching was also important to teachers recognizing and identifying the significance of how students connected to school as an institution. Conversations collected from teacher-participants highlighted that teachers believed there was a distinct connection between teacher–student relationships, students' connections to the text, and students' connections to the institution of school. This was the case from the beginning of the professional development series.

During a discussion about the factors contributing to student success or failure, Jackie spoke about a personal scenario with her own daughter's experience in school. Although Jackie never explicitly stated it, the nature of our conversation led me to assume that her daughter was also African American and that the reason she agreed to introduce personal testimony was to emphasize and support the notion that African American students connect to school and school content through the personal relationships with their teachers. Jackie indicated that because her daughter struggled in school and had trouble with school-related content, she disconnected from school:

> I mean, I have to be honest. I have a daughter, and my daughter is 19. And she just struggled with testing anxiety. She knew her content. You discussed it, she got it. When it came down to the actual test, she struggled. So for her, graduating with a C average, knowing all the content, was just horrendous on her psyche. And we saw it play out as the years went on. And it just crippled her. Now she's doing exceptionally well. She's [in college] where she's carrying a 3.8 GPA. But that—it took a year of her saying that, "Oh, I can do this and I am great at this." You know? So I think that years of being told—whether it's at home or at school or— just not being validated—is just really bad.

What Jackie illustrated for the teachers in the room was that her daughter had not experienced school success because her identity and agency were not aligned to the school environment; thus, her efficacy to do well in school was negatively affected. This idea of the real ramifications of identity and agency is important for teachers to understand, but they can only be understood and properly addressed if teachers have a strong connection to their students.

Connections to the Text

Teachers in this study indicated that one of the things they felt was most important in helping students develop appropriate school literacy was to make sure that students found some connection to the texts they were expected to read. Teachers' thoughts on the need for students to connect with texts aligned with Rosenblatt's (1978) assertion that the author talks to the reader through the text and the reader speaks to the author when he can generate meaning from the text. However, before we could engage in conversations about how students directly connected to texts, the teachers were given space to explore their perceptions of students and the connections between those perceptions and their pedagogy and text selections for students. This particular line of reflective inquiry is relevant to my first research question, which asks how teachers' knowledge and accompanying perceptions of their African American male students evolved as they participated in the professional development series of the study, which was designed to help them understand the in-school literacies of their students. Dialogue taken from group discussions helped me answer questions about what the teacher-participants thought about their students.

For instance, when the literacy achievement and overall achievement of African American male students was compared to that of their White counterparts, the teacher-participants were astonished by the disparities. Data from the Children's Defense Fund (2014), National Center for Education Statistics (NCES; 2011), Schott Foundation for Public Education (2010), and Kunjufu (2002, 2005) outlined how African American males fared on state and national assessments that measured literacy proficiency, graduation rates, rates of discipline, and college acceptance and compared those data to the data of their White counterparts. I asked the teachers in my study to participate in an activity called "See/Think/Wonder" in which they engaged in a conversation with their tables about what they saw in the data, what the data made them think about, and what they wondered about the data that was not ostensibly addressed.

Teachers questioned and challenged one another about whether there was a relationship between the socioeconomic background of students and their ability to connect with school academic content. There were opposing opinions as to why students do not connect with school-based literacy. One school of thought was that homes that were low on the socioeconomic continuum were also homes where literacy was not emphasized; thus, students who came from such homes tended to reject literacy at school. The other school of thought was more related to a line of inquiry that did not pinpoint the problem, but rather asked why students did not connect with school-based literacy. These participants suggested that teacher perceptions were one of the reasons why students rejected school literacy. One of the teachers, Jill, who engaged in this conversation, commented:

> If you weren't raised reading to your children—and so we've had some conversations about that at our school, about—well that's a piece of it. But [Sally], when you said that it was this notion of socioeconomic, you know there's one statistic that jumps out at me that maybe kind of challenges that, is this notion of there are 609,000 African American males enrolled in college, compared with 1.4 million African American females. So, if the issue is socioeconomics, why are there more than twice as many African American females? I think there's definitely some sort of issue more relevant to males and perceptions.

Although Jill did not question the specific relationship between teachers' perceptions of students and in-school literacy, she challenged the notion that students' connection to academia and academic content is more related to socioeconomics than to how teachers perceive their students. Furthermore, Jill implied in her quote that African American males are not successful in school, which results in a lack of access to postsecondary schooling, which one may argue starts with how they are perceived in school by their teachers.

A DEEPER LOOK AT TURMOIL:
HOME-BASED AND SCHOOL-BASED ADVERSITIES
THAT IMPACT STUDENT LEARNING OUTCOMES

A fundamental part of the inquiry outlined in this book is to delve deeper into the topic of turmoil. The teachers in this study understood on a surface level the role that turmoil plays in the lives of African American males and how it affects their learning and connection to school-based academic activities. Some of the teachers in the study also understood that African American males experienced turmoil at the hands of their teachers, whether or not they had experienced it at home or outside of school. Educational researchers like Tatum talked about the turmoil that African American male students face and its deep roots in American history. Educators can also look to medical practitioners and researchers like Harris (2018) and Felitti and colleagues (1998), who have done empirical research on the psychological, physiological, and neurological impact of adversity on children. I would caution readers not to assume that turmoil is something that is native to, or experienced by, African American children alone. Nonetheless, because this book focuses on the sociocultural ramifications on literacy for African American male students, we need to discuss the role that turmoil plays in their lives and how it can serve as a barrier to access to the dominant narrative often found in school-based texts.

In Felitti and colleagues' (1998) Adverse Childhood Experience (ACE) Study, they identified several different types of exposure to adversity among patients that were treated in a local health system. The study identified the most common adversities experienced by the participants in their childhoods. Seven categories of ACEs were studied:

- Psychological abuse
- Physical abuse
- Sexual abuse

- Violence against mother
- Living with household members who were substance abusers
- Living with household members who were mentally ill or suicidal
- Living with household members who had ever been imprisoned (Felitti et al., 1998)

In the ACE Study, the data collected from patients allowed the researchers to demonstrate a strong relationship between exposure to childhood adversity and risky behaviors (such as smoking, illicit drug use, and multiple sex partners) known to be linked to several of the leading causes of death for adults (Felitti et al., 1998).

Harris (2018) built upon the work of the ACE Study and questioned whether the rates at which she was treating her patients for asthma and ADHD had anything to do with toxic stress that they may have experienced in childhood. Harris, a pediatrician and medical researcher who was practicing medicine in the Bayview neighborhood in San Francisco, California, at the time, saw several patients with abnormal health conditions. She was compelled to research toxic stress further after she encountered Diego, a child patient who was quite small for his age. At first glance, Diego had the stature of a 4-year-old, but Harris was flabbergasted to find out that he was actually 7. When she did further research, she found that Diego's bone age was also that of a 4-year-old: He had simply stopped growing. Harris did further inquiry about Diego's childhood experiences and found that he had been sexually abused at the age of 4, about the time that he stopped growing.

Her treatment of Diego inspired her to participate in similar inquiries about her patients' history with trauma and stress, leading her to make the connection between stress and their health conditions. Harris used the ACE indicators from the ACE study and developed a protocol to scan incoming patients for childhood adversities. She began collecting data from her patients and found that many of the children she treated experienced one or more ACEs. Although Felitti et al. (1998) were attempting to make a connection between morbidity in adults and adverse experiences that children had experienced before they reached the age of 18, Harris was observing morbidity and comorbidities in children who had experienced one or more of the adverse childhood experiences.

After understanding some of the connections between diseases and behaviors and ACEs, Harris began to survey all of her patients at her clinic and documented that recurrent toxic stress identified by one or more of the ACEs not only led to morbidity in children and adults, but also had neurological and genetic ramifications. She found that the stresses that caused neurological issues (for example, people who experienced toxic stress were found to have trouble sleeping, had negative behaviors at school and at home, and were more often obese) also had the potential to change the way that DNA was transcribed. Our bodies "read" our genetic code and use those readings to produce proteins, reproduce cells, and heal. When we are exposed to ongoing toxic stress, our bodies' genetic code–reading response changes to adapt to heightened levels of stress in the body.

Harris used the insights of her research to implement healing practices in her clinic. Not only did Harris treat her patients for the many health-related issues for which they originally visited the clinic for treatment, she and her colleagues also gave patients access to physiological and psychological treatment, including a therapeutic component that involved parent–child sessions, mindfulness and yoga, and an exercise and nutrition program to address certain physical manifestations (e.g., obesity) of toxic stress on the body. After the implementation of these programs in Dr. Harris's clinic, she saw profound positive results in academic achievement, school and home behaviors, and weight loss among the children she treated.

Harris's (2018) research gave educators a scientific basis for speaking about how trauma impacts the lives of African American students. However, in order to fully understand the academic repercussions of trauma, educators must engage in inquiry that allows them to know their students on deep levels. In order to engage in inquiry about the behaviors of children and adolescents, particularly the observed behaviors in schools, educators should engage in conversations about brain development. Part of the brain's development includes the maturation and evolution of the prefrontal cortex, the part of the brain that controls reasoning and decision making and is the last part of the brain to fully mature. It has been documented that the decisionmaking process in human beings does not always have the benefit of being controlled by optimal neurological functioning, even in a normal maturation process. Additionally, when children endure ongoing stress and turmoil, the impact on this part of the brain can be particularly devastating. Although Harris found that the effects of toxic stress happened across racial, economic, and cultural lines, African American children in inner-city and suburban schools have higher reported rates of traumatic events (Roberts, Gilman, Breslau, Breslau, & Koenen, 2011). African Americans have the highest lifetime prevalence rate of post-traumatic stress disorder (PTSD) compared to their White,

Latina/o, and Asian counterparts—that is, African Americans are more likely to have suffered from PTSD at some point in their life than any other group. Moreover, "Blacks and Hispanics had higher risk of child maltreatment, chiefly witnessing domestic violence, and Asians, Black men, and Hispanic women had higher risk of war-related events than Whites" (Roberts et al., p. 71).

Knowing that African Americans are more likely to suffer from PTSD at some point in their lives than any other group and that they are among those most at risk of childhood trauma gives us valuable context for thinking about the trauma and turmoil that African American students may experience. Harris (2018) made a connection to how ACEs impact learning:

> It seemed that learning was the proverbial canary in the coal mine. The fact that our patients with four or more ACEs were 32.6 times likely to have been diagnosed with learning and behavioral problems signaled to us that ACEs had an outsize effect on children's rapidly developing brains. (p. 152)

Although there is a connection between toxic stress and learning, this does not let schools off the hook. The problematic part of this new understanding about ACEs and how they affect the brain's functioning is that although school personnel intuitively understand the dynamics of research such as Harris's, schools and their officials react in punitive ways toward African American students (as the data documented earlier about disproportionality prove). African American males in particular are disciplined at higher rates, even if there is evidence that students have experienced turmoil (Johnson, 2016). When African American students' behavior (academic and social) does not match up with the expected norms or mores of the dominant cultural narrative, they become subject to harsh disciplinary practices, one of the main factors identified as the catalyst to the school-to-prison pipeline.

Additionally, as pointed out by teachers in this study, even if students may not have been exposed to any of the ACEs outside of the school environment, schools' negative reactions to African American males often serve as an agent of turmoil or stress. Accordingly, schools have exacerbated this interrelationship between adversity and a lack of connection with school. It is not a coincidence that African American children have the lowest rate of achievement in the areas of reading and math and are disciplined at twice and sometimes three times the rates of their White and Asian counterparts. The persistent and ongoing racist social and educational practices enacted upon African American male students can either add to the ACEs that they already have or introduce new ones where no other adversities existed.

In 2018, as a part of an antiracism institute that I facilitated with a colleague, we showed the documentary *13th* by director Ava DuVernay to a group of educators. We put together a panel of African American female students to talk about the connection between the prison–industrial complex and the school-to-prison pipeline. We took note of what the students were saying, and below are the accounts of how African American students in a predominantly White school district are treated:

> One student said, "I don't have hope that you will make [schools] better for me but I hope you get it right for my little brother."

> Another student said, "Black kids wake up every day and face racism. We have to decide whether to fight or just give up and submit to it. When we come to school we shouldn't have to fight it. You all just watched *13th* and pat us on the back and say 'that's terrible' . . . but this is what we live every day."

> Another student said, "The Black boys have given up hope that schools will get better for them. The girls have to be the backbones and keep giving them hope and encouraging them to keep going on."

> This question was posed to the group of teachers by the students, challenging them, "What are *you* going to change as a result of participating in this work?"

These accounts are just general accounts of how schools can impact the lives and learning of African American students; however, we can see that schools can impact them in profound ways.

If we can agree that adverse experiences have a physiological, psychological, and neurological impact on students, particularly African American students, and if we can agree that schools have been instrumental in perpetuating racist practices in their structures, discipline practices, and instructional practices, then we may be able to further agree that schools have played a part in adding to the traumatic experiences that African American students face. Thus, students' traumatic experiences and the research behind how trauma affects the learning process show that the way African American students are treated in school can lead to diminished learning outcomes for them.

Furthermore, if we can qualify daily exposure to racism as ongoing and persistent trauma, then we can make the claim, based on multiple data points, that school is just one of many institutions that reify racist thoughts and practices.

One might question the validity of the claim that the institution of school has perpetuated racist practices and that those acts have the potential to affect African American students physiologically and neurologically. Because discipline and achievement data are predictable along racial lines, it is relatively simple to establish this claim that schools engage in racist practices. What is more difficult is to classify the impact of racism as trauma for African American students and to determine its implications on learning.

Let us start with the notion that ongoing exposure to the social construct of racism has the potential to produce the kind of maladaptation observed in African American students. Common sense would tell us that if we accept the premise that schools support the dominant cultural narrative, regardless of whether they are heterogeneous (all Black) or are predominantly White, African American students would have difficulty connecting to that narrative. Accordingly, the dominant cultural narrative supports the use of texts that undergird that narrative, which often has little relevance to, or even devalues, the lives of African American students. While some might not regard this disconnect between students' lives and the dominant narrative that runs in opposition to it as racist, the notion warrants further dialogue. As we proceed along this line of inquiry, we must continue to explore any possible connection between racism and its significance to the African American psyche (not inferring that this is a monolith), and the connection of that psyche to the school environment and school-related texts.

Because of the work of people like Harris and others who have done extensive research on toxic stress and its effect on physiological and neurological functions in human beings, especially children, the American Psychiatric Association is considering several proposed changes to the *DSM-5* (the fifth edition of the *Diagnostic and Statistical Manual of Mental Disorders*). One of these proposed changes would codify the language about persistent trauma (or *toxic stress*, if Harris's term is used) and suggest that persistent trauma be regarded and treated in the same way as post-traumatic stress disorder because the two conditions have similar symptoms. The American Psychiatric Association defines PTSD as:

> a psychiatric disorder that can occur in people who have experienced or
> witnessed a traumatic event such as a natural disaster, a serious accident,

a terrorist act, war/combat, rape or other violent personal assault. . . . A diagnosis of PTSD requires exposure to an upsetting traumatic event. However, exposure could be indirect rather than first hand. (American Psychiatric Association, 2017)

According to the American Psychiatric Association, the symptoms of PTSD fall into four main categories:

1. Intrusive thoughts such as repeated, involuntary memories; distressing dreams; or flashbacks of the traumatic event. Flashbacks may be so vivid that people feel they are reliving the traumatic experience or seeing it before their eyes.
2. Avoiding reminders of the traumatic event may include avoiding people, places, activities, objects, and situations that bring on distressing memories. People may try to avoid remembering or thinking about the traumatic event. They may resist talking about what happened or how they feel about it.
3. Negative thoughts and feelings may include ongoing and distorted beliefs about oneself or others (e.g., "I am bad," "No one can be trusted"); ongoing fear, horror, anger, guilt, or shame; much less interest in activities previously enjoyed; or feeling detached or estranged from others.
4. Arousal and reactive symptoms may include being irritable and having angry outbursts; behaving recklessly or in a self-destructive way; being easily startled; or having problems concentrating or sleeping. (American Psychiatric Association, 2017)

The recommendation of the changes to the *DSM-5* further proposes that persistent trauma not be classified as adjustment disorder just because the symptoms may fall below the symptomatic threshold for PTSD (American Psychiatric Association, 2017), but to be considered for the diagnosis of PTSD, as the symptoms of adverse experiences are similar. Accordingly, if exposure to ongoing trauma or turmoil results in symptoms similar to PTSD and if we believe African Americans are targets of racist thoughts and acts (including in the school environment), then we can make the case that school environments often serve as one of the contributing factors to African American students experiencing toxic stress.

If African Americans experience toxic stress—whether that toxic stress is a result of ACEs or racism or both—we can make the case that because of that toxic stress, many African American students exhibit the symptoms of PTSD. Schools should look into treating the underlying causes of PTSD (within their control) rather than using discipline to control the behaviors of students. Furthermore, these understandings must be used to combat perceptions that African American male students are apathetic about their education or unable to understand or connect with school-based content.

Thus, postulations such as these beg the need for more research on ACEs experienced by African American students in particular, including how they are mistreated in schools and how the repeated exposure to conscious bias, unconscious bias, and other racist acts affects their learning. The implication for schools is that these adverse experiences encountered in school have the potential to impact students' psychological, physiological, and neurological functioning.

WHAT CAN TEACHERS DO RIGHT NOW?

- Incorporate ongoing and regular activities where teachers and students can build relationship and community.
- Engage in regular inquiry about teacher identities and perceptions of African American students. Use discourse analysis to determine which themes emerge from those conversations.
- Build restorative classrooms by allowing students to design the code of conduct and classroom rituals.
- Use bridge texts to connect school-based literacy to whatever students are reading.
- Use music or other popular media as texts in the classroom.
- Design afterschool activities around literacy events (e.g., poetry slam, storytelling, forensics).
- Allow students to be "16 and Black and have an opinion."

WHAT CAN ADMINISTRATORS DO RIGHT NOW?

- Dedicate a space in the school for showcasing African American literacy (e.g., authors, artists, or writers).
- Start open and honest dialogues about toxic stress in students (don't just assume that all trauma is home-based).
- Advocate for the hiring of restorative justice personnel.
- Allow longer-term discipline to be decided by a committee comprised of outside-of-school-district staff.
- Use staff PLC time for book clubs dedicated to learning about teaching for social justice.

CHAPTER 8

Literacy Is . . .

Looking at Literacy Through a Different Lens

Once you learn to read, you will forever be free.

—Frederick Douglass

TEACHERS' EXPANSIONS OF THEIR DEFINITIONS OF LITERACY

One of the themes that emerged from the teacher conversations I facilitated with my study was how they construed and defined literacy. Teachers' individual conceptions of literacy were important because their personal thoughts about literacy had the potential to have an impact on their perceptions of their students' literacy and the pedagogy and texts that they selected. One of the guiding questions of this study asked whether teachers experienced a progression in thought with regard to their perceptions of the efficacy of their African American students and whether they reconceptualized their definitions of literacy. I wanted to determine whether participation in the professional development series led to the teachers redefining literacy to include the sociocultural nature of literacy and the various ways that African American male students display literate behaviors.

In the opening activity of the professional development, I asked teachers to provide their own written definitions of literacy without context and without influence of the activities they would engage in as part of the study. I wanted their beginning conceptions to be authentic and representative of their individual thoughts. I compared their beginning definitions of literacy to their subsequent definitions after a close reading of our guiding text and supplementary texts, and self-reflections of their teaching.

My experiences as an educator have taught me that literacy is often regarded as a one-dimensional, nonrecursive static event. Literacy is often defined not as a process but rather as a set of actions with which one engages. This assertion has been substantiated through dialogue I have had with teachers, including some of those who participated in this study. If teachers are allowed to participate in inquiry and reflection into their practices, as they did in this study, they have the opportunity to refine, redefine, and reconceptualize their definitions of literacy. As an example, one teacher initially defined literacy as "the ability to read and comprehend information, the ability to write coherently using logic and support." Another defined literacy as "reading and deciphering text and symbols (and codes)." A third teacher defined literacy as "[being] competent and proficient in reading (decoding and comprehension) (verbal and written)." Although each one of the initial conceptions provided by the teachers were solely activity based, the teachers' conceptions of literacy spoke of actions using varying systems of communication; thus, many of the teachers' conceptions of literacy could be considered activity-based, semiotic-based (e.g., dealing with systems of communications), or both. During the analysis of the data, I assigned codes to each piece of the participants' data, allowing me to document their evolution in thought from the initial activities through the focus group interview.

Initially, many of the teachers included in their definitions the multiple ways that students can communicate, but many did not include how students interact with one another during literacy events, how students connect to texts, the historical and sociocultural nature of literacy for African American students, or how the relevance of the content of school-related literacy plays a part in their lives. If literacy is defined solely as the ability to understand and decode texts, then the function of literacy and the idea that it can serve as a means to open one's ability to interact with the world will be lost on many African American students.

I found that many of the initial conceptions of literacy were not multifaceted; the definitions did not include thoughts about sociocultural, sociopolitical, and economic conceptions of literacy and participating in literacy events. I also found that none of the initial definitions included thoughts about the relationship between the reader and the teacher and the reader and the text. Throughout the study, I supported the premise that literacy is sociocultural in nature and that literacy is a social act. If we assume this premise is true, then the argument can be made that many of the teachers in this study did not give definitions that aligned with what the literature and research say about how students develop literacy and participate in literacy events. However, teachers recounted that they believed in the importance and the influence of how sociocultural variables impact their students' connection to school-based literacy.

As a result of the discrepancy between their definitions of literacy and their philosophies and pedagogical actions, I was able to further support my postulation that many educators often view literacy as a one-dimensional, nonrecursive static process.

Although I collected concrete examples of two definitions of literacy from each teacher-participant, it was the final interview that provided me with answers about teachers' feelings about the variance between their two conceptions of literacy. In the focus group interview, I asked, "Has your definition of literacy changed since the inception of the class? If so, please let me know how." Before providing analysis about the participants' thoughts about how they expanded their definitions of literacy, it is important to provide a few more examples of teachers' beginning conceptions of literacy and how those conceptions changed after they engaged in 5 days of professional development.

Many of the teachers' initial conceptions of literacy were activity-based definitions; however, I used several of the different codes from discourse analysis to identify the essential components of participants' thoughts and feelings regarding literacy. In this analysis, I identified the activity-based components of each of the participants' conceptions and noted the development between the first iterations of their definitions of literacy and the second definitions. Additionally, the data that focus participants provided in the final interview helped me determine if they had expanded their definitions. For example, Julia's beginning definition of literacy was as follows:

> the ability to read and comprehend written language—aspects of understanding as essential. Literacy development [is] supporting growth and fluency within—letter recognition, letter sounds, word meaning, reading fluency, comprehension.

Initially, I regarded the components of Julia's conception of literacy as having an interdependent relationship between different parts of a sign system, or having a semiotic relationship. In discourse analysis, semiotic building refers to participants using communicative systems and other systems of knowledge to convey events of the past, present, and future. Although somewhat action-oriented, Julia's initial conception of literacy provided a glimpse into her thinking about the multiple components and facets of literacy. Her progression in thinking was documented after she provided her second definition of literacy: "the ability to intellectually engage with, and make meaning from, various forms of communication—written language, art, music, spoken language, culture." Although Julia's second definition also showed a semiotic relationship between the components of literacy, rather than focusing on specific actions, she spoke about the promise of literacy and the multiple ways one can ingratiate oneself into the process of literacy.

Like the other teachers, Julia did not believe that she reconceptualized her definition of literacy; rather, she believed it expanded as a result of her participation in the study. This is important because the objective of the professional development series was not for teachers to adopt any one specific viewpoint without critical analysis; instead, it was to provide teachers with opportunities to reflect and consider multiple points of view and integrate new understandings into their own beliefs and practices in ways that made sense to them.

In response to the question posed in the final interview about whether or not their definitions of literacy changed as a result of participating in the study, Julia responded:

> My definition of literacy did not change, because I felt already very aware and very comfortable about it. What I found to be interesting is others' perceptions and the methods other teachers use. Like what you just said about doing the different books [referring to the practice of allowing students to choose books that they liked]. I thought that was really—that's really nice that you did that. It also gave the [students] the opportunity to share that connection.

Julia felt that she had a firm grasp on what literacy was and what it meant for her students. When I reviewed Julia's two conceptions of literacy, I was able to observe that her understanding of literacy became more nuanced and complex over the course of the study. In her final interview, she indicated that she believed that the professional development series was valuable to her as she sought to expand her conception of literacy to be inclusive of her students' literacy behaviors.

Julia was not the only teacher who felt that the professional development series helped with the reconceptualization and expansion of their initial conceptions of literacy. Lynn brought up some of the same themes as Julia. Even though Lynn could have been considered a fledgling teacher when her years of service were compared to the years of service of the other teachers, she was nonetheless one of the most vocally assertive teachers and her voice provided rich data for my analysis.

Lynn specifically spoke about how she believed her conception of literacy developed and expanded as a result of her participation in the study. At the beginning, Lynn defined literacy as "the ability to read, write, speak, listen, and act in a way that anyone in the same discipline would be able to understand." Her initial conception of literacy was activity-based, as she documented that literacy was the ability to perform certain tasks. However, Lynn's reconceptualized thoughts about literacy at the end of the study showed a more expansive definition:

> Literacy is the ability to read, write, speak, listen, act in a manner that an expert in any discipline would be able to understand what you are communicating. To be literate means to be engaging in literacy, be it reading, writing, speaking, listening, or acting. With each attempt our literacy skills are improved. Literacy is developed through the sociocultural paradigm—literacy and literacy development cannot happen in isolation, but rather must happen in a social and cultural context that is relevant and meaningful to the learners.

Lynn's reconceptualized ideas about literacy represent a metamorphosis from her previously activity-based conception. Her new conceptualization was an affirmation of how students connect to literacy and make human connections, and how literacy includes social constructs linked to literacy engagement. She still included the initial activity-based functions of literacy in her reconceptualization, but she expanded her definition and spoke about how students develop literacy and how literacy is a social act, influenced by one's social and cultural identity. She also spoke about the relevance of literacy events to readers.

Lynn's reconceptualization of literacy showed growth. Additionally, her reconceptualization of literacy, as well as her understanding of literacy as a multifaceted, social act, helped to connect the ideas of the definition of literacy to her understanding of it. In her focus group interview, Lynn spoke about how her definition of literacy had expanded:

> Um, I don't know that my definition has changed, but it's certainly expanded. And I—I talked about this at our last session as well. I think, you know, going into it I had this conception of literacy as we read, and we write, and we understand those things that we read and we write. And I think that that has expanded to include the—the listening, the speaking, the, you know, kind of world literacy of understanding social cues, and the kind of code-switching that our students do every day. All of that is included in literacy. So, it's all that decoding that they have to do on a

daily basis. So, I definitely think it's—my definition has expanded since—since we started the class.

It was refreshing that the teachers found that their participation in the professional development series encouraged them to think more deeply about the nature of literacy and its implications for African American male students. However, while I was listening to the recorded sessions and reading through the transcripts, I wondered if the ethnicity of the teacher and the ethnicity of the students with whom the teacher had experience was a factor in how teachers reconceptualized literacy. Several of the teachers taught in affluent districts where African American students come with different life experiences, compared to African American students in predominantly African American districts. Therefore, with regard to the reconceptualization of literacy, I thought it was important to compare the findings from other teacher-participants with findings from Jackie, an African American teacher working with a student population that was 98% African American, to determine whether or not there was some congruence in the thoughts about what literacy is and the promise of literacy for African American students specifically.

When the theme of reconceptualizing literacy emerged, I wondered if Jackie's background and experiences might have contributed to her different initial perspectives and beliefs about what literacy was and what it meant for her students. I wondered if the activities and the text used in the study were as valuable for her as they seemed to be for her colleagues who had different ethnic backgrounds, taught in different districts, and worked with a different population of students. Jackie's conceptualizations about literacy were integral in helping the theme of teachers' expansion of their definitions of literacy to emerge. One of the major findings evident across all teacher-participants emerged through the discussions about their developing understandings about literacy and how those understandings led to their reconceptualized understandings and definitions of literacy.

Jackie's beginning definition of literacy was "the ability to read, write, think, and understand. I believe this includes words, graphics, people, and circumstances." In my ongoing analysis of the teacher dialogues, I found that Jackie's written definition of literacy was not as expansive as her understandings of the roles of in-school and out-of-school literacy as she expressed them in class. I coded her beginning conceptions of literacy as activity-building. With regard to literacy, in discourse analysis, activity-building does not speak to the expansive and multifaceted nature of literacy. It simply denotes the specific language about the actions one engages in during a task or event. Simply put, activity-building with regard to literacy is linked to the action or function of reading rather than the connection between ideas, the sociocultural context in which literacy is situated, or the possibilities that arise from participation in literacy events. Jackie's thoughts reminded me that one of the purposes of this study was to help teachers reflect on their understandings of literacy, their pedagogy, and how the text selections they choose for students can open up a world to which students otherwise might not have been privy.

In Jackie's second definition at the end of the study, she defined literacy in the following manner:

> Literacy is one's ability to read, comprehend, and apply one's understanding of a text, whether it is written, verbal, or an artistic representation. Furthermore, during the process of literacy development, one learns to decode text in any form in order to find meaning. Literacy exists in the sociocultural paradigm and embraces one's diverse cultural background to assist or connect students to a given text.

I thought that Jackie's second definition described how literacy is the relationship among all of its subcomponents. When compared to her first definition, there seemed to be a development of her thoughts and ideas. In discourse analysis, semiotic building refers to using cues to identify a system of knowledge. Although Jackie's thoughts about what literacy was differed slightly in language, when compared to her understanding of in-school and out-of-school literacy practices, I believe she had a clear understanding and an improved development of ideas of the multiple components of literacy and that her understandings of literacy developed as a result of participating in the study.

Jackie could not be present at the focus group interview, but she answered the question "Has your definition of literacy changed since the inception of this class?" She responded in the following manner:

> I do not believe my definition of literacy has changed since the beginning of the class. I have always believed that literacy is one's ability to read, comprehend, and interpret text, whether the text is words, symbols, etc. Furthermore, literacy incorporates one's ability to articulate the text in written or verbal form.

Although Jackie did not believe that she had reconceptualized her ideas about literacy, it was evident to me that her initial conception of literacy had developed from being an activity-based function to a broader idea of literacy that was inclusive of possibilities, actions, students' surrounding environments and culture, and the inclusion of other genres of expression of thought beyond the mechanics of reading. After I reviewed Jackie's initial conceptions and reconceptions about what literacy was and compared them to other teachers' definitions, I also found that Jackie had seen the value in participating in the study and that it had an influence on how she conceptualized literacy. I also found that the theme about teachers' understandings of students' literacy and the expansions of their definitions of literacy was essential to helping all the other themes to emerge. I came to this understanding as I realized that all the themes that emerged from the data analysis were borne out in the notion that teachers had a firm understanding about their own understandings of literacy and what literacy meant to students' lives.

THE NECESSITY OF TEACHERS' USE OF EVIDENCE-BASED INSTRUCTIONAL STRATEGIES

In my duties as a school district administrator and through my involvement with organizations at the regional, state, and national levels, I have frequent conversations with teachers from numerous districts in multiple regions. During these conversations, I hear teachers' points of view regarding instructional programming and what should be provided for students. I often hear from teachers that, in order to give students the help they need, teachers need to be trained in how to use literacy strategies that aid in their instruction of African American male students. Teachers often ask for strategies that they can use the very next day.

Teachers' feelings about their efficacy in understanding African American male students' out-of-school literacies and how to help them was also evident in the surveys that I asked them to complete. The initial survey was geared heavily toward collecting data about teachers' perceptions of their African American male students, their own efficacy as teachers to help their African American male students connect to in-school literacy, and their preparedness and preparation. Conversely, the second survey was geared heavily toward assessing teachers' thoughts about students' interests related to literacy. Teachers overwhelming thought that the use and knowledge of evidence-based instructional strategies was closely tied to teacher efficacy and student agency. Some of the strategies that teachers reported using in their classrooms included the following:

- Word walls
- Talking to the text
- Journals and quick writes
- Use of culturally relevant texts
- Prereading
- Listening to students' interests
- Accessing metacognition using anchor charts
- Reading apprenticeship

Although teachers used these strategies and others to help to engage their African American students, many recounted that these strategies either did not improve the connection to school-expected literacy for their students or that they had not had recent and relevant experiences that built their skill levels to impact the literacy of their African American students.

TEACHERS' IMPROVED UNDERSTANDINGS OF STUDENTS' LITERACY PRACTICES

Teachers' understandings of the out-of-school literacy practices of African American male students, the sociocultural paradigm in which those practices exist, and the connection to the expected in-school literacy practices of those same students was key to understanding the conversations in which teachers engaged. The research questions sought to make meaning of teachers' beginning perceptions of their African American male students and how those perceptions related to their pedagogy and text selection and their understandings of African American male students' in-school and out-of-school literacy practices. Specifically, one of the questions asked, "In what ways might teachers' developing understandings about the in-school and out-of-school literacies of African American males contribute to their decisions about pedagogy and curriculum in ways that are culturally relevant and meaningful to the African American male students they teach?" When seeking to answer a question like this one, it was necessary to think about how teachers' understanding of their students' literacy practices help them develop positive or negative perceptions, and how the two influenced their pedagogy, relationships, and text selections.

Although teachers' beginning and expanded definitions of literacy showed the progression in thinking, there was also a direct relationship between their expanded definitions to their enhanced understandings of student literacy practices. A striking and insightful revelation came from Lynn as we were considering how teachers' definitions of literacy impacted their feelings about their students' efficacy and the sociocultural factors that influenced their literacy in school and beyond, and how they understood those. Lynn stated:

> So, you know, I think most of us—I mean, I look around this table and I think most of us have, you know, a set of skills—or a repertoire of skills—that are pretty much scientific, evidence-based—these are skills and strategies that work to encourage reading and comprehension. And I think we do a good job of that. We do a good job at teaching skills. I mean, the CCSS [Common Core State Standards] has a lot of that skill-based stuff built into it, too. So, where we've definitely been lacking—and we talked about this in previous sessions—is, how much does the literature that we bring to the classroom, or allow students—maybe that's the more important thing—allow students to bring to the classroom—how much of it is truly reflective of them? And how much do they see themselves in that text? Does it—does it matter to them? Because we can teach all the best strategies in the world, but if the kids don't care about what they're applying the strategies to, it's not going to matter. And I go back to this notion of, "Conditioning to see themselves as inferior beings." Right? And then that notion of turmoil, and in the sense of controlling your own destiny, feeling in control and out of control. How are we—how are we representing that?

As Lynn's thoughts demonstrate, once teachers began to expand their definitions, they saw literacy as more than just an activity with which one participates in school; instead, they began a line of professional inquiry about how literacy could bolster the academic and personal confidence in students.

The discussions about the Tatum text elicited responses from teachers that brought forward this notion that their definitions of literacy had expanded over the course of the study. The study results indicate that it was important for teachers to use their expanded definitions and understandings as a basis to understand students' literacy practices in and out of school. I used the Tatum text as a means to help me answer the research questions and to gather data about the impact of a book club as a professional development model and instructional model.

Furthermore, I provided a list of questions to the teachers, from which they identified the most essential questions to answer for themselves and for their individual group discussions. The following guiding questions that I provided to the groups helped the theme about teachers' improved understandings of student literacy practices to emerge:

1. How do variables outside of schools affect students' access to and attainment of literacy?
2. How do you choose texts? How important is contextual understanding to literacy?
3. How has your thinking changed from the time that we started until now?
4. Do you believe turmoil plays a factor in the literacy development of Black males? If so, what do you do to mitigate this factor?
5. What cultural competencies do you believe Black boys should have to be successful in school?
6. What does the promise of literacy "do" for young Black males?
7. Does viewing literacy as a social act and through the sociocultural paradigm change how you view students' literacy connections?
8. As a teacher, how can you help validate students' identities?

Prior to the study, I had expected many of the guiding questions to be generated and developed by the teachers as a result of the reading and processing of the text. However, I chose to develop the guiding questions, and I led the discussions using those questions, which were linked to one or more of my research aims.

The questions I asked the teacher-participants were integral in helping me understand their thoughts. They also helped the theme of teachers' improved understandings of student literacy emerge. Since the study was based on a book club model, as a part of the book club discussion methodology, participants were expected to engage in inquiry that might not have otherwise happened in any other instructional practice. As the study progressed, I noticed that, although engagement was hard to measure and the teachers' future intent to further engage their students was impossible to ascertain, the teacher-participants started on the journey with the intention of questioning and challenging their perceptions and practice.

My analysis of the teachers' dialogues and the identification of the major themes helped establish the conclusions, assertions, and implications of teachers' perceptions and their relationship to how students connect to expected school literacy. Accordingly, I found that teachers felt their involvement in the study encouraged a progression and evolution of their perceptions and understandings of the in-school and out-of-school literacies of the African American male students that they taught.

WHAT CAN TEACHERS DO RIGHT NOW?

- Explore the idea that students may experience turmoil at school at the hands of school personnel.
- Engage in inquiry that allows you to expand your definitions of literacy.
- Survey students about their experiences in school.
- Allow students to engage in the construction of instructional activities that engage them.
- Provide opportunities for students to submit anonymous feedback.
- Record your conversations about your instructional practices on literacy and your perceptions of students, and use Gee's (1999) discourse analysis to code your thoughts about students' literacy practices.
- Answer the questions posed in this chapter (p. 160).

WHAT CAN ADMINISTRATORS DO RIGHT NOW?

- Put together student focus groups where the central questions are about the education of African American male students and where students are allowed to guide the work in the following ways:
  - » They provide the school with feedback about how to teach them.
  - » They affirm their identities as leaders and scholars.
  - » They set the terms of the research that will be conducted by the adults.
- Provide professional development on current trends in literacy.
- Consult with preeminent researchers in the field and use data collected from surveys, conversations, and research studies to build systemic interventions.
- Use the talents of the staff within the district to inform instructional and district practice.

CHAPTER 9

The Choice Is Yours

"Giving a Damn" as a Strategy for Improving Student Outcomes

And I think just asking them—like, I think that makes those connections which seems to be—my takeaway so far from this whole course, is that, like, the strategy we need is to connect with our students. So just make those connections. Like, that's the whole like, "give a damn" strategy. That's the damn strategy. Like, find out what they need. Like, come to where they are."

—Julia, middle school teacher

A key piece of data for my study emerged during the activity where the group discussed Tatum's (2005) nesting ground framework. In this activity, I asked participants to talk with their table groups about how their individual practices aligned to each category of strands described in the framework (e.g., theoretical, instructional, and professional development strands). Julia's group quickly began a conversation about instructional strategies they used in their classrooms. Julia talked about her belief that just "giving a damn" about the kids was the only strategy that teachers need.

Although Julia was perhaps searching for the right words to articulate her understanding, she made an important realization about the lives of Black males. She challenged herself and her colleagues to find ways for the identities of Black male students to garner some privilege and voice in the classroom setting. Her response to the question about how to connect to students' out-of-school literacy and to African American male students as learners spoke specifically to the research questions of this study. Many educators enter the profession with the notion that they can employ a number of strategies to "fix" literacy and learning outcomes for African American male students. Additionally, teachers who have been practitioners in the field for numerous years are at a loss as to what to do to help their African American male students. The following is an actual email from a teacher seeking help from an administrator:

> I met with the English department that was present briefly on Friday and wanted to share a common request for support I heard and echo myself. Most of us have had conversations with you, both individually and as a group, about the need to close the gap in our district for our minority students. We feel your passion and recognize that there are potential inequities both in our school and district-wide. We want to help this problem and are looking for your guidance with doing so. Speaking candidly, [Richard], we agree that inequities can exist, but we don't know what moves we need to make to fix this. We are struggling with how to solve the problem. As a department, we want to do what's best for ALL students. We have the best of intentions as professionals. We are experts at our curriculum and experienced in our pedagogy, but we seem to be falling short of your expectations and need some tangible support and guidance on real moves we should be making in the classroom. I have always welcomed our discussions as a point of reflection to better my practice and ensure equity for all students. I feel I've walked away with some insights but know I could be learning more.
>
> I would love to schedule a time for you to talk to the department, or maybe we could do a full building training, on some real moves we could be making. I am a solutions-based person. I see the problem, so I want to work with you to find some solutions that we could all start implementing.

Teachers around the country are asking for strategies to help their students. Even the teachers who participated in the study documented in this book indicated in their initial surveys that they were searching for instructional strategies to use for their African American male learners.

The conversation that educators have failed to emphasize and put our full participation into, with regard to engaging African American students, has everything to do with how they are treated in school, not just the strategies that we use for them. Furthermore, educators and politicians need to pay much more attention to the historical, societal, and cultural ramifications of schooling for African American children. Irrespective of their family incomes, African American students do not come to school with the same background experiences, affiliations, access to content, language, and resources as their White counterparts.

Moreover, African American students are less likely to be encouraged or given opportunities to engage with rigorous content through honors level, Advanced Placement, or International Baccalaureate programming. Although these things might seem like obvious concepts to grasp, not enough care is being given to helping African American students connect with school.

This idea that America owes an educational debt to African American students comes with a wide array of implications. The educational debt not only demands improvements in economic equality and equity in funding and resource allocation in American schools for African American students; it requires us to accept the responsibility to ameliorate the damage done through hundreds of years of educational neglect, particularly through the denial of access to literacy. One could argue that the educational debt is one of the main ingredients of the school-to-prison pipeline. Winn and Behizadeh (2011) supported this argument by stating that "the notion of an educational debt is inextricably linked to the building as well as to the potential dismantling of the school-to-prison pipeline" (p. 158). If the school-to-prison pipeline is a manifestation of the failure to pay the educational debt that American society and the American institution of school owes to African American children, then school failure and the disconnect from school literacy becomes a violation of African American students' civil rights.

As it is with the payment of any immense debt, the education debt that American society owes to African American children should be paid strategically and with intentionality. I don't think one could imagine paying off the U.S. national debt in one fell swoop; we need to view the education debt in the same manner. If closing achievement and opportunity gaps are a real concern for this nation, then the education debt must be paid, starting with actions such as these:

- Engaging in wide-scale inquiry and conversations about the historical and political implications of schooling for African American students
- Allowing students to choose texts that are relevant to their lives and interests
- Developing activities to get to know students' cultural backgrounds and the various other sociocultural components of their lives
- Researching and implementing evidence-based instructional strategies to use with students

- Allocating finances, time, and human capital to address the specific needs of African American students
- Committing to antiracist instruction, courses and course materials, and school policies and structures
- Reeducating teachers, administrators, boards of education, and community members about providing equity for African American students
- Providing access to rigorous content and courses for African American students
- Creating a culture where the ill treatment of African American students can be challenged by any member of the organization

When we view African American students' connection to school and literacy through this lens, it becomes even more problematic to assert that adherence to silver-bullet strategies will improve their academic lives. As researchers like Ladson-Billings (2006) compel us to explore this idea of the educational debt, we should also explore how the other institutions of this country have excluded African American participants. Since the inception of this nation, African American people have been denied participation in economic prosperity, socialization, and hundreds of cultural institutions, which has all led to social and economic poverty. The lack of social and economic power has been a greater barrier to the promise of a prosperous life offered through literacy and academic engagement than the lack of strategies.

One pioneer in the effort to pay the enormous educational debt owed to African American students was Julius Rosenwald. Rosenwald joined the Sears and Roebuck Company after serving as a major clothing supplier and rose through the ranks to become the company's president in 1908, serving until 1924. As Rosenwald brought the company to great financial success through the advent of the Sears catalog, he also amassed great personal wealth. Booker T. Washington approached him with a vision to build schools in southern states that would be learning centers to teach African American children. Their partnership sparked a relationship in which Rosenwald used his immense financial resources to build more than 5,300 schools, vocational shops, and teacher's homes across 15 states in the South and Southwest from 1912 to 1932 (National Trust for Historic Preservation, 2018).

At the apex of the building campaign, many of the schools were attacked and burned down by those who were participating in the type of emotional, physical, and academic terrorism described earlier in this book. Rosenwald rebuilt the schools each time the schools were burned down, and he didn't let the attacks discourage him from building more schools to provide access to a greater number of students across the rural South ("Rosenwald," 2018).

Rosenwald was able to "give a damn" on a large scale and did so. Rosenwald provided an example of what Julia had described in her study comments as the essence of "giving a damn": finding out what African American students need and meeting them where they are. In building schools and answering terrorism with determination, he did more than provide buildings and settings for education to take place; he also provided a highly visible message for his time: that Black lives matter. In his own way, he set about addressing the education debt. His example was one that enabled African Americans to feel more respected and enabled, and he set an example for other Americans.

Actions like Rosenwald's (and those of thousands of other advocates and activists) support Tatum's (2005) assertion that the implementation of silver-bullet strategies alone will not improve how African American males connect to school and school-expected literacy practices. The purpose of highlighting the philanthropy of people like Rosenwald is not to suggest that the only way that teachers, administrators, or other educators can "give a damn" is to donate money or build schools. The point is to emphasize that in order to engage African American male students fully in the schooling process, one must do it with passion, intentionality, and the donation of one's talents and skills. While teachers will still need to have access to relevant professional development and access to evidence-based instructional strategies to address students' literacy, this is not enough. Before we can engage African American male students with any sort of strategy, we have to connect them to the school as an institution, to the academic content and language that is expected of them, and to caring adults, including teachers. The teachers from the study articulated that, in order to engage African American male students in school (which results in engagement in expected school literacy practices), it is important for teachers and schools to do the following:

1. Help them make connections to the school, the teacher(s), and the text(s).
2. Reconceptualize or expand their definitions of literacy.
3. Engage in inquiry to improve their understandings about how students develop literacy.
4. Research and implement evidence-based instructional strategies for literacy.

The "What Teachers Can Do Right Now" and "What Administrators Can Do Right Now" sections give educators concrete ways to accomplish these suggestions in a practical setting. Even when they understand that literacy development is sociocultural in nature, the teacher-participants frequently spoke about the need to have evidence-based instructional strategies to use with their students. This study supported that evidence-based instructional strategies that are supported by student data are part of educators' desire to help their students; however, analyzing literacy data of African American students is not enough. I have heard educators ask questions such as, "How many of these students are special ed?" or "Which of these students came from Detroit?" Questions like these intimate that schools as institutions bear little responsibility for student results on achievement assessments or reading inventories, or for the relationships that students have with school. Furthermore, the coded language behind questions such as "which of these students came from Detroit" are often based on racist and biased assumptions that students from Detroit are not academically capable to perform well in settings outside of Detroit (e.g., suburban school districts).

WHAT CAN TEACHERS DO RIGHT NOW?

- At the upper grade levels, watch the movie *13th* and engage in conversations with students and other teachers about the school-to-prison pipeline.
- Engage in conversations with colleagues about the education debt, and begin to enact suggestions such as the ones listed in this chapter.
- Suspend the use of coded language.
- Analyze the proficiency *and* growth data for African American males, and use the data to change instructional practice.

WHAT CAN ADMINISTRATORS DO RIGHT NOW?

- Use school time, resources, and facilities to educate staff and the community about the effects that the current state of the country is having on young Black males.
- Plan events/groups that specifically target engaging African American families in the school environment.
- Establish a list of "look fors" when observing teacher behavior toward African American male students.

CHAPTER 10

Are We on Ten Yet?

Reconceptualizing Schools for African American Students

A child cannot be taught by anyone who despises him, and a child cannot afford to be fooled.

—James Baldwin

The data regarding the dropout rates, graduation rates, and reading proficiency of African American students are alarming. Schools and politicians have made feeble attempts at fixing the problem regarding success in school for African American children, but little has been done to produce measurable and sustainable results. Furthermore, the reading proficiency of African American male students has been measured through the use of standardized assessments, which tell educators very little about students' actual proficiency with texts and their participation in literacy events as a whole. The most common response to Black students' failure and lack of proficiency in reading on standardized assessments is to provide reading specialists, assign students to remediation groups, or certify students for special education services. Because standardized assessments test less for fluency and word recognition and more for students' familiarity with the values, events, and social codes of dominant culture, many interventions that lack a sociocultural component that helps students connect to literacy often fail.

The study outlined in the preceding chapters provided the foundation for the two purposes of this book: to help teachers build school environments that promote literacy development for their African American students and to provide potential solutions to the problems of school disenfranchisement and the rejection of school-based literacy by African American male students. Above all else, the study and review of the relevant literature highlighted the fact that it is necessary to continue to engage teachers in conversations that allow them to reflect on their perceptions of African American students' literacy and encourage them to use instructional practices and modes of inquiry that allow them to understand and connect with their students.

TEACHERS' RECOGNITION OF THE IMPORTANCE OF AND RELATIONSHIP TO STUDENTS' CONNECTIONS TO TEACHERS, SCHOOL, AND TEXTS

Data gathered from the teacher-participants in the study showed the need for teachers to better understand their students' backgrounds and identities. Teachers' thoughts around this also supported the notion that there is an education debt that is owed to African American students that can be repaid through genuine relationships between students and their teachers. Furthermore, what I was able to find during the analysis of the teacher data was that students told their teachers stories of ill treatment they had received from other teachers. The idea that students feel victimized by their teachers in contemporary school environments is in line with how African American students have been treated throughout their history in this nation, particularly in institutions of learning after schools were integrated. Thus, it did not come as a surprise that there was an overwhelming sense among the teacher-participants that their students rejected school because of negative experiences with their teachers.

The teacher-participants also found that when students did not have meaningful relationships with their teachers, not only did students reject school as an institution, they rejected school-related content. They recounted that they were able to get their students to connect with school-related texts when they took the time to get to know them and when they valued their identities and their language by integrating it with the academic language of school. Conversely, the teachers in this study talked about how their students' other teachers marginalized them and devalued their identities, which led to their diminished agency and efficacy. Furthermore, teachers spoke about how the structure of their schools served as barriers to access to literacy for their students. When seeking to understand students' identities and how they link to school, one can support the notion that school structures often provide yet another barrier for access to the school-related content and literacy for African American males.

Teachers talked extensively about the importance of developing relationships with their students and about what they did to accomplish establishing those relationships. In order to begin to pay back the education debt that is owed to students, teachers have to continue to examine their perceptions of their students and their abilities. They also have to reflect on how those perceptions are influenced by the larger dominant culture, inquire about the ways in which their instructional practices are culturally relevant to their students, and engage in ongoing inquiry about their pedagogy and how they could improve it to make it relevant to their students. Teachers' conversations should also include discussions about using evidence-based models as appropriate instructional practices.

Within this theme, teachers also talked about what they know about African American students' identities and how those identities often run counter to the values found in expected school literacy. Ideas about students' identities sparked conversations about the need for teachers to understand their students, and as one participant declared, "students should be allowed to be 16, and Black, and have an opinion." Without students' connection to the teachers, the school, and the text, it would not matter what teachers' beliefs were about student literacy and which strategies they used to help students to connect.

TEACHERS' EXPANSIONS OF THEIR DEFINITIONS OF LITERACY

In one of the beginning activities, I asked teachers to provide their written definitions of literacy. The purpose of this activity was to establish a foundational understanding of teachers' beginning perceptions of literacy and to determine how their participation in the activities of this study may have influenced them to reconceptualize their definitions and aid in their progressive understanding of literacy in the lives of their students. As a means to gauge teachers' overall growth in their understandings of African American students' literacies, a second opportunity was provided to them to submit a written definition of literacy. Finally, in the focus group interview, participants were asked to talk about their growth in understanding about their definitions of literacy and whether they felt they had reconceptualized their definitions as a result of participating in this study. The group overwhelmingly felt that they had not reconceptualized their definitions, but had expanded them. The teachers in this study felt that the activities of the study allowed for their definitions to be inclusive of the multifaceted ways that literacy is represented rather than conceive it as a monolithic or limited concept.

I used discourse analysis by Gee (1999) to review and code teachers' conversations with one another. Many of the teachers' beginning definitions were coded using the activity building code, which established that many of the teachers viewed literacy as a set of activities. Teachers' expanded definitions of literacy included other building codes: activity building, socioculturally situated identity and relationship building, and world building. The difference in how teachers' definitions of literacy expanded represented a growth in thought and how they conceived literacy. Teachers' expansion in their definitions of literacy served as the underpinning for establishing their improved understandings of students' literacy practices. They talked about how they expanded their definitions of literacy and their overall understandings of students' literacy practices as a result or participating in this study. Accordingly, their data helped to establish that their participation in inquiry encouraged them to use their improved understandings to change their instructional practice and to develop culturally relevant instruction.

TEACHERS' IMPROVED UNDERSTANDINGS OF STUDENTS' LITERACY PRACTICES

The participants used the conversations and activities in the study to spark inquiry into their practice and speak about the need to develop better understandings about their students' out-of-school literacy practices. After gaining a better understanding of their students' out-of-school literacy practices, they were able engage in discussions about how to develop instruction that linked those practices to expected school-related literacy. Some of the students' out-of-school literacy practices included participation in rap battles, writing poetry and song lyrics, reading websites connected to their interests, and storytelling. One elementary teacher allowed an African American student to create an African American superhero and write a whole story featuring the superhero. She helped the student "publish" his text and allowed him to read it to the class. Some of the high school teachers held poetry or rap battles in class, while others helped students participate in writing intensives. One teacher even joined a group of her students at a poetry reading as they read works written in her class. As they engaged their African American male students in some of these activities, the teachers spoke about the need to further understand the lives of their students through a sociocultural paradigm. They spoke about students' varied lives, understandings, and opportunities to make connections to their literacies. With these understandings, teachers were able to eloquently speak about what they could do and be responsible for that would help improve the literacy connections for their students.

THE NECESSITY OF TEACHERS' USE OF EVIDENCE-BASED
INSTRUCTIONAL STRATEGIES

Even though teachers need evidence-based strategies to help connect their African American students' out-of-school literacy experiences to school-expected literacy, conversations about how to engage those students must include opportunities for teachers to engage in ongoing inquiry about their instructional practices for African American male students. Also, teachers must reflect on their perceptions, beliefs, and mindsets while presenting those evidence-based instructional practices.

In the initial survey, teachers were asked which instructional strategies they used in their classrooms to improve student literacies. Teachers provided lists of strategies that they used, but many of them documented that the use of many of the strategies was met with minimal success. Proceeding with this notion in mind, the data analyzed from the participants in this study supported the assertion that the confluence of the themes that emerged from the activities in this study are necessary components for the identification of appropriate instructional strategies. Teachers should use this knowledge to build effective instructional frameworks to address the complex literacy needs of African American male students. Participants talked about the value of the dialogues and about their plans to develop book clubs with their students and to employ other instructional interventions that they gleaned from their colleagues, including the following:

- Student reflections about school-based texts
- Student book clubs
- Allowing students to translate the language of traditional texts into language that they understand
- Promoting multivariate literacies (comic books or graphic novels, magazines, articles, and blogs)

THE EDUCATION DEBT . . . REVISITED

The notion of an education debt owed to African American children has the potential to be a controversial issue. Many school officials, legislators, and laypeople think African American underachievement lies solely with the student and family. Millions of dollars, thousands of hours of human labor, and years of conversations about how to reform schools has led to minimal change in the achievement levels for African American children. I would think that, since none of those things has worked, we would be engaged in national conversations about how those dollars might be better spent and what the right things to do would be. Instead, I hear sentiments such as these: "If Black students would just conform to schools, do their homework, and study for tests, everything would be okay," or "If Black parents cared about their child's education, then teachers wouldn't have such a hard time." Comments like these are not only common, they are damaging. African American parents care about their students' education just as much as White or Asian parents. As a Black administrator, I am often asked by parents how they should navigate school environments. Regardless of income, many parents do not have the social capital to be successful in their advocacy of their children. Furthermore, since the institution of school is rooted in the sociocultural paradigm (including social, economic, political considerations), classrooms must include opportunities to assert families' out-of-school identities inside the classroom. Conversely, as African American male students do this, they must learn how to morph their identities to fit into different spaces. Aside from the sociopolitical, economic, and social constructs that are the building blocks to the White dominant power structure, schools often serve as incubators that help nurture the destructive beliefs that are branded on the fabric of our society.

I receive a stark reminder of the education debt when I drive through the city of Detroit. Within an hour's drive, one can juxtapose the gentrification currently under way in the city's arts, sports, and entertainment district with the economic depression in the residential areas. As mentioned earlier, Detroit is approximately 82% African American with 40% of its residents living in poverty (U.S. Census Bureau, 2010). Although Detroit is currently experiencing revitalization efforts, African American residents are not active (or invited) economic participants in the city's economic growth, despite the fact that the city's economic growth and renaissance has a direct link to the education landscape in the city and the region.

If we looked at the current situation with a blind eye, it would be easy to conclude that Detroit's economic revitalization is occurring independent of an educational revitalization. Any major city that seeks to grow in size and attract residents must have a flourishing school system. It is easy to surmise that the absence of African American residents from this process, coupled with the ongoing and longstanding underachievement of African American students in the public school system, is evidence that the economic and academic malpractice and maleficence against African American children is continuing.

The Detroit school structure has been under constant political and physical restructuring (state takeover, financial management, and incorporation of a statewide school system) for the past several decades. The most recent iteration of the takeover of Detroit Public Schools occurred in 2009 while Governor Jennifer Granholm was in office. It involved the institution of an emergency financial manager, Robert Bobb, who took over all financial and academic decisions for the district. At the time of the takeover, the district had a student population of roughly 167,000 and a $100 million fund balance (Black, 2016; Guyette, 2015). After 6 years under state control with a revolving door of several different emergency financial managers, the Detroit Public Schools system found itself with approximately 120,000 fewer students and more than half a billion dollars in debt. To add to that, between the years of 2009 and 2016, the state of Michigan was trying its hand at several different reform tactics, including a statewide reform district called the Education Achievement Authority (EAA). The idea of the EAA was to take over the lowest 5% of underperforming schools. Thus, the state had to develop a new accountability system where schools were labeled as a "reward," "focus," or "priority" school, and the lowest of these would be subject to further scrutiny. Furthermore, as the new structure was put in place, so were multiple and ever-changing state assessments. Although all of the aforementioned events have helped perpetuate the miseducation of African American children, none is as shameless as the physical conditions that African American children in Detroit have had to endure.

Thus far, we have concentrated on the instructional, cultural, and social inequities that African American students have had to face, but we've talked very little about the physical conditions. Additionally, the data collected from teachers in my study came from teachers in the suburbs who have had to struggle with only a fraction of the economic, physical, and psychological issues African American children have had to endure, absent the psychological ramifications of trying to assimilate in majority-White school environments. Many of the teachers who are teaching in the Detroit Public Schools Community District (formerly Detroit Public Schools) are underpaid and ill prepared to handle the multitude of issues that many of the students bring to school. Although many give their best effort, they have difficulty helping students overcome structural barriers to learning. In some cases, the school buildings themselves are structurally unsound and represent unfit learning environments. In fact, in 2016, teachers in the Detroit Community School District led several sickouts to bring attention to the deplorable conditions in many of the schools. The conditions made international news as teachers anonymously posted pictures of mushrooms growing in school spaces (see Figure 10.1), rat and mouse droppings, moldy lunches served to students, exposed piping, holes in drywall and plaster, and many, many others on social media.

Figure 10.1. Mushrooms growing in a hallway of a Detroit school, 2016

Source: Anonymous photo submitted to clickondetroit.com

The images that were posted by teachers about their classroom conditions are reminiscent of the atrocious conditions documented in Jonathan Kozol's (1991) *Savage Inequalities*, where he presented a scathing (and true) account of the disgraceful physical and instructional conditions in public schools all across the nation. Kozol spent 2 years traveling the country and collecting data about how the nation educates our children, particularly African American and Latino/a students who were living in urban areas and who lived in poverty (it is important to point out that race and poverty are not synonymous). Kozol documented, with evidence, what we already knew: that even after *Brown v. Board of Education*, African American children have been receiving an inferior education. Kozol (1991) wrote:

Of an entering ninth grade class of 20,000 students in Detroit, only 7,000 graduate from high school, and, of these, only 500 have the preparation to go on to college. Educators in Detroit, *The New York Times* reports, say that the "financial pressures have reached the point of desperation." In 1988, according to a survey by the Free Press, the city spent some $3,600 yearly on each child's education. The suburban town of Grosse Pointe spent some $5,700 on each child. Bloomfield Hills spent even more: $6,250 for each pupil. Birmingham, at $6,400 per pupil, spent the most of any district in the area. "Kids have no choice about where they're born or where they live," says the superintendent of another district, which has even less to spend per pupil than Detroit. "If they're fortunate [enough] to [have been] born in . . . Birmingham, that's well and good." Their opportunities, he says, are very different if they're born in a poor district. (p. 198)

Kozol also compared the conditions of public schools in urban areas and the type of education that students of color were receiving to the instruction and environments found in wealthy communities. One had to be in total denial not to recognize the academic disparities Kozol pointed out. Even more depressing is that little has been done to correct these ills in the years since the original publication of his book. Politicians and educators have not been able to improve schools and the outcomes for African American children, and the disparity in achievement between White and Black students is widening.

In regions like southeast Michigan, African American families have worked hard since the Great Migration to the North to provide a better life for their children. In the past 30 years or so, many families pooled their economic resources and, in many instances, bought homes in the surrounding suburban areas that Kozol talked about. They felt that moving to suburban school districts would give their children the long-awaited educational equity that African American parents and their children so desired and deserved. They wanted to escape the inequitable education that they received in the South and in poor and depressed communities. What scores of African American families quickly found was that even though they worked countless hours to be able to afford housing in middle-class suburban areas, those communities and school districts sent blatant and covert messages to the families and children that the students were unwanted. I've heard tale after tale, observed with my own eyes and ears, and watched news story after story where African American students were physically, socially, and psychologically abused. A few of my own family members experienced such treatment, and in one suburban Detroit school district in 1989, the superintendent automatically retained large numbers of African American male students who came from Detroit Public Schools. Actions like these have had lasting negative effects on my friends and family members. In some instances, the students questioned their parents about why they had to repeat a grade.

Because many African American families have experienced inferior educational practices and environments for their students, they have had to take multiple measures to ensure that their students receive a quality education in high-performing school districts. Much to their chagrin, similar to the Great Migration of African Americans seeking refuge from the tyrannical social, economic, and academic practices of the South, African American children faced racism and racist practices in suburban school districts in suburbs surrounding cities like Detroit, St. Louis, Chicago, Boston, Los Angeles, and Cleveland.

RECOMMENDATIONS

In order for teachers, administrators, schools, and districts to develop appropriate literacy interventions for African American males, the historical implications and analyses of the sociocultural components of literacy and students' identities should be central to their understandings. This book has shown how the institution of slavery, Jim Crow laws, school desegregation, and the negative perceptions of African American males that are woven into the cultural, political, and social fabric of this country have had a devastating effect on the literacy of African American males.

In order to help African American male students connect and buy in to school-based literacy, educators *must* use different approaches from what they have attempted in the past. Students' home mores, cultural ethoses, and identities must be appreciated and valued in the school context before students can be expected to connect to school values, mores, and the types of social paradigms and political thought encouraged in the school context. It is possible to help students to make connections to these ideals through their exposure to appropriate texts, access to culturally relevant content, and the assurance of equity.

Although instructional strategies such as book club are among the widely used evidence-based instructional models with the specific aim of improving the reading comprehension of students, there is a dearth of studies that document literacy interventions for specific use with African American students (Lindo, 2006; Morgan & Mehta, 2004). The themes that emerged from teachers who participated in this study helped establish the importance of using effective literacy interventions for students to help them connect to school-based literacy expectations. Vygotsky's social learning theory was used as the theoretical model, and book club was used as the practical model to engage teachers in ongoing dialogue. The accompanying activities and research on the sociocultural paradigm was used to develop the Black Male Literacy Paradigm, a model for literacy instruction. Moreover, the research on collaboration, improving schools' culture, and professional learning communities provides a framework for ongoing professional development and collaboration time for teachers.

IMPLICATIONS

It is problematic to continue to support the idea that schools have no responsibility for adjusting their practices and policies to accommodate the needs of African American male students. If African American male students continue to be expected to change their identities to fit the values of the school, then students will continue to feel disconnected from their schools. Educators should participate in inquiry that involves the restructuring and reconceptualization of the institution of school and challenge the model introduced by Thomas Jefferson (1781), where he asserted that school is for (White) boys who show the most promise and that the "rubbish" should be discarded. Challenging this paradigm would entail recognizing the idea that there is an education debt that needs to be paid to African American students and that we need to explore strategies on how to pay that debt.

The way the institution of school is structured has changed only slightly since its inception, prompting the question of whether school will ever be able to accommodate the needs of African American male students. When public schooling was first introduced, African Americans were still captives and it was illegal for them to learn how to read or participate in any academic endeavors. Thus, school was never designed to accept or accommodate the culture, language, or literacy of African American people. The institution of school was set up as a system based on meritocracy. In order to begin to address the needs of African American children, schools must become more egalitarian in nature.

The idea that African American boys refuse to connect or buy in to school culture should continue to be reviewed, and researchers should continue to explore the reasons why this occurs. The teacher-participants in my study established that African American male students find it difficult to connect with school culture, regardless of the school or school districts they attend. What was missing from the data was a discourse about how teachers could influence a whole-scale structural change of the institution of school to help these students connect. Though this study directly addressed how teachers helped students connect to in-school literacy, one of the tertiary discourses that it initiated was how the convergence of the lives of African American students and how they connect to school are related to how teachers' perceptions of them impact their school success.

We must also continue the dialogue about the view that is held by many, that we need to help students buy in to the structures of already-established school cultures. This notion presupposes that the existing cultures of schools are, in fact, right for African American male students. When we situate literacy within the sociocultural paradigm, it becomes clear that we need to consider how school cultures impede African American males' ability to access school-based literacy.

The teacher-participants in the study indicated that, although they believed that their understandings of African American male literacy can be improved through greater access to evidence-based strategies, not enough professional development was available to engage them in the types of discussions they needed to help them improve their practice. Also, other practitioners often recognize that there is a dearth of professional learning opportunities that seek to meet the complex needs of students, particularly those specifically geared toward African American male students. The teachers indicated that even the infrequent experiences they had with professional development aimed at improving students' literacy was not effective. The Black Male Literacy Paradigm has professional learning for teachers embedded into it, and teachers can use it to understand the students that they teach as they participate in ongoing learning and inquiry about who their students are and how they connect to school. Although many districts provide teachers with the time to converse with their fellow teachers, they do not encourage or require dialogue, inquiry, and actions that align with theory, nor are teachers given the capacity to collect or review data to determine the impact of their new learning on the achievement of their students. Teachers should be given the opportunity to engage in new learning that addresses multiple models and frameworks that are evidence-based.

Another implication of understanding the impact of the sociocultural paradigm for literacy involves recognizing and acknowledging how teachers' treatment of African American students can affect those students in negative ways. Teacher-participants indicated that many of their students felt disconnected from school because their teachers have victimized them. One of the case study participants indicated that educators often feel that the turmoil that many African American male students face occurs outside of school; however, students often encounter turmoil as a result of the relationships, or lack thereof, with their teachers and the school environment. This is an important point to drive home. I frequently hear educators talk about the turmoil that students bring to school, but rarely do I hear educators talk about how school and school relationships negatively impact students' lives. While students' turmoil may be real and may occur outside of school, educators should understand and respond to how students may experience turmoil at school and at the hands of school personnel.

In order to authentically address the literacy needs of African American male students, educators must be willing to address their own biases toward their students. While teachers should be participating in collaborative inquiry about evidence-based literacy strategies, they should be simultaneously participating in individual and collaborative inquiry about their perceptions of students and how those perceptions influence their instruction, treatment, and text selections for African American male students. Furthermore, the significance of the race and culture of the teacher, the race and culture of the student, and the cultural context of school and literacy should also be a part of teacher and school conversations.

The teachers who participated in the dialogue initiated by this study questioned their own practices and perceptions as well as the practices and perceptions of their colleagues. The study gave them a safe space and opportunity to grapple with race, culture, and instructional practices and the expectations of African American male students. As educators use their improved understandings of their Black male students to influence classroom and school structures, we must continue to engross ourselves in this most important work. The challenge of this work of changing school environments and improving literacy instruction will be to resist defaulting to the belief that students' skill sets alone are the things to be addressed. If educators do not move beyond accessing and discussing data about the failure rates of African American male students and begin to do in-depth analyses of in-school expectations, discipline practices, and how race serves as a predictor of a student's life and academic trajectory, then students will continue to find difficulty connecting to school-based literacy and school-based content.

Finally, like many of the teachers with whom I come in contact, the teacher-participants in this study indicated that they often feel they cannot be honest about their feelings with their colleagues about colleagues' racist or insensitive comments. If we hope to move beyond harboring negative perceptions of African American male students, teachers must feel comfortable enough to address, correct, and interrupt negative, racist, and biased assumptions about African American male students. Teachers can participate in such dialogue within the construct of professional learning communities or other structured and unstructured learning conversations.

CHALLENGES TO THIS WORK

There are challenges to the work of changing school culture that might impede readers from assessing its potential impact on the achievement of African American male students. Although the teacher-participants' data supported the idea that their engagement in professional learning helped them progress in their understanding of the nature of literacy and how African American male students connect to school-based literacy, there were not enough data to demonstrate that the teachers changed their actual practice. Research such as the study outlined in this book might be fully supported in teachers' school environments over a specific period of time with a component that allows researchers or school officials to observe teachers in their classroom environments. Furthermore, research studies and practices should be grounded in ongoing discourses, within the context of a community such as a school professional learning community, to provide the opportunity for teachers to align their instructional practices, discourses, and student data.

Educators should consider creating cohorts within a school building or district to allow teachers to participate in inquiry about how to make larger structural changes to the institution of school. To effect organizational change, professional learning for teachers should be aligned to districts' visions, missions, and instructional activities, and should become a part of the common practice, lexicon, and mindset of school districts. Therefore, classroom teachers, superintendents, and other instructional staff should participate in ongoing professional learning and should participate in activities that support evidence-based instructional frameworks upon which they can rely.

. . . UNTIL WE MEET AGAIN

The literacy development of African American male students does not occur in a vacuum; rather, it is part of their maturation and is aligned to their social experiences. To ignore the unique way that literacy is intertwined with other aspects of the lives of African American male students is tantamount to education malpractice, social and academic marginalization, and ineptitude on the part of educators and education policymakers. Over the past several decades, hundreds of studies have been conducted about how to improve literacy. Those studies should be analyzed and used to design instruction for African American males. This book supports actions such as these and makes a strong case for educators to view the literacy practices of African American male students through a different lens.

Teachers need to be given tools to address the chasm between the in-school and out-of-school literacy practices of African American male students. Those in the field of education must start by addressing the hegemony of dominant-culture narratives within school environments. Teachers and schools must also help students feel as though their primary discourses are valued, because their identities are concomitant with their culture and language. Since students bring their identities to literacy events, they must know and feel encouraged to link their identities with expected school literacy.

Schools must seek new ways to help African American male students connect to the institution of school. As the data supports, African American male students reject school and school content because they do not have positive relationships with their teachers; thus, they experience school failure as a result. The data highlighting the rate of school failure among African American male students should spark outrage and be viewed as an educational epidemic. The best way to address school failure among African American male students and improve their connection to school-based literacy is to understand that the achievement gap is a representation of an education debt that is owed to them. We can help educators understand this by providing appropriate professional learning opportunities for them that allows them to (1) address their negative perceptions and beliefs about African American male students, (2) have access to evidence-based instructional strategies, and (3) participate in meaningful dialogue about pedagogy. Lastly, results from research studies should serve as a theoretical foundation and should be a catalyst to spark educators to begin the necessary dialogues.

WHAT CAN TEACHERS DO RIGHT NOW?

- Seek out longitudinal data about the students you teach:
  » Ask the students about how they learn in order to improve your understanding of their assessment data.
  » Seek to understand students' lives and find out if there is a correlation between their school performance and out-of-school environment.
- Recognize that you have biases that impact your instruction, discipline of students, and text selections for them—and work actively to change them!
- Become active on a political level to advocate for more equitable funding of schools, and join a regional or national content-based organization or political action committee to allow your voice to be heard.

WHAT CAN ADMINISTRATORS DO RIGHT NOW?

- Challenge teachers to broaden their definition of literacy.
- Invest in resources/texts that students will connect with in the classroom and beyond.
- Build master schedules that ensure the most effective teachers are with the kids who need them most, regardless of seniority or personal preferences.
- Analyze the demographics of advanced classes, and the students being identified as needing an intervention or individualized education program (IEP).
- Begin to pay back the education debt to African American male students.

Epilogue

On that balmy spring day back in 1985, I was 10 years old and wore size 10 Adidas Top Tens. I walked in my own kicks, and sometimes I didn't even want to. I often think about the psyche of a young Black boy who aims a 9-millimeter pistol at the head of an even younger Black boy and demands his shoes. I think about what it would have been like for that young man to walk in my shoes, even for a short period. What would he have dreamed he could become? Where would those shoes have taken him? If he had new shoes, would he have thought that he was somebody, that he could accomplish anything?

When I think of the red, white, and blue high-tops with the spongy tongue, I think of America. These were the type of shoes that spawned a worldwide movement, that inspired b-boys and b-girls to put brightly colored fat laces in them, that inspired the most famous rap group in the world, RUN DMC, to write the most noticeable 16 bars dedicated to an article of clothing. I understood fully why that boy with the black 9-millimeter wanted my shoes so badly. But I was but a boy, and he could not walk in my shoes, not even as he threatened my life. Not only could *he* not walk in *my* shoes, but even at that young age, I often had to walk in shoes made for others . . . for grown men. I wore size 10 shoes at 10 years old, and I sometimes had to walk in the types of responsibilities assigned to the men who probably fit my shoes.

My new kicks gave me character, they gave me notoriety, they helped me pick at that crack in my shell until my brand-new soul emerged. I used my new kicks to walk proudly as I wore the responsibilities of grown men as a badge of honor. I was a third parent to my two younger sisters. I provided the emotional support to my grandmother that she never received from her husband. I critically analyzed my lot in life as a human, as a Black boy growing up in Detroit, as the beneficiary of talents bestowed upon me by the almighty God. Ever since I can remember, I have felt the burden of caring for others. I don't know if my teachers intuitively discovered this or if it was the fact that they felt the pressing need to engage young African American males in literacy. Whatever the reason, the way my teachers helped me engage

184

in literacy helped me bear my cross. I was the one who needed to be encouraged. I was the one who needed to be nurtured. I was the one who needed someone to notice who I was. I was the one who needed that book that spoke to me, that spoke to my life. I walked in my own kicks down that path, and some of my teachers chose to walk with me.

Literacy would not have saved me from the bullet of that gun had it been expelled from its dull, black barrel, but it did save my life on countless other occasions. I think about the time it saved me when I was 16 and I was pulled over by a cop who attempted to search my mother's car without provocation. I knew my constitutional rights were being violated because of the miniature copy of the U.S. Constitution that I carried around with me, given to me by my American history teacher.

Or what about my educational path? I was exposed to so many texts, contexts, words, and experiences through literacy that this Black boy from the west side of Detroit, who came from the type of neighborhood that does not produce a lot of PhDs, was able to attend renowned public schools that were recognized at the regional, state, and national levels. Years later, I walked across the stage in my brand-new shoes as they announced my name, "Aaron M. Johnson . . . dissertation . . . *Understanding the In-School Literacies of African American Males Through a Sociocultural Paradigm: Implications for Teacher Professional Development."*

What about the Vocabulary Skill Building (VSB) program developed by my heroine master teacher, Mrs. Willie Bell Gibson? She told us, "As long as you know the meanings of words, their histories, and their synonyms and antonyms, no one will *ever* be able to talk over your head." She saved my life.

What about the countless times that literacy saved my life as I spent hour after hour, Saturday after Saturday, away from my neighborhood, in the Detroit Public Library? My mother would drop me off at the downtown branch of the library and I would get lost in the stacks. Before the advent of cellphones and other technology, my mother would drop me off and tell me, "Go do your homework and go read." I couldn't even call her and tell her when I was ready. So I read. And I read. I read about how the possession of the Panama Canal would transfer in ownership from the United States back to Panama in 1999. I read about the bubonic plague in Europe, and about how California had the largest population, but Alaska was the largest state geographically. I read about Easter Island, and how the Native Americans "sold" Manhattan Island, and the habited and uninhabited islands that make up the Hawaiian Islands. I fell in love with Marguerite Johnson (Maya Angelou), and Chloe Ardelia Wofford (Toni Morrison), and Bigger Thomas, and Langston, and Malcom, and Pecola Breedlove, and the beautiful song that James Weldon Johnson wrote for Black people so that *we* could feel comfortable standing for our own anthem. I read about Henry Ford and how he took his quadricycle on an inaugural run down Woodward Avenue. I read about Black Bottom and the 1943 and 1967 riots and how Detroit's first Black mayor started off just as my grandfather had, building up the wealth of this nation in an automobile plant.

I didn't know it at the time, but on that balmy day on that playground in 1985 when I stared down the barrel of that black 9-millimeter, held by a teenage soldier who wasn't in school and who needed a new pair of combat shoes, I was to become the dream of my great-grandfather, a Black man who drove a car for White folks in Prattville, Alabama, but who owned more than 40 acres of land that he had to forfeit to the county in payment for $1,000 in taxes he owed. I was to become the dream of my mother, who admitted that her dream was for me to just go to college and that she had no idea how I would be able to finish or that I would ever go as far as I had gone. I was to become the dream of my great-great-grandfather, the Autauga Indian who married a White woman in an age where loving the wrong person could get you killed.

I have walked in the shoes of the generations before me. I have walked in the shoes of my grandmother Annie Belle Humphrey and my grandfather Winston Humphrey and my mother, Lila Humphrey, and my absent father, James Johnson, and his absent father, James Johnson. I chose to be present and became the present. I am the dream that they could not dream.

My kicks—the red . . . the white . . . the blue—represented freedom. They represented the prosperity, the hope, and the dream promised by America. My kicks connected me to a culture, and that culture connected me to a history, which connected me to a drive to build a new history, a new legacy, to build a new dream, to encourage my own son that he can believe that his intelligence, his beauty, the pain and suffering of his ancestors affords him the goddamn right to be treated fairly, equally, and equitably.

It's balmy today in America, and a shadowy figure stands on a vast, green playground off in the distance. A pop fly lands and rolls out by his feet and someone in his new red, white, and blue kicks approaches him to retrieve the ball.

The shadowy figure reaches into his pocket.

Click-clack.

"Check in those kicks, America. I know a few million people who need to walk in them for a lil' bit."

Afterword

Johnson's *A Walk in Their Kicks* is a mosaic articulation of the African American male schooling experience. It takes a deep dive into the quagmire of school-based literacy development for African American males. Johnson unapologetically confronts the history of schooling in this country and how this history has disenfranchised African American males in their schooling experiences and has created a pipeline of disconnection to literacy, leading to the maleducation of this student population. He challenges educators to move beyond their quest for simple remedies to the complexities of educating African American male students by offering a framework for improving literacy instruction in particular and schooling in general for our most vulnerable students. The Black Male Literacy Paradigm described in this book is a comprehensive approach to literacy acquisition designed specifically with African American males in mind. The author's framework covers a wide spectrum of constructs that must become a part of the pedagogy of teachers if we are serious about reversing the malpractice so endemic to the educating of African American males in our schools. The theories introduced in this paradigm can be used as a blueprint for overcoming the barriers that prevent African American males from having a liberating and culturally responsive education that connects to their identities, culture, and lived experiences.

Johnson is an emerging preeminent thinker, writer, scholar, and leader in the area of African American male literacy development. *A Walk in Their Kicks* elucidates what's possible for educators and what's essential to the schooling of African American males in our quest to eliminate the gaps in opportunity, access, equity, equality, culture, relationships, placement, discipline, rigor, and more that manifest themselves as the gaps in achievement so prevalent among this student population. This thought-provoking text provides practical solutions to reversing the educational trajectory for African American male students.

—Jay B. Marks, PhD, diversity and equity consultant,
Oakland Schools, Michigan

References

Alfaro, M. J. M. (1996). Intertextuality: Origins and development of the concept. *Atlantis,* 268–285.

American Psychiatric Association. (2017). What is posttraumatic stress disorder? www.psychiatry.org/patients-families/ptsd/what-is-ptsd

Anderson, J. (1988). *The education of Blacks in the south, 1860–1935.* Chapel Hill, NC: The University of North Carolina Press.

Bakhtin, M. (1981). *The dialogic imagination.* Austin: University of Texas Press.

Bakhtin, M. (1986). The problem of speech genres. In C. Emerson & M. Holquist (Eds.), *Speech genres and other late essays* (pp. 60–102). Austin, TX: University of Texas Press. (Original work published 1953)

Bandura, A. (1997). *Self-efficacy: The exercise of control.* New York, NY: W. H. Freeman.

Bandura, A. (2000). Exercise of human agency through collective efficacy. *Current Directions in Psychological Science, 9*(3), 75–78.

Bandura, A. (2001). Social cognitive theory: An agentic perspective. *Annual Review of Psychology, 52,* 1–26.

Binet, A., & Simon, T. (1916). *The development of intelligence in children.* Baltimore, MD: Wilkins and Wilkins Company.

Black, S. M. (2016). *An examination of urban school governance reform in Detroit public schools, 1999–2014.* Available from ProQuest Dissertations & Theses A&I. (1790627273). Retrieved from search.proquest.com.proxy.lib .wayne.edu/docview/1790627273?accountid=14925

Blalock, H. M. (1967). *Toward a theory of minority-group relations.* New York, NY: John Wiley & Sons, Inc.

Bloome, D., & Bailey, F. M. (1992). Studying language and literacy through events, particularity, and intertextuality. In L. Beach, J. J. Green, M. L. Kamil, & T. Shanahan (Eds.), *Multidisciplinary perspectives on literacy research* (pp. 181–210). Urbana, IL: National Council of Teachers of English

Bond, H. M. (1966). *The education of the negro in the American social order.* New York, NY: Octagon Books. (Original work published 1934)

Brown v. Board of Education, 347 U.S. 483 (1954).

Brown, C. (1965). *Manchild in the promised land.* New York: NY: Scribner.

Bryk, A. S., & Driscoll, M. E. (1988). *The high school as community: Contextual influences and consequences for students and teachers.* Madison, WI: National Center on Effective Secondary Schools.

Campano, G., & Vasudevan, L. (2009). The social production of adolescent risk and the promise of adolescent literacies. *Review of Research in Education, 33*(1), 310–353.

Cazden, C. B. (1988). *Classroom discourse.* Portsmouth, NH: Heinemann.

Chavous, T. M., Bernat, D. H., Schmeelk-Cone, K., Caldwell, C. H., Kohn-Wood, L., & Zimmerman, M. A. (2003). Racial identity and academic attainment among African American adolescents. *Child Development, 74*(4), 1076–1090.

Children's Defense Fund. (2014). The state of America's children 2014. Retrieved from www.childrensdefense.org/library/state-of-americas-children/education.html

Coates, T. (2009). *The beautiful struggle.* New York, NY: Spiegel and Grau. Coates, T. (2015) *Between the world and me.* New York, NY: Spiegel and Grau.

Cumming v. Richmond County Board of Education, 175 U.S. 528 (1899).

Csikszentmihalyi, M. (1990). *Flow: The psychology of optimal experience.* New York, NY: Harper & Row.

Delpit, L. (1996). *Other people's children.* New York, NY: New Press.

Dewey, J. (1909). *Moral principles in education.* Boston, MA: Houghton Mifflin Company.

Dewey, J. (1916). *Democracy and education: An introduction to the philosophy of education.* New York, NY: The MacMillan Company.

Dewey, J. (1956). *The school and society & the child and the curriculum.* Chicago, IL: The University of Chicago Press.

Douglass, F. (2003). *Narrative of the life of Frederick Douglass, an American slave.* Boston, MA: Bedford/St. Martin's.

Du Bois, W. E. B. (2009). *The souls of Black folk.* Oxford, England: Oxford University Press. (Original work published 1903)

DuFour, R., & Eaker, R. (1998). *Professional learning communities at work.* Bloomington, IN: National Educational Service.

Elmore, R. F. (2003). *Knowing the right thing to do: School improvement and performance-based accountability.* Washington, DC: NGA Center for Best Practices.

Ernst-Slavit, G., & Mason, M. R. (2011). "Words that hold us up": Teacher talk and academic language in five upper elementary classrooms. *Linguistics and Education, 22*(4), 430–440.

Fanon, F. (1963). *Wretched of the earth.* New York, NY: Grove Press.

Felitti, V. J., Anda, R. F., Nordenberg, D., Williamson, D. F., Spitz, A. M., Edwards, V., Koss, M. P., & Marks, J. S. (1998). Relationship of childhood abuse and household dysfunction to many of the leading causes of death in adults. *American Journal of Preventative Medicine, 14*(4), 245–258.

Fisher, E. J. (2005). Black student achievement and the oppositional culture model. *The Journal of Negro Education, 74*(3), 201–209.

Flake, S. (2010, February 16). You don't even know me [Video file]. *YouTube.* Retrieved from youtu.be/Gy4u44FZk94

Fordham, S., & Ogbu, J. U. (1986). Black students' school success: Coping with the "burden of 'acting White.'" *Urban Review, 18*(3), 176–206.

Franzak, J. K. (2006). A review of the literature on marginalized adolescent readers, literacy theory, and policy implications. *American Educational Research Association, 76*(2), 209–248. Retrieved from www.jstor.org/stable /3700589

Freeman, L. L. (2011). *Effective language arts teachers of urban African American middle school students in the greater Detroit area.* Available from ProQuest Dissertations & Theses A&I. (903797089). Retrieved from pqdtopen.proquest .com/doc/903797089.html?FMT=AI

Gary et al. v. Snyder et al., No. 2:2016cv13292 - Document 112 (E.D. MI. 2018).

Gee, J. P. (1989). Literacy, discourse, and linguistics: Introduction. *Journal of Education, 17,* 5–17.

Gee, J. P. (1998). "What is literacy?" In V. Zamel & R. Spack (Eds.), *Negotiating academic literacies: Teaching and learning across languages and cultures* (pp. 51–59). New York, NY: Routledge.

Gee, J. P. (1999). *An introduction to discourse analysis: Theory and method.* London, England: Routledge.

Gee, J. P. (2001). Identity as an analytic lens for research in education. *Review of Research in Education,* 99–125.

Greene, J. P., & Winters, M. A. (2006). Leaving boys behind: public high school graduation rates. *The Manhattan Institute of Policy Research* (Civic Report 48). Retrieved from www.manhattan-institute.org/html/cr_48.htm

Guerra, J. (2007). Out of the valley: Transcultural repositioning as a rhetorical practice in ethnographic research and other aspects of everyday life. In P. Enciso, C. Lewis, & E. B. Moje (Eds.), *Reframing sociocultural research on literacy: Identity, agency, and power* (pp. 137–162). Mahwah, NJ: Lawrence Erlbaum Associates.

Guyette, C. (2015). After six years and four state-appointed managers, Detroit Public Schools' debt has grown even deeper. *Metro Times, 35*(20).

Harris, N. B. (2018). *The deepest well: Healing the long-term effects of childhood adversity.* Boston, MA: Houghton Mifflin Harcourt.

Hattie, J. (2012). *Visible learning for teachers: Maximizing impact on learning.* New York, NY: Routledge.

Hattie, J. (2016). *Visible learning into action: International case studies of impact.* New York, NY: Routledge.

Heath, S. B. (1989). Oral and literate traditions among Black Americans living in poverty. *American psychologist, 44*(2), 367.

Herrnstein, R. J., & Murray, C. (1994). *The bell curve: Intelligence and class structure in American life.* New York, NY: The Free Press.

Hirsch, E. D. (2003). Reading comprehension requires knowledge—of words and the world. *American Educator, 27*(1), 10–13.

History.com Editors. (2018, September 20). Great Migration. *HISTORY*. Retrieved from www.history.com/topics/Black-history/great-migration

James, D. R. (1989). City limits on racial equality: The effects of city-suburb boundaries on public-school desegregation, 1968–1976. *American Sociological Review, 54*(6), 963–985. Retrieved from www.jstor.org/stable/2095718?seq=1#metadata_info_tab_contents

Jefferson, T. (1781). *Notes on the state of Virginia*. Retrieved from docsouth.unc.edu/southlit/jefferson/jefferson.html#p138

Johnson, A. M. (2016). *Understanding the in-school literacies of African American males through a sociocultural paradigm: Implications for teacher professional development*. Available from ProQuest Dissertations & Theses A&I. (1790628128). Retrieved from search.proquest.com.proxy.lib.wayne.edu/docview/1790628128?accountid=14925

Kirkland, D. E., & Jackson, A. (2009). We real cool: Toward a theory of Black masculine literacies. *Reading Research Quarterly, 44*(3), 278–297.

Koffka, K. (1935). *Principles of gestalt psychology*. London, England: Lund Humphries.

Kozol, J. (1991). *Savage inequalities: Children in America's schools*. New York, NY: Harper Perennial.

Kristeva, J., & Moi, T. (1986). *The Kristeva reader*. New York, NY: Columbia University Press.

Kucer, S. B. (2009) *Dimensions of literacy: A conceptual base for teaching reading and writing in school settings*. Mahwah, NJ: Lawrence Erlbaum Associates.

Kunjufu, J. (2002). *Black students. Middle class teachers*. Chicago, IL: African American Images.

Kunjufu, J. (2005). *Keeping Black boys out of special education*. Chicago, IL: African American Images.

Ladson-Billings, G. (2006) From achievement gap to educational debt: Understanding achievement in U.S. schools. *Educational Researcher, 35*(7), 3–12.

Learning. (n.d.). *Merriam-Webster*. Retrieved from www.merriam-webster.com/dictionary/learning

LeCompte, M. D., & Schensul, J. J. (1999). *Analyzing & interpreting ethnographic data*. Walnut Creek, CA: Altamira Press.

Lee, J. (2002). Racial and ethnic achievement gap trends: Reversing the progress toward equity? *Educational Researcher, 31*, 3–12.

Lewis, C. (2001). *Literacy practices as social acts*. Mahwah, NJ: Lawrence Erlbaum Associates.

Lewis, C., Enciso, P., & Moje, E. B. (Eds.) (2007). *Reframing sociocultural research on literacy: Identity, agency, and power*. Mahwah, NJ: Lawrence Erlbaum Associates.

Lincoln, Y. S., & Guba, E. G. (1985). *Naturalistic inquiry*. Thousand Oaks, CA: Sage.

Lindo, E. (2006) The African American presence in reading Intervention experiments. *Remedial and Special Education, 27*(3), 148–153.

Lortie, D. C. (1975). *Schoolteacher: A sociological study.* Chicago, IL: University of Chicago Press.

Luke, A. (2003). Literacy and the other: A sociological approach to literacy research and policy in multilingual societies. *Reading Research Quarterly, 38*(1), 132–141.

Marzano, R. J., & Pickering, D. J. (2005). *Building academic vocabulary: Teacher's manual.* Alexandria, VA: Association for Supervision and Curriculum Development.

Marzano, R. J., Waters, T., & McNulty, B. A. (2005). *School leadership that works: From research to results.* Alexandria, VA: Association for Supervision and Curriculum Development.

Maslow, A. H. (1943). A theory of human motivation. *Psychological Review, 50,* 370–396.

McMahon, S. I., Raphael, T. E., Goatley, V. J., & Pardo, L. S. (Eds.). (1997). *The book club connection: Literacy learning and classroom talk.* New York, NY: Teachers College Press.

Meinke, S. (2011, September). *Milliken v. Bradley*: The northern battle for desegregation. *Michigan Bar Journal.* Retrieved from www.michbar.org/file/journal/pdf/pdf4article1911.pdf

Michigan Department of Education. (2016). 2015 significant disproportionality list. *Michigan Department of Education.* Retrieved from www.michigan.gov/mde/0,4615,7-140-6598_48005-428529--,00.html

Milliken et al. v. Bradley et al., 418 U.S. 717 (1974).

Morgan, S. L., & Mehta, J. D. (2004). Beyond the laboratory: Evaluating the survey evidence for the disidentification explanation of Black-White differences in achievement. *Sociology of Education, 77*(1), 82–101.

National Center for Education Statistics, U.S. Department of Education (NCES). (2011). The condition of education 2011. Retrieved from nces.ed.gov/pubsearch/pubsinfo.asp ?pubid=2011033

National Center for Educational Statistics, U.S. Department of Education (NCES). (2013). The condition of education 2013. Retrieved from nces.ed.gov/programs/coe/indicator_coi.asp

National Center for Educational Statistics, U.S. Department of Education (NCES). (2014). The condition of education 2014. Retrieved from nces.ed.gov/pubs2014/2014083.pdf

National Center for Educational Statistics, U.S. Department of Education (NCES). (2016). The condition of education 2016. Retrieved from nces.ed.gov/pubs2016/2016144.pdf

National Trust for Historic Preservation. (2018). Rosenwald schools. Retrieved from savingplaces.org/places/rosenwald-schools#.WK8jqxIrImr

Newkirk, T. (2002). *Misreading masculinity: Boys, literacy, and popular culture.* Portsmouth, NH: Heinemann.

Noguera, P. A. (2003). The trouble with Black boys: The role and influence of environmental and cultural factors on the academic performance of African American males. *Urban Education, 38*(4), 431–459.

Obama, B. (2006). *The audacity of hope.* New York, NY: Three Rivers Press.

Ogbu, J. (1991). Minority coping responses and school experience. *Journal of Psychohistory, 18,* 433–456.

Oliver Brown et al. v. The Board of Education of Topeka, Kansas, Shawnee County et. al., 347 U.S. 483 (1954).

Olzak, S., Shanahan, S., & West, E. (1994). School desegregation, interracial exposure, and antibusing activity in contemporary urban America. *American Journal of Sociology, 100*(1), 196–241.

Payne, R. K. (1995). *A framework for understanding poverty.* Highland, TX: Aha! Process.

Plessy v. Ferguson, 163 U.S. 537 (1896).

Porowski, A., O'Conner, R., & Passa, A. (2014). *Disproportionality in school discipline: An assessment of trends in Maryland, 2009–12.* (REL 2014–017). Washington, DC: U.S. Department of Education, Institute of Education Sciences, National Center for Education Evaluation and Regional Assistance, Regional Educational Laboratory Mid-Atlantic. Retrieved from ies.ed.gov/ncee/edlabs/regions/midatlantic/pdf/REL_2014017.pdf

Roberts, A. L., Gilman, S. E., Breslau, J., Breslau, N., & Koenen, K. C. (2011). Race/ethnic differences in exposure to traumatic events, development of post-traumatic stress disorder, and treatment-seeking for post-traumatic stress disorder in the United States. *U.S. National Institutes of Health's National Library of Medicine, 41*(1), 71–83.

Rosenblatt, L. M. (1978). *The reader, the text, the poem: The transactional theory of the literary work.* Carbondale, IL: Southern Illinois University Press.

Rosenblatt, L. M. (2004). Transactional theory of reading and writing. *Theoretical Processes of Reading, 48,* 1363–1398.

Rosenholz, S. J. (1985). Effective schools: Interpreting the evidence. *American Journal of Education, 93,* 352–388.

Rosenwald: The remarkable story of a Jewish partnership with African American communities. (2017). Retrieved from rosenwaldfilm.org/rosenwald/about/

Rowan, B. (1990) Commitment and control: Alternative strategies for the organizational design of schools. *Review of Research in Education, 16,* 353–389.

Schoenbach, R., Braunger, J., Greenleaf, C., & Litman, C. (2003). A special section on reading: Apprenticing adolescents to reading in subject-area classrooms. *Phi Delta Kappan, 85*(2), 133–138.

Schott Foundation for Public Education. (2010). Yes we can: The Schott 50 state report on public education and Black males. Retrieved from schottfoundation.org/report/yes-we-can-schott-50-state-report-public-education-and-Black-males

Skiba, R. J., & Rausch, M. K. (2006). Zero tolerance, suspension, and expulsion: Questions of equity and effectiveness. In C. M. Everston & C. S. Weinstein (Eds.), *Handbook of classroom management* (pp. 1063–1100). New York, NY: Routledge.

Smith, M. W., & Wilhelm, J. D. (2002). *Reading don't fix no Chevys: Literacy in the lives of young men.* Portsmouth, NH: Heinemann.

Somers, C. L., Owens, D., & Piliawsky, M. (2008). Individual and social factors related to urban African American adolescents' school performance. *High School Journal, 91*(3), 1–11.

Steele, C. M. (1992). Race and the schooling of Black Americans. *Atlantic Monthly, 4*(1), 68–78.

Swann v. Charlotte Mecklenberg, 402 U.S. 1. (1971).

Tatum, A. (2005). *Teaching reading to Black adolescent males.* Portland, ME: Stenhouse Publishers.

Tatum, A. (2006). Engaging African American males in reading. *Educational Leadership, 63*(5), 44–49.

Tatum, A. (2008). Toward a more anatomically complete model of literacy instruction: A focus on African American male adolescents and texts. *Harvard Educational Review, 78*(1), 155–180.

Thurmond, V. A. (2001). The point of triangulation. *Journal of nursing scholarship, 33*(3), 253–258.

U.S. Census Bureau.(2010). *2010 Census.* Retrieved from factfinder.census .gov/

U.S. Constitution. Amend. XIII, §1.

U.S. Constitution. Amend. XIV, §1.

Vygotsky, L. (1978). *Mind in society: The development of higher psychological processes.* Cambridge, MA: Harvard University Press.

Welch, F., & Light, A. (1987). *New evidence on school desegregation.* Prepared for the United States Commission on Civil Rights. Los Angeles, CA: Unicon Research Corporation.

Winn, M. T., & Behizadeh, N. (2011). The right to be literate: Literacy, education, and the school-to-prison pipeline. *Review of Research in Education, 35*(1), 147–173.

Wood, D., Kaplan, R., & McLoyd, V. C. (2007). Gender differences in the educational expectations of urban, low-income African American youth: The role of parents and the school. *Journal of Youth and Adolescence, 36*(4), 417–427.

Woodson, C. G. (1933). *The mis-education of the negro.* Washington, D.C.: The Associated Publishers.

Wright, B. L., & Counsell, S. L. (2018). *The brilliance of Black boys: Cultivating school success in the early grades.* New York, NY: Teachers College Press.

Wright, R. (1945). *Black boy (American hunger).* New York, NY: Harper & Brothers/Harper Perennial.

X, M., & Haley, A. (1965). *The autobiography of Malcom X.* New York, NY: Grove Press.

Index

Academic achievement gap, 70–77
  dropout rates, 72, 80, 168
  education debt vs., 74–77
  graduation rates, 70, 72, 114
  reading proficiency scores, 72–74
  schools and, 4–5
  socioeconomic status and, 70–71
ACE (Adverse Childhood Experience)
  Study, 142–149
Achievement gap. *See* Academic
  achievement gap
ACT, 105, 115
Adidas Top Ten high-tops (new kicks),
  1–2, 184–185, 186
Administrators
  reconceptualizing schools for
    African American students,
    168–177
  What Can Administrators Do Right
    Now? strategies, 30, 67, 83, 97,
    116, 149, 161, 167, 183
Advanced Placement (AP) courses,
  164
Adverse Childhood Experience (ACE)
  Study, 142–149
Aesthetic stance (Rosenblatt), 40–41
African American(s). *See also* African
  American males
  dominant culture and, 28
  dropout rates, 72, 80, 168
  and education debt. *See* Education
    debt
  historical background, 15–29, 51,
    131, 132, 176–177

impact of No Child Left Behind
  (NCLB), 51–56
and slavery. *See* Slavery
and sociocultural nature of learning,
  33–42, 81–82
standardized assessment and, 61–66
text selection and, 36, 37, 39–42,
  65, 80–81, 96–97
verbal forms and literary history of,
  64
African American males. *See also* Black
  Male Literacy Paradigm (BMLP);
  Education debt
damage caused by literacy
  development practices, 3–4,
  8–9, 52–56, 62–64
devaluation of African American
  identity and language, 46–47
disidentification with school, 28,
  87–92, 138–139
engaging in literacy, 117–142
flow theory and, 31–32
graduation rates, 70, 72, 114
home-based/school-based
  adversities faced by students,
  127, 131–134, 136–137, 142–
  149
impact of stereotypes, 114
need for evidence-based
  instructional practices, 118,
  157–158, 172
reconceptualizing schools for
  African American students,
  168–177

African American males *(continued)*
  socialization of, 79
  and sociocultural nature of learning.
    See Sociocultural nature of
    learning
  special education services, 17, 52,
    53, 80, 128
  standardized testing and, 61–66,
    79–80, 141
  strategy for improving student
    outcomes, 107, 162–167
  teacher expansions of definition of
    literacy, 29, 50–51, 63–66, 76,
    92–97, 118, 150–157, 170–171
  teacher perceptions of student
    connections to school, 138–140,
    169–170
  teacher perceptions of student
    connections to teachers, 120–
    138, 169–170
  teacher perceptions of student
    connections to text, 118, 140–
    142, 169–170
  teacher preparation to teach, 44,
    58–59, 75
  teacher understandings of student
    literacy practices, 118, 158–161,
    171
  text selection and, 7–8, 36, 37, 39–
    42, 65, 80–81, 96–97
  violence aimed at, 1–3, 6–7, 76,
    184–185, 186
Agency
  in Black Male Literacy Paradigm
    (BMLP), 44, 57
  defined, 34, 80
  efficacy in, 37–38
  in literacy development practices,
    33–34, 37–42
  modes of, 41
  and stereotype threat theory
    (Steele), 90
  student identity and, 85
  students linking identity to text, 44,
    57, 140–142, 169–170

and transcultural spaces (Guerra),
    47, 57, 61, 86–87
Alfaro, M. J. M., 48, 70
American Psychiatric Association,
    147–149
Anda, R. F., 142–146
Anderson, J., 23–24
Angelou, Maya (Marguerite Johnson),
    185
Assessment of literacy. *See*
    Standardized testing
Assimilation, 85
Autobiography of Malcolm X (Malcolm X
    and Haley), 8

Bailey, F. M., 47, 68, 81
Bakhtin, M., 40, 57, 70, 86
Baldwin, James, 9, 76, 117, 168
Bandura, A., 10, 32–38, 41, 42, 69, 79,
    90, 91
Baraka, Amiri, 9
Beautiful Struggle,The (Coates), 8
Behizadeh, N., 164
Bernat, D. H., 89, 90
Between the World and Me (Coates), 3–4,
    5, 8, 29
Binet, Alfred, 62
Binet-Simon Scale, 62
Black, S. M., 174
Black Boy (R. Wright), 5, 8
Black Codes, 20–21, 22, 25, 51, 132
Black Gen-Xers, 2
Black Lives Matter, 166
Black Male Literacy Paradigm (BMLP),
    43–59
  challenges to, 180–181
  contextual understanding, 44, 47–
    48, 80, 96–97
  culture and socialization, 44, 48–56,
    77–82
  home vs. school language, 44, 45–
    47, 68–69, 108
  implications, 178–180
  key assumptions, 43
  nature of, 43–45

origins of, 34–35, 42, 43, 45, 107–108

power, agency, and identity, 44, 57, 68–70, 77–82, 84–97

steps in using, 108

summary and recommendations, 29–30, 59, 66–67, 82–83, 115–116, 149, 161, 167, 182–183

teacher-participants in developing, 101–115

teacher perceptions of African American male students, 44, 56–57, 85, 92–97, 120–142, 169–170. *See also* Key themes of study

teacher preparedness, 44, 58–59, 75

visual representation of, 43–45

Blacks. *See* African American(s); African American males

Blalock, H. M., 27

Bloome, D., 47, 68, 81

Bobb, Robert, 174

Bond, Horace Mann, 18–19, 20

Book club model

of professional development, 58, 106, 159, 160, 177

for students in classroom, 34, 69, 106, 172, 177

Bradley, Vera, 26–27

Braunger, J., 74, 137

Breedlove, Pecola, 185

Breslau, J., 144–145

Breslau, N., 144–145

Brilliance of Black Boys, The (Wright & Counsell), 114

Brown, Claude, 5, 8

Brown, Michael, 3

Brown v. Board of Education of Topeka, 22–26, 175

Bryk, A. S., 75, 134

Busing of students, 27–29

Caldwell, C. H., 89.90

Call-and-response traditions, 50

Campano, G., 87

Castile, Philando, 2

Cazden, C. B., 40, 81, 108

"Chalk Talk" activity, 121–123

Chavous, T. M., 89, 90

Children's Defense Fund, 141

Civil Rights Act of 1964, 22

Civil War, 20, 23, 131

Coates, Ta-Nehisi, 3–5, 8, 29

College Board, 62, 115

Common Core State Standards (CCSS), 159

Condition of Education Reports (National Center for Education Statistics), 72–74, 79–80, 141

Contextual understanding

in Black Male Literacy Paradigm (BMLP), 44, 47–48, 80, 96–97

intertextual nature of language and, 47–48, 70

social power and, 69–70

in student identity, 86

Counsell, S. L., 114

Culture. *See also* Socialization

and home vs. school language, 44, 45–47, 68–69, 108

and literacy development, 8–9

and transcultural spaces (Guerra), 47, 57, 61, 86–87

Cumming v. Richmond County Board of Education, 21

Curriculum

in early ideas of public schooling, 16, 18, 19

and student disidentification with school, 87–92, 138–139

Czikszentmihalyi, Mihaly, 10, 31, 138–139

Deficit model, 38–39, 64, 66, 74

De jure segregation, 26–27

Delpit, Lisa, 28, 29, 77, 78–79, 81

Democracy, education as foundation for, 18, 19–20

Democracy and Education (Dewey), 18

Desegregation, 22–29
  busing of students, 27–29
  de jure segregation and, 26–27
  disciplinary practices and, 53
  opposition to, 27–29
  suburbanization and, 25, 27–28, 53
Detroit Board of Education, 26–27
Detroit Public Schools Community
    District (formerly Detroit Public
    Schools), 26–27, 50–51, 52, 55,
    173–177
Dewey, John, 18, 19–20
Diagnostic and Statistical Manual of
    Mental Disorders (DSM-5), 147–148
Diallo, Amadou, 3
Discipline policies, 52–54, 128
Discourse analysis framework. See also
    Teacher-participants in study
  building tasks, 117–118
  key themes, 118–161, 169–177
Discourse/language
  contextual understanding and, 44,
    47–48, 80, 96–97
  defined, 45
  home vs. school, 44, 45–47, 68–69,
    108
  intertextuality and, 47–48, 70
  multiple types of, 46
  and reading vs. literacy, 49–50
  in socialization process, 49
  standardized testing and, 61–66
  student discourse communities,
    86–87
  vocabulary and, 68–69
Dominant culture. See also
    Socialization; Student identities
  concept of, 28, 36
  devaluation of African American
    identity and language, 46–47
  hegemony of, 181–182
  and home vs. school language, 44,
    45–47, 68–69, 108
  literacy development practices vs.
    other cultures, 28–29

perceptions of Black males in, 49
  and racism, 147
  reading proficiency and, 72–74
  socialization process and, 48–50,
    78–79
  standardized testing and, 61–66
  student assimilation into, 85
  and student disidentification with
    school, 89–90, 138–139
  teachers and, 132–133
  text selection in schools and, 47
Douglass, Frederick, 6, 150
Driscoll, M. E., 75, 134
Dropout rates, 72, 80, 168
Drug trade, 2–3, 5, 6–7
DSM-5 (Diagnostic and Statistical Manual,
    fifth edition), 147–149
Du Bois, W. E. B., 15
DuFour, R., 75
DuVernay, Ava, 146

Eaker, R., 75
Economically disadvantaged, as term,
    54, 112
Education Achievement Authority
    (EAA, Michigan), 55, 174
Education debt, 74–77, 172–177
  connections to school-related
    literacy, 74–75, 120–142,
    169–170
  education as civil right, 75–76
  nature of, 74
  Rosenwald schools and, 165–166
  and strategy for improving student
    outcomes, 107, 162–167
  What Can Administrators Do Right
    Now?, 30, 67, 83, 97, 116, 149,
    161, 167, 183
  What Can Teachers Do Right Now?,
    29, 66, 82, 97, 115, 149, 161,
    167, 182
Education of the Negro in the American
    Social Order, The (Bond), 18–19
"educator's oath" (Johnson), 99–100

Edwards, V., 142–146
Efferent stance (Rosenblatt), 40–41
Efficacy
    in agency, 37–38
    defined, 37, 80
    nature of, 37–38
    student identity and, 41, 85, 137–138
Elmore, R. F., 82
Enciso, P., 8, 32, 57, 79, 86–87
Ernst-Slavit, G., 80
Evidence-based instructional practices, 36, 118, 157–158, 172
    What Can Administrators Do Right Now?, 30, 67, 83, 97, 116, 149, 161, 167, 183
    What Can Teachers Do Right Now?, 29, 66, 82, 97, 115, 149, 161, 167, 182
Ewing, Patrick, 1–2
Expulsions, 52–54, 128

Fanon, Frantz, 9
Felitti, V. J., 142–146
Ferguson, John, 20–21, 22, 24
Finding Forrester (movie), 128
Finger, John, 24
Fisher, E. J., 64, 77, 87–88, 89, 90, 92
Flake, Sharon, 121–123
Flow (Czikszentmihalyi), 31–32
Flow theory (Czikszentmihalyi), 10, 31–32
Ford, Henry, 186
Fordham, S., 90–91
Fourteenth Amendment, 21, 23, 75
Franzak, J. K., 61, 63, 70, 77
Freeman, L. L., 26
Freire, Paulo, 9

Gary v. Snyder, 50–51, 52
Gee, James Paul, 32, 37, 40, 45, 46, 57, 68, 78, 85, 86, 93, 117–118, 170–171

Gender
    and early ideas of public schooling, 15, 19
    and literacy development, 8–9
Generational poverty, 38–39
Gestalt theory (Koffka), 33, 38, 80
Gibson, Willie Bell, 185
Gilman, S. E., 144–145
Goatley, V. J., 41
Graduation rates, 70, 72, 114
Granholm, Jennifer, 174
Grant, Oscar, 3
Great Migration, 25–27, 176–177
Green, Malice, 3
Greene, J. P., 72
Greenleaf, C., 74, 137
Guba, E. G., 109
Guerra, J., 47, 57, 86, 87
Gun violence, 1–3, 6–7, 184–185, 186
Guyette, C., 174

Haley, A., 8
Harris, N. B., 142, 143–145, 147–148
Hattie, J., 56–57, 71
Heath, S. B., 37, 63–66, 137, 138–139
"Here's What, So What? Now What?" activity, 134–135
Herrnstein, R. J., 61–63, 71
Hierarchy of needs (Maslow), 36–37, 138
Hirsch, E. D., 49
Historically Black Colleges and Universities, 25
History.com, 25
Hughes, Langston, 185
Humphrey, Lila, 186
Humphrey, Winston, 186
Humphrey Annie Belle, 186

Iceberg metaphor, 39–40, 46
Identity. See Student identities; Teacher-participants in study
International Baccalaureate (IB) courses, 164

Intersectionality, 84–87
Intertextuality, 47–48, 70
IQ tests, 61–62

Jackie (teacher-participant), 105,
    111–112, 131, 133–137, 138–140,
    155–157
Jackson, A., 77–78, 81, 139
James, D. R., 27–28
Jane (teacher-participant), 95, 96,
    103–104, 112–113, 131, 137–138
Jefferson, Thomas, 15–19, 178
Jim Crow laws, 10, 20–21, 22, 25, 51,
    132, 177
Johnson, Aaron M., 18, 20, 27, 34,
    36–37, 52, 58, 62, 63, 65, 86,
    145. See also Black Male Literacy
    Paradigm (BMLP)
    ". . . on the state of the west side,"
        13–14
    early literacy practices, 5–7
    "educator's oath," 99–100
    personal background, 1–2, 5–7,
        184–185, 186
Johnson, James (father and
    grandfather), 186
Johnson, James Weldon, 185–186
Julia (teacher-participant), 104–105,
    113–115, 128–130, 152–153, 162,
    166
Justice, in public education, 18–19

Kaplan, R., 77
Key themes of study, 118–161,
    169–177
    home-based/school-based adversities
        faced by students, 127, 131–134,
        136–137, 142–149
    need for evidence-based
        instructional practices, 118,
        157–158, 172
    teacher expansions of definitions of
        literacy, 29, 50–51, 63–66, 76,
        92–97, 118, 150–157, 170–171

    teacher perceptions of student
        connections to school, 118,
        138–140, 169–170
    teacher perceptions of student
        connections to teachers, 118,
        120–138, 169–170
    teacher perceptions of student
        connections to text, 118, 140–
        142, 169–170
    teacher understandings of student
        literacy practices, 118, 158–161,
        171
Kirkland, D. E., 77–78, 81, 139
Koenen, K. C., 144–145
Koffka, K., 33, 35, 38, 80
Kohn-Wood, L., 89, 90
Koss, M. P., 142–146
Kozol, Jonathan, 175–176
Kristeva, J., 47–48, 70
Kucer, S. B., 32, 34–35, 36–37, 41, 42,
    43, 45, 60, 63, 68
Ku Klux Klan, 22
Kunjufu, J., 141

Ladson-Billings, G., 8, 74, 165
Language. See Discourse/language
Learning. See also Literacy
    development practices
    in agency, 41
    in behavioral perspective, 32
    defined, 32
    as social construct, 32–38
Leaving Boys Behind (Greene &
    Winters), 72
LeCompte, M. D., 109
Lee, J., 74
Lewis, C., 8, 28, 32, 34–35, 36–37, 41,
    43, 57, 60, 63, 65, 68, 69, 70, 79,
    80, 86–87, 89, 95, 137
Light, A., 27
Lincoln, Y. S., 109
Lindo, E., 73, 74, 81, 177
Literacy development practices. See
    also Black Male Literacy Paradigm

(BMLP); Schools and schooling;
Standardized testing; Teacher(s)
agency and, 33–34, 37–42
basic tenets, 79
damage to Black men and boys, 3–4,
8–9, 52–56, 62–64
defining literacy, 151–157, 158–159
desegregation of schools and, 22–29
of dominant culture vs. other
cultures, 28–29
engaging African American males
in, 117–142
expanding understanding of literacy,
29, 50–51, 63–66, 76, 92–97,
118, 150–157, 170–171
historical background, 15–29, 51
importance of, 8–9
learning as social construct, 32–38
literacy as social construct, 32–38,
63
and opposition to school integration,
27–29
potential positive impact of, 5–8
premises of study of, 9–10
and reading vs. literacy, 49–50
reconceptualizing schools for
African American students,
168–177
rejection by African American
males, 28
as social acts, 80
sociocultural nature of learning,
33–42, 48, 81–82, 101–103
sociopolitical barriers to literacy
development, 50–51
strategy for improving student
outcomes, 107, 162–167
student identity and, 31–32
teacher identities and, 108–115
teacher understandings of student
literacy practices, 118, 158–161,
171
text selection, 7–8, 36, 37, 39–42,
65, 80–81, 96–97

transactional theory of reading and
writing (Rosenblatt), 10, 38–42,
135
Literacy Practices as Social Acts (Lewis),
69
Litman, C., 74, 137
Lortie, D. C., 75
Luke, A., 49
Lynn (teacher-participant), 94, 104,
105, 110, 119, 126–128, 129,
153–154, 159

Malcolm X, 8, 43, 185
Manchild in the Promised Land (Brown),
5, 8
Marks, J. S., 142–146
Marks, Jay B., 187
Marshall, Thurgood, 22–24
Martin, Trayvon, 3
Marzano, R. J., 108
Maslow, A. H., 36–37, 42, 90, 91, 138
Mason, M. R., 80
McLoyd, V. C., 77
McMahon, S. I., 41
McNulty, B. A., 108
Medical model of education, 61–62
Mehta, J. D., 70–72, 77, 89–90, 91–92,
138, 177
Meinke, S., 26
Meritocracy, 16–17, 19, 178
Merriam-Webster, 32
Michigan. *See also entries beginning with*
"Detroit"
Education Achievement Authority
(EAA), 55, 174
Gary v. Snyder, 50–51, 52
graduation rates, 72, 114
waiver of No Child Left Behind
mandates, 55, 174
Michigan Department of Education,
110, 111–112, 114–115, 128
Milliken, William, 26–27
Milliken v. Bradley et al., 26–28
Mind in Society (Vygotsky), 33

MI School Data (Michigan Department
    of Education), 110, 111–112,
    114–115
Mis-Education of the Negro, The
    (Woodson), 9, 23–24
Misreading Masculinity (Newkirk),
    48–49
Moi, T., 47–48, 70
Moje, Elizabeth Birr, xi–xii, 8, 32, 57,
    79, 86–87
Moral Principles in Education (Dewey),
    18
Morgan, S. L., 70–72, 77, 89–90,
    91–92, 138, 177
Morphemic awareness, 39
Morrison, Toni (Chloe Ardelia
    Wofford), 9, 185
Motivation
    in agency, 41
    and hierarchy of needs (Maslow),
        36–37, 138
Murphy, Judge, 50
Murray, C., 61–63, 71
Music, 50, 65, 184

Narrative Life of Frederick Douglass, The
    (Douglass), 6
National Assessment of Educational
    Progress (NAEP), 62–63, 72–74,
    79–80
National Center for Education
    Statistics (NCES), 72–74, 79–80,
    141
National Trust for Historic
    Preservation, 165
Nesting Ground Framework (Tatum),
    79, 93–94, 124, 139–140, 162
Newkirk, T., 8, 48–49, 134, 137, 139
No Child Left Behind (NCLB), 51–56
    adequate yearly progress (AYP), 51
    basic mandates, 51
    disaggregation of student data, 51
    school closures, 51–52, 54–55
    standardized testing, 52, 54–55

    state waivers of original mandates,
        55, 174
    zero tolerance discipline policies,
        52–54, 128
Noguera, P. A., 77, 81
Nordenberg, D., 142–146
Notes on the State of Virginia (Jefferson),
    15–19

Obama, Barack, 84, 132
O'Conner, R., 52–53
Ogbu, J. U., 28, 64, 78, 87–88, 89,
    90–91, 134, 138
Olzak, S., 27–28
". . . on the state of the west side"
    (Johnson), 13–14
Opportunity gap. *See* Academic
    achievement gap
Oppositional culture model (Ogbu),
    87–88, 89, 90–91
Oral traditions of storytelling, 29, 50,
    65, 76
Other People's Children (Delpit), 29
Owens, D., 77

Pardo, L. S., 41
Passa, A., 52–53
Payne, R. K., 71
Phonemic awareness, 39
Pickering, D. J., 108
Piliawsky, M., 77
Plessy, Homer, 20–21, 22, 24
Plessy v. Ferguson, 20–21, 22, 24
Poetry writing, 50, 65
Porowski, A., 52–53
Porter, John, 26
Post-traumatic stress disorder (PTSD),
    144–145, 147–149
Poverty. *See* Socioeconomic status
Power. *See* Social power
Prison–industrial complex, 146, 164
Professional development
    book club model, 58, 106, 159, 160,
        177

teacher preparation to teach African American males, 44, 58–59, 75
Psychometric exams, 62–63

Race. *See also* Dominant culture
  and early ideas of public schooling, 16–19
  and intelligence, 61, 62, 71
  and literacy development, 8–9
  and teacher perceptions of students, 7
Racism
  dominant culture and, 147
  institutional, 102
  persistence and permanence of, 39, 147
Raphael, T. E., 41
Rap music, 50
Rausch, M. K., 53–54
Reading proficiency
  dominant culture and, 72–74
  expanding understanding of literacy and, 29, 50–51, 63–66, 76, 92–97, 118, 150–157, 170–171
  and reading vs. literacy, 49–50
  transactional theory of reading and writing (Rosenblatt), 10, 38–42, 135
Reconstruction Era (1865-1877), 19, 20, 25, 132
Reflex theory, 37–38
Rice, Tamir, 3
Roberts, A. L., 144–145
Rosenblatt, L. M., 10, 38–41, 42, 135, 140
Rosenholz, S. J., 130
Rosenwald, Julius, 165–166
Rowan, B., 130
RUN DMC, 184

SAT (Scholastic Aptitude Test), 62, 115
Savage Inequalities (Kozol), 175–176
Schensul, J. J., 109
Schmeelk-Cone, K., 89, 90

Schoenbach, R., 74, 137
Scholastic Aptitude Test (SAT), 62, 115
Schools and schooling. *See also* Literacy development practices; Teacher(s)
  and achievement/opportunity gaps, 4–5
  busing of students, 27–29
  damage to Black men and boys, 3–4, 8–9, 52–56, 62–64
  democracy and, 19–20
  desegregation, 22–29
  Jefferson's vision of, 15–19
  as meritocracy, 16–17, 19, 178. *See also* Standardized testing
  potential positive impact of, 5–8
  race in teacher perceptions of students, 7
  as refuges, 3
  rules of engagement in, 4
  school failure and, 119–120, 138
  special education services, 17, 52, 53, 80, 128
  standardized testing. *See* Standardized testing
  teacher perceptions of student connections to, 138–140, 169–170
  violence in, 53–54
School-to-prison pipeline, 146, 164
Schott Foundation for Public Education, 141
Scott, Walter, 3
Sears Roebuck Company, 165–166
"See/Think/Wonder" activity, 141
Segregation
  de jure, 26–27
  and desegregation, 22–29, 53
Self-esteem, and student disidentification with school, 89–92, 138–139
Self-fulfilling prophecy, 2
"Separate but equal" doctrine, 20–21, 22, 24, 25
Shanahan, S., 27–28

Shaw, Errol, 3
Simon, T., 62
Skiba, R. J., 53–54
Slavery, 6
    Civil War, 20, 23, 131
    and early ideas of public schooling,
        17, 19
    and education debt, 76
    and the Thirteenth Amendment, 20,
        21, 75
Smith, M. W., 8, 31, 36, 60, 63, 64, 65,
    88, 89, 134, 139
Snyder, Richard, 50–51, 55
Social development theory (Vygotsky),
    10, 32–38, 41–42, 79, 80, 177
Socialization, 44, 48–56, 77–82
    cultural connections in, 77–78
    dominant culture and, 48–50, 78–79
    environmental factors in, 77
    language in, 49
    social power and, 69, 77–82
Social learning theory (Bandura), 10,
    33–38, 41–42, 79
Social power
    in Black Male Literacy Paradigm
        (BMLP), 44, 57, 68–70, 77–82,
        84–97
    social codes and, 69–70
    student identities and, 92–97
    student socialization and, 69, 77–82
    and transcultural spaces (Guerra),
        47, 57, 61, 86–87
Sociocultural nature of learning,
    33–42, 81–82
    agency and identity in, 33–34,
        37–42
    importance of sociocultural factors,
        77
    intertextuality and, 47–48, 70
    social development theory
        (Vygotsky), 10, 32–38, 41–42,
        79, 80, 177
    social learning theory (Bandura),
        10, 33–38, 41–42, 79

standardized testing and, 61–66
teacher understanding of student
    literacy practices, 101–103, 118,
    158–161
transactional theory of reading and
    writing (Rosenblatt), 10, 38–42,
    135
Socioeconomic status
    and academic achievement gap,
        70–71
    economically disadvantaged, as
        term, 54, 112
    generational poverty, 38–39
    standardized testing and, 61, 70–71
Somers, C. L., 77
Special education services, 17, 52, 53,
    80, 128
Spitz, A. M., 142–146
Standardized testing, 17, 60–66
    and academic achievement gap,
        70–74
    ACT, 105, 115
    African American males and, 61–66,
        79–80, 141
    culturally biased, 71
    IQ tests, 61–62
    and No Child Left Behind (NCLB),
        52, 54–55
    psychometric exams, 62–63
    of reading proficiency, 72–74
    SAT (Scholastic Aptitude Test), 62,
        115
    self-esteem and, 90
Steele, C. M., 28, 78, 87, 88–89,
    90–91, 138
Stereotype threat theory (Steele), 87,
    88–89, 90–91
Sterling, Alton, 2
Student identities
    in Black Male Literacy Paradigm
        (BMLP), 44, 57, 84–97
    concept of, 86
    and connections to school, 138–140,
        169–170

and connections to text, 118, 140–
    142, 169–170
and connections with teachers, 120–
    138, 169–170
contextual understanding and, 86
devaluation of African American
    identity and language, 46–47
discourse communities in, 86–87
disidentification with school, 28,
    87–92, 138–139
efficacy and, 41, 85, 137–138
"fear of acting White," 90–91
intersectionality and, 84–87
in literacy development practices,
    39–42
oppositional culture model (Ogbu),
    87–88, 89, 90–91
self-esteem in, 89–92
social power and, 92–97
stereotype threat theory (Steele),
    87, 88–89, 90–91
students linking identity to text, 44,
    57, 140–142, 169–170
text selection and, 39–40, 96–97
and transcultural spaces (Guerra),
    47, 57, 61, 86–87
Suburbanization, 25, 27–28, 53
Suspensions, 52–54, 128
Swann v. Charlotte Mecklenberg, 24

Tatum, Alfred, 7–8, 28, 29, 31, 32, 43,
    60, 62, 63, 64, 68, 75, 80, 89, 96,
    106–108, 131–134, 136, 137, 159,
    166
    Nesting Ground Framework, 79,
        93–94, 124, 139–140, 162
Teacher(s). *See also* Literacy
    development practices; Schools
    and schooling
    biases of, 7, 8–9, 120–142, 169–170,
        179–180
    book club model of professional
        development, 58, 106, 159,
        160, 177

as central figures in schooling, 18
and dominant culture, 132–133
"educator's oath" (Johnson), 99–100
expanding understanding of literacy,
    29, 50–51, 63–66, 76, 92–97,
    118, 150–157, 170–171
impact of engagement in classroom
    subject-area work, 74–75
and importance of student
    connections to teachers,
    schools, and texts, 118–142,
    169–170
Nesting Ground Framework (three-
    pronged approach), 79, 93–94,
    124, 139–140, 162
participants in study. *See* Teacher-
    participants in study
perceptions of students, 7, 8–9,
    44, 56–57, 85, 92–97, 118,
    120–142, 169–170. *See also* Key
    themes of study
preparation to teach African
    American male students, 44,
    58–59, 75
and reasons for school failure, 119–
    120, 138
reconceptualizing schools for
    African American students,
    168–177
text selections of, 7–8, 36, 37, 39–
    42, 65, 80–81, 96–97
understandings of student literacy
    practices, 118, 158–161, 171
use of evidence-based instructional
    practices, 118, 157–158, 172
and valuing of student identities,
    92–97
What Can Teachers Do Right Now?
    strategies, 29, 66, 82, 97, 115,
    149, 161, 167, 182
Teacher-participants in study, 101–
    115, 179–181
    Jackie, 105, 111–112, 131, 133–137,
        138–140, 155–157

Teacher-participants in study
(continued)
Jane, 95, 96, 103–104, 112–113,
131, 137–138
Julia, 104–105, 113–115, 128–130,
152–153, 162, 166
Lynn, 94, 104, 105, 110, 119, 126–
128, 129, 153–154, 159
Teaching Reading to Black Adolescent
Males (Tatum), 29, 93–94
Text selection, 7–8
African Americans and, 36, 37,
39–42, 65, 80–81, 96–97
dominant culture and, 47
iceberg metaphor for, 39–40
and teacher perceptions of student
connections to text, 118, 140–
142, 169–170
13th (film), 146
Thirteenth Amendment, 20, 21, 75
Thomas, Bigger, 185
Thurmond, V. A., 109
Till, Emmett, 76
Toxic stress, 142–149
Transactional theory of reading and
writing (Rosenblatt), 10, 38–42,
135
aesthetic stance, 40–41
efferent stance, 40–41
text selection and identity, 39–42
Transcultural spaces (Guerra), 47, 57,
61, 86–87
Trauma, 142–149
Triangulation of data, 109

Understanding the In-School Literacies of
African American Males Through a
Sociocultural Paradigm (Johnson),
44, 56–57, 92–97, 185. See also
Black Male Literacy Paradigm
(BMLP)
discourse analysis framework,
117–118, 125, 134, 149, 152,
155–156, 170

key themes, 118–161, 169–177
teacher-participants, 103–115. See
also Teacher-participants in
study
U.S. Census Bureau, 173
U.S. Constitution
Fourteenth Amendment, 21, 23, 75
literacy development practices and,
19
Thirteenth Amendment, 20, 21, 75
U.S. Department of Education, 52–53,
62–63
U.S. Supreme Court
Brown v. Board of Education of Topeka,
22–26, 175
Cumming v. Richmond County Board of
Education, 21
Milliken v. Bradley et al., 26–28
Plessy v. Ferguson, 20–21, 22, 24
Swann v. Charlotte Mecklenberg, 24

Vasudevan, L., 87
Violence
against Black males, 1–3, 6–7, 76,
184–185, 186
guns and, 1–3, 6–7, 184–185, 186
school, 53–54
zero tolerance discipline policies
and, 52–54, 128
Virginia Conventions, 124–125
Vocabulary Skill Building (VSB)
program, 185
Vygotsky, L., 10, 32–38, 41, 42, 68, 69,
79, 80, 134, 177

Walker, David, 9
Washington, Booker T., 165
Waters, T., 108
Welch, F., 27
Welsing, Frances Cress, 9
West, E., 27–28
What Can Administrators Do Right
Now? strategies, 30, 67, 83, 97,
116, 149, 161, 167, 183